PRIVATE PRISONS AND POLICE

RECENT AUSTRALIAN TRENDS

Edited by

Paul Moyle

PLUTO PRESS
AUSTRALIA

Dedication

To Julie, Jamie and Alex

P. M.

First published in September 1994 by
Pluto Press Australia Limited,
PO Box 199, Leichhardt, NSW 2040

Cover design: Trevor Hood

Index: Neale Towart

Typeset, printed and bound by
Southwood Press, 80 Chapel Street, Marrickville, NSW 2204

Australian Cataloguing in Publication Data

Private prisons and police

Bibliography.
Includes index.
ISBN 1 86403 013 5.

1. Corrections — Contracting out — Australia. 2. Corrections —
Contracting out. 3. Police, Private — Australia. 4. Police,
Private I. Moyle, Paul.

365.994

Contents

Acknowledgments

The involvement of commercial interest in the criminal justice system can give rise to a conflict between private interests and the public interest in ensuring an open and accountable system. Researches in this area have encountered unique obstacles to accessing information held by various public and private agencies. Without this information, a proper analysis can be difficult to undertake. An Australian Institute of Criminology Conference entitled 'Private Sector and Community Involvement in the Criminal Justice System' held in Wellington, New Zealand, November 30-December 2, 1992 provided, for the first time, an opportunity for greater accountability and openness by private companies and correctional authorities involved in prisons and police. A clearer understanding of the rationale, philosophy and operational objectives of these groups emerged from this conference. This book updates and re-conceptualises some material that was presented at this conference.

The collection and editing of these contributions benefited from the generosity and support of many persons. Thanks are due to Richard Harding, George Zdenkowski, George Winterton, Alex Amankawah, Tom Middleton, Paul Finn, John Braithwaite, Kenneth Sutton, Brian Dickson, Allan Wilson (now deceased), David Biles, Duncan Chappell, John Myrtle, Mary Burgess, Tony Keyes, Laurie Cullinan, Rod Broadhurst and Anna Ferrante. Thanks are also due to Ric Sissons from Pluto Press who was very supportive of this project in what is a new and emerging area of criminology.

I owe a great debt to the many inmates, custodial officers, middle level managers, and program and training staff at several correctional centres, both private and public. These people spoke frankly about their experiences and views on often difficult and sensitive issues.

Five institutions have generously provided fellowships, access to facilities and some funding during the twelve months it has taken for this book to be edited. They are the Faculty of Law, James Cook University; the Division of Law, Research School of Social Sciences, Australian National University; the Australian Institute of Criminology, Canberra; the Crime Research Centre, University of Western Australia, special thanks are due to Rev Dr Noel Kentish the principal of St Columba College and the support of the College council is warmly acknowledged.

I am also indebted to private and government organisations which include, Corrections Corporation of Australia, Prisoners' Legal Service (Qld) and Queensland Corrective Services Commission, especially its Deputy Director General, Stan Macionis. Mr Macionis has taken the step of releasing parts of the contract, audit and tender documents concerning the Queensland government's decision to privatise Borallon Correctional Centre. He did so despite the fact that release of such information would subject the Commission to greater scrutiny and criticism. This demonstrates a quality which is often lacking in senior levels of bureaucracy.

Finally, I must express my deep appreciation to Julie Carlton who more than any other person has provided advice, word processing, computing and other support in preparing this manuscript.

Paul Moyle
Crime Research Centre, University of Western Australia

March 1994

Contributors

THE EDITOR

Paul Moyle is currently an Honorary Research Fellow at the Crime Research Centre, University of Western Australia and is completing a PhD on the privatisation of prisons in Queensland, Australia through the Faculty of Law, University of New South Wales. He has published widely on legislative reform of the administration of corrections and private sector involvement in corrections in various journals including *The Howard Journal of Criminal Justice, British Journal of Criminology and The Criminal Law Journal*. He has acted as an adviser to the Public Sector Management Commission in its review of the efficiency and effectiveness of the Queensland Corrective Services Commission (1993). He has also acted as a consultant to various criminal justice agencies including the Federation of Community Legal Centres and the State Public Services Federation. He is currently coordinator of a national corrections network group and is completing a book examining the introduction of Australia's first private prison, Borallon Correctional Centre, in Queensland, Australia (forthcoming 1995).

THE AUTHORS

Eileen Baldry is a lecturer in Social Policy and Welfare at the School of Social Work, University of New South Wales. She is actively involved in support services for offenders, ex-offenders and their families.

David Belton is National Secretary of the Prison Officers' Association of Australasia and State Secretary of the West Australian Prison Officers Union of Workers. He has been closely involved in award restructuring which led to the West Australian government rejecting the option of private sector involvement in corrections (1994).

Allan Brown is a senior lecturer in Economics at the School of Economics, Faculty of Commerce and Administration, Griffith University. He is the author of *Commercial Media in Australia: Economics Regulation and Technology* (1986), University of Queensland.

Wayne Calabrese is the Chief Executive Officer of Australasian Correctional Management Pty Ltd. He is also Senior Vice President, Business Development, Wackenhut Corrections Corporation, Florida, USA.

Terry Craig is Manager, Inmate Programs, Correctional Operations, Department of Justice, New Zealand. He has been actively involved in correctional management for the past ten years.

Janet Chan is a senior lecturer in the School of Social Science and Policy, University of New South Wales. Her research interests are in criminal justice reforms and innovations. She is the author of *Doing Less Time: Penal Reform in Crisis* (1992), Institute of Criminology, Sydney University.

Debra Diplock is General Manager, Human Resources, Australasian Correctional Management Pty Ltd. She is a member of the Australian Human Resources Institute.

Richard Harding is a professor and is Director of the Crime Research Centre, University of Western Australia. He was formerly director of the Australian Institute of Criminology. Some of his books include *Police Killings in Australia* (1970), Penguin and *Fire Arms and Violence in Australian Life* (1981), UWA Press. His most recent publication is *Repeat Juvenile Offenders: The Failure of Selective Incapacitation in Western Australia* (1993), Crime Research Centre, UWA, Report No. 10.

Donna Keogh is an associate lecturer in Social Sciences at the Queensland University of Technology. Her research interests are in political science and public policy in the areas of health, education and criminal justice.

Robyn Lincoln is a PhD candidate in the School of Social Sciences at Queensland University of Technology. Her research focuses on Aboriginal criminal justice issues, juvenile justice and comparative criminology. She is a founding member of the Bond University Crime Research Unit.

Stan Macionis is Deputy Director General of the Queensland Corrective Services Commission. He has been involved with private sector management of corrections since 1990 and his responsibilities have included contract development and negotiation for private sector operations in Queensland, Australia.

Mick Ryan is Professor of Penal Politics at the University of Greenwich, London. Among other publications he has co-authored, with Tony Ward, *Privatization and the Penal System: The American Experience and the Debate in Britain* (1989), Open University Press. He was a consultant to the Parliamentary Labour Party during the passage of the 1991 Criminal Justice Act which sanctioned private prisons.

Rick Sarre is a senior lecturer, School of Law, Faculty of Business and Management, University of South Australia. He is a barrister and solicitor and has lectured in law in South Australia and Iowa, USA over the past twelve years.

Paul Wilson is a professor and Dean of Humanities and Social Sciences at Bond University, Queensland. He is also Director of the Bond University Crime Research Unit. His most recent book, co-authored with Duncan Chappell, is entitled *Australian Criminal Justice System* — the mid 1990s (1994), Butterworths.

George Zdenkowski is a former Australian Law Reform Commissioner and is an Associate Professor of Law at the Faculty of Law, University of New South Wales. He co-authored *The Prison Struggle* (1982), Penguin with David Brown and writes regularly on criminal justice issues in *The Bulletin*.

Foreword

George Zdenkowski

Australian policy-makers in the criminal justice sphere are frequently headstrong in introducing initiatives, often borrowed from foreign shores, without carrying out adequate research and without evaluating the suitability of the measures for Australian conditions.

Yet making ill-judged criminal justice policy decisions can have profound effects on people—not only those directly affected by such decisions but those to whom bureaucrats and politicians are ultimately accountable, the community as a whole.

No-one can claim to have perfected solutions for criminal justice reforms and all familiar with the problems in this area freely acknowledge their complexity. But if hasty reforms have an adverse impact and such reforms have not been subjected to the consultative processes and scrutiny demanded by the democratic system, then those responsible for the reforms must be held accountable.

Perhaps the paramount exemplar of this tendency of ad hoc criminal justice policy in recent times is the privatisation of prisons in Australia. Given the fundamental shift in public policy this involved, the manner in which this change in Australian penal administration was introduced was both arrogant and breathtaking.

In effect, it has been privatisation of corrections by stealth. For the shallow research, desultory consultation and half-hearted media discussion which preceded the decisions to privatise could not be dignified by the description 'policy debate'. Yet Queensland and New South Wales, within a short span, have implemented a privatisation policy with the result that about eight per cent of prisoners in Australia are currently detained in this manner. Victoria has called for tenders to finance, design and construct three private prisons (one of which will be for women). Other Australian jurisdictions are actively considering the option. New Zealand is in the final stages of considering tenders for two private prisons. It is an Australasian issue.

A robust debate of the complex issues surrounding privatisation is precisely what is called for. This pioneering volume will provide the platform for this urgently needed discussion.

The editor, Paul Moyle, has succeeded in attracting a wide range of distinguished contributors including academics, administrators (from the public and private sectors) and a prison officers' representative. Not surprisingly, there is a diversity of views! Yet, as Moyle notes, the collection is avowedly eclectic. The approach to the material also varies considerably so that the discussion deals, at different times, with empirical, theoretical, practical and policy issues.

Although several contributions in the book are critical of the manner in which Australian prisons have been privatised, it is by no means a uniformly critical polemic against privatisation per se. Refreshingly, the notion of privatisation itself is dissected and contextualised. A note of caution is sounded against freely translating, for example, North American concepts to Australasia.

The ethical issues entangled with punishment for profit are examined. This is an essential dimension of the debate that has been largely buried by the fiscal imperative. The relative financial and political accountability of public and private sector prisons are also assessed.

One of the key planks in favour of prison privatisation is the argument based on cost. Privatisation, it is said, would lead to greater efficiency and fiscal benefits would endure to the benefit of the community. The studies in this volume would seem to indicate that the cost-benefit advantages of private sector institutions are at least equivocal. Difficulties of comparison of such institutions and the use of different accounting methodologies are highlighted. Certainly more research in this area is warranted.

Another argument advanced in support of private prisons is the undeniably abysmal track record of public sector prisons. But to assert that privatisation is the only answer is logically flawed and confuses two dimensions of the problem — prison policy and delivery of that policy.

If the policy is demonstrably unsound then the introduction of privatisation — a different instrument to play the same tune 'more efficiently'— will not solve the problem. If the policy is acknowledged to be flawed, then why cannot public sector prisons deliver the new policy just as effectively?

There appears to be some evidence to date that enlightened programmes and policies in some private prisons have proved to be more humane and led to fewer management problems than is the case generally, in some public sector prisons. To what extent are such programmes and policies inexorably linked to private prisons? One can point to the benefits of such policies in public sector prisons such as Lotus Glen in north Queensland and the Special Care Unit in Long Bay Prison Complex in Sydney.

Ironically, the introduction of private prisons may prove to be the catalyst for the introduction of enlightened programmes and policies in public sector prisons which had hitherto met with staunch resistance from prison officers.

Interestingly, several contributors argue that the issue may not be whether privatisation is desirable or not. Rather the questions become: which progressive changes may flow from a privatisation policy? How, when and where might private interests be positively involved in the development of penal policy? These issues take the debate to a more sophisticated level than previous arguments about dollars and cents.

A welcome bonus in this book is that the analysis of privatisation is extended beyond prisons to police. The private security industry has been part of the Australian landscape for much longer than private corrections. Yet the powers of private security agents are little understood and have not been the subject of sustained academic analysis in this country. The chapters on private policing provide an illuminating overview of the major issues and allow the reader to make connections between the policy concerns, relating to privatisation, which link policing and corrections.

The book will have several positive effects. At the least it provides a scholarly yet practical foundation for important public policy debate. It identifies significant areas for further research. It may, indeed, lead to a reversal or substantial modification of privatisation policies espoused to date in relation to prisons and police. Jurisdictions considering privatisation may be encouraged to reflect in greater detail on their policy options.

In any case, the editor, the authors and the publisher are to be congratulated for their timely and substantial contribution to this important sphere of social policy debate in Australasia.

Introduction

Privatisation of prisons and police: recent Australasian developments

Paul Moyle

In recent years there has been intense interest in the private sector's role in aspects of the criminal justice system. This attention has been fuelled by the fact that large multinational corporations are now seeking business opportunities in the management of correctional centres and the performance of policing roles. Over the past four years there has been a remarkable expansion of private sector involvement in a range of areas relating to the administration of criminal justice. Because of this there has been heightened public interest in the process yet, unfortunately, the private sector has caught many regulatory agencies unaware, consequently they find themselves poorly prepared to deal with the complex issues that such involvement raises. Examples of these deficiencies are plenty.

In 1993 for example the Queensland Public Sector Management Commission (PSMC) noted that qualitative comparisons had not yet been attempted between public and private prisons and that qualitative indicators 'have not been subject to close consideration' (PSMC 1993, p. 118). The report went further indicating that the Queensland Corrective Services Commission (QCSC) had not developed a legislative approach to contract management. A legislative approach occurs in New South Wales identifying 'mandatory conditions; minimum performance standards; monitoring; and reporting' (PSMC, p. 118). The PSMC noted that there was an urgent requirement to develop:

> a methodology for evaluating contract management of custodial and community corrections centres which includes:
> - the basis on which costs should be compared;
> - the basis on which quality of service can be assessed; and
> - the overall financial and other impacts on the State and the State correctional system of contract-managed centres. (PSMC, p. 119)

With such an important and visible policy initiative as contract managing correctional facilities, citizens have a right to ask why it should take four years to develop basic quality indicators to measure and compare the performance of the private sector.

There are other examples of a lack of necessary preliminary work before involving the private sector in the criminal justice system. In Queensland, private companies now exercise what have been traditional powers of government: powers such as performing the remand and reception function which involves classifying an inmate; identifying and determining major and minor breaches under corrective services legislation; initiating transfers within the corrective services system; and providing information which has a direct impact on parole and remission determinations.

To allow private companies to perform these functions without public debate or community discussion and input is not only inexcusable in principle but indicates a more fundamental problem with the introduction of the private sector in corrections. It is the obligation of regulatory agencies to ensure involvement by private commercial groups in the criminal justice system occurs in a democratic and open way. Contracts for the management of private prisons are currently transparent (unavailable to the public) which leads to considerable uncertainty about companies' obligations and the responsibilities of states. Early evidence suggests Freedom of Information legislation is proving inadequate as a method to allow access to audit reports, financial data, tender documents and contracts. Private companies have attempted to reduce the publication of research results and discussion in the popular media about issues surrounding their involvement in corrections. All this, rather ironically, has occurred in the context of claims by the private sector that their involvement will lead to increasing correctional reform and change, greater accountability and openness in decision making and a more effective and efficient corrective services system. (See Moyle 1994a.)

Anomalies are not limited to private sector involvement in corrections. Government authorities have also been inefficient in discharging their legal obligations to citizens, especially those imprisoned. Recently, the QCSC has been criticised by the judiciary for failing to provide natural justice when administering corrections. It has done so by unreasonably relying on public interest immunity to limit the availability of information and seeking to apply managerial discretion in areas that should be subjected to judicial review (CLJ 1993b, pp. 284-291). In some cases it has exceeded its statutory discretion to administer remissions by taking irrelevant considerations into account. (See Moyle 1993a, pp. 358-364, 1993c and 1994b.) Whilst these practices are not acceptable, they have been subjected to close judicial scrutiny by the Supreme Court of Queensland. Part of the explanation for the level of this scrutiny has been that the QCSC is a statutory authority subject to ministerial accountability. The same level of accountability has not occurred with private sector operators. To date documentation about decision making within private sector prisons has been difficult to obtain and therefore not subjected to the same judicial scrutiny.

This difference in accountability is in part a logical consequence of the sensitivity and secrecy that surrounds a company's operations when it is competing for increased market share within the criminal justice system. Academics are seen to be meddling, perhaps even hindering, the economic expansion of companies. It has become difficult to raise critical issues in this highly sensitive area without being subject to pressures from private companies. It is difficult to know where to draw the line in terms of direct engagement in public discussion about the advantages and disadvantages of private sector involvement in corrections. (See chapter 1.)

This book is a collection of chapters that combine empirical, policy, theoretical and practical analysis of a range of issues in a dynamic area. An eclectic approach has been adopted for two reasons. First, a need to focus upon the specifics of the Australian and New Zealand experience identifying unique developments within our criminal justice system. Too often Australian and New Zealand experiences have been glossed over or, worse still, assumed to be universal, ahistorical and an extension of North American developments. North America, England, Australia and New Zealand do not necessarily share similar experiences, outcomes or responses to private sector involvement in corrections or policing. It is important to treat jurisdictions as specific by building a detailed understanding of the issues that face policy makers within particular environments. In this sense, it is not a weakness to admit the complexities of views concerning the advantages and disadvantages of private sector involvement in prisons and police.

Second, to exclude participants who have a variety of approaches would make the same mistake that many bureaucracies and private companies have done when developing and implementing this policy. (See above.) In the early stages of the policy initiative is it important to draw upon different sources for analysis including government officials, industrial groups, private companies, community and voluntary groups and specific interest groups such as prisoner representative groups. The community should build a variety of theoretical and practical perspectives based upon different assumptions which must be tested against empirical results. These readings present a variety of perspectives in one collection allowing the reader to readily compare the latest developments in this area. Despite these contributions there is an urgent need for greater information accountability. The responsibility rests with regulatory agencies. Only after this is satisfied can more sophisticated and refined analysis be undertaken. This book challenges agencies to improve accountability by providing more documentation about private sector involvement in the criminal justice system. It also outlines important issues concerning this involvement.

This book is divided into five parts. The first identifies the boundaries for private sector involvement in corrections using three approaches. Chapter 1 by Paul Moyle explores some practical issues that have emerged from the Queensland experience. He relates these issues to the current move by the Victorian government to finance, design, construct and manage three private prisons. It is a general discussion delivered to a broad audience. It raises comparative issues regarding the adequacy of legislation for private prisons, the uncertainty of costs, the difficulties of linking private sector involvement with improvement in work practices and the need for more community consultation when implementing private sector involvement.

Janet Chan in chapter 2 explores some models for private sector involvement including the historical development of this policy in the United States. The author outlines some of the promises of privatisation, indicating difficulties in the scope for efficiency and problems of evaluation and accountability. Chan challenges researchers to directly engage in a systematic evaluation of these initiatives. She concludes 'the possibility that progressive changes may result from the privatisation initiative' are still open. This chapter provides a useful discussion of the relationship between privatisation and decarceration.

A significant area of concern has been the models of accountability for the contract management of prisons. Richard Harding in chapter 3 identifies some key elements of accountability, stressing the importance of governments' regulatory role. He warns that 'public interest' would be threatened if certain criteria were not satisfied. The central issue becomes avoiding the hazards of private management of prisons, such as allocating punishment and capture (a situation where regulators become more concerned with serving the interests of the industry rather than serving public interests). Harding stresses the need to promote competition and interaction between the private and public sector. Finally, a model to avoid these hazards is provided.

Chapters 4 and 5 deal with the industrial issues that underpin private sector involvement in corrections. Whilst these issues remain largely unresolved, these chapters take a significant step towards allowing them to be more clearly understood.

David Belton in chapter 4 describes the Prison Officers Association of Australasia's objectives and relates these to its policy on private sector involvement in corrections. He outlines the basis for the union's opposition to private sector involvement. He goes on to examine the West Australian Prison Officers Union as exemplifying a response that opposes privatisation yet supports the industrial and safety concerns of all prison officers, public and private.

Chapter 5 by Debra Diplock and Wayne Calabrese identifies the history of Australasian Corrections Management's (ACM) role in corrections and in particular, its industrial relations strategy at its two Australian centres (Arthur Gorrie and Junee Correctional Centres). ACM's correctional philosophy is outlined and the background and objectives for the management of Junee and Arthur Gorrie Correctional Centres, including how the company performs its remand and reception responsibilities, is provided. Enterprise agreements for custodial and non-custodial officers are outlined with particular reference to coverage disputes between ACM and the Queensland State Service Union (in Queensland) and the Public Service Association (in New South Wales). The basic contradiction between enterprise agreements and industrial based agreements is highlighted. Chapters 4 and 5 provide the clearest indication of the views of industrial interests in corrections so far in the Australasian debate.

The next four chapters, in Part II, discuss specific case studies on aspects of private sector involvement in corrections in Queensland, and to a lesser extent, New South Wales.

Eileen Baldry, in chapter 6, analyses the involvement of corporations in corrections from a socio-political perspective. She identifies sellers and buyers and describes a need for US companies to locate off-shore to countries such as Australia because of a growing market in corrections. Baldry draws comparisons with electrical power, chemical and medical industries noting that these corporations have actively promoted and sold their services. She concludes that US international entre-preneurial activities have not always been in the interest of receiving countries and their citizens. The attempt to link macro issues to specific jurisdictional experiences is important and useful. It is an area of scholarship that has recently received international interest which involves examining the operations of specialised subsidiaries of large conglomerates. (For example see Lilly 1991, Lilly and Knepper 1992, and Shichor 1993.)

In chapter 7 Paul Moyle publishes the results of a preliminary case study examining Australia's first private prison. After identifying the justifications for private contract management, its legislative basis, regulatory arrangements and operational standards, he outlines industrial and work issues, the quality of the correctional environment, accountability, monitoring and performance. A preliminary frame-work is offered to re-examine these issues when studying private sector involvement in corrections. (For an analysis of Corrections Corpor-ation of Australia's attempts to influence the research process and control dissemination of results, see chapter 'Introducing Private Prisons in Queensland — Legal, Political and Policy Issues' in *Private Contract Management of Prisons in Queensland Reform or Regression?*, 1995, forthcoming.)

Chapters 8 and 9 deal with the important issue of cost comparisons between Borallon and Lotus Glen Correctional Centres in Queens-land. Governments consider cost savings to be an important justifica-tion for contract management. Given this, both chapters are topical. A theme in these chapters is the continuing uncertainty about whether cost savings are achieved by contract management. The reason for this uncertainty is based upon a lack of external audits and deficiencies in the methodology and practise of identifying relative costs across the two areas.

Chapter 8 by Stan Macionis was a response to the publication (Moyle 1992) of the QCSC's expenditure statements from July 1, 1990 to May 31, 1991. This data indicated Borallon Correctional Centre was over budget whereas Lotus Glen Correctional Centre was under budget. It also suggested Borallon's net expenditure exceeded the net expenditure of Lotus Glen for the same period while the net daily costs per offender at Borallon were more than that for Lotus Glen. The article raised questions about the adequacy of the method the Commission used to apportion costs between public and private centres. Macionis attempts to refine these expenditure statements by arguing that after further revision of Lotus Glen's gross rather than net budget, the cost for Borallon for 1992/3 was approximately 10 per cent lower per offender than Lotus Glen.

Allan Brown in chapter 9 questions the assertion that only the private sector can significantly improve its efficiency with the delivery of corrective services. He examines the effects of corporatisation and commercialisation on the public sector noting that several empirical studies indicate publicly owned providers of goods and services can substantially improve economic performance over a short period of time. It would appear that award restructuring would also allow for significant improvements in the economic efficiencies in correction centres. This is supported by recent developments, for example the West Australian Prison Officers Union developed a restructuring plan which would save the West Australian prison system (fully operated by the state) $8m per year. The plan involved foregoing overtime payments, cut back in holiday entitlements and sick leave, and working 80 extra hours per year for a higher base salary. (See Pollard 1994.) In relation to Macionis' cost comparisons Brown notes that it is not entirely satisfactory for the Commission to issue a brief statement of figures and expect them to be accepted on face value.

It is clear from the work of Macionis and Brown that extravagant claims of economic efficiency need to be treated suspiciously until such time as full information is provided for independent evaluation.

Part III consists of Terry Craig's examination of the New Zealand experience which has developed rapidly over the past three years. It is interesting to note that private contract management of prisons has received a range of responses from New Zealand governments and senior policy makers within the Department of Justice. These have varied from endorsement and support, actively encouraging private sector involvement in the penal system (see Eagleson 1991 and Smith 1992), to the rejection of the notion of full privatisation (see Department of Justice 1988 and Roper Report). Despite contradictions in policy since 1991, the New Zealand government has called for expressions of interest to finance, design, build and operate a 350 bed regional (minimum/medium security) correctional facility and a 250 bed remand facility on the North Island.

Terry Craig builds upon this history by calling for a clarification of the objectives, issues and constraints of the prison system. He challenges the utility of a bipolar model of service provision in the New Zealand context and proposes a model based on a mix of service providers within a structure that is sensitive to desired outcomes.

Part IV by Mick Ryan gives an international perspective of private sector involvement in corrections. This perspective is tempered by an understanding of the comparative subtleties and of the jurisdictional differences in the implementation of the policy. Ryan argues that a central issue in the privatisation movement will be the re-conceptualisation of the nature and scope of the role of the states within various political structures. Future evaluation of private sector involvement will not depend upon 'a crude struggle between public and private, but rather a debate about exactly where, and on what terms private interests should be involved'.

Part V explores the important area of private sector involvement in policing functions. There are obvious areas of overlap between policing and incarceration. For example, in both areas multinational security corporations are attempting to expand their market share. This provides scope for comparing the differences and similarities in key areas such as the source of authority to use force and protect property.

The legal powers of private police and security providers are explored by Rick Sarre in chapter 12. He identifies a piecemeal array of legal rights, privileges and assumptions. 'No single legislation delineates or grants legal authority . . . whatever coercive powers private security personnel assume, they are not based in statute'. He explores how best to implement regulation of both private and public police, concluding the powers of both need to be 'more tightly defined and delineated'.

The final chapter in Part V, by Paul Wilson, Donna Keogh and Robyn Lincoln, outlines factors leading to an increase in the use of private security to perform traditional policing functions. The authors argue that three options for regulation exist — wholly deregulated free market, introduction of government controls and licensing or self-regulation by the industry. They reject self-regulation primarily because of the diversity of industries, deficiencies in training and the voluntary nature of a code of ethics. They argue that a national approach is needed towards training, focussing on efficiencies, evaluation, accountability, use of force, public access, standards and fee setting involving a Government Standing Commission regulating private security in each state. They note a lack of coordinated action will allow the private sector to shift authority from the state into its own sphere, allowing unjustified input into setting and monitoring standards.

The aim of this book is to provide the basis for a more detailed discussion concerning the broader theoretical and practical issues that private sector involvement raises in policing and corrections. By presenting a variety of theoretical perspectives and empirical works, it is hoped that the reader will gain a better understanding of some of the central issues emerging from this new phenomenon. Constructive reform can only be implemented if a commitment to greater openness and accountability is demonstrated by those in positions of power and authority. This book raises issues which authorities must respond to in a constructive and useful way.

References

Department of Justice 1988, *Privatising Prisons*, New Zealand.

Eagleson, W. 1991, Report on Visit to Penal Institutions in the United States of America: August-September 1991, National Parliamentary Research Unit, House of Representatives, New Zealand.

Lilly, J. 1991, 'Power, Profit and Penality: A Beginning', Paper presented at the Annual Meeting of the American Society of Criminology, San Francisco.

Lilly, J. and Knepper, P. 1992, 'An International Perspective on the Privatisation of Corrections', *Howard Journal of Criminal Justice*, vol. 31, no. 3, pp. 174-191.

Ministerial Committee of Inquiry into the Prisons System 1989, *Prison Review Te Ara Hou: The New Way*, New Zealand.

Moyle, Paul 1992, 'Privatising Prisons The Underlying Issues', *Alternative Law Journal*, vol. 17, no. 3, pp. 114-119.

— 1993a, Felton Case Note, *Criminal Law Journal*, vol. 17, no. 5, pp. 357-364.

— 1993b, Fritz Case Note, *Criminal Law Journal*, vol. 17, no. 4, pp. 282-292.

— 1993c, Hogan Case Note, *Criminal Law Journal*, vol. 17, no. 1, pp. 67-70.

— 1994a, 'Contracting for Private Prisons in Queensland, Australia—Lessons for penal policy', Paper presented to the Prisons 2000 Conference, University of Leicester, April in *Socio-Legal Bulletin*, no. 12, Autumn, pp. 16-22.

— 1994b, Bulger Case Note, *Criminal Law Journal*, vol. 18, no. 3, pp. 176-180.

Pollard, J. 1994, 'Jail Officers Cut Overtime', *Sunday Times*, May 15, p. 11.

Public Service Management Commission 1993, *Review of the Queensland Corrective Services Commission*, Queensland Government Printer, Brisbane.

Roper Report. *See* Ministerial Committee of Inquiry into the Prison System.

Shichor, David 1993, 'The Corporate Context of Private Prisons', *Crime, Law and Social Change*, vol. 20, pp. 113-138.

Smith, M. 1992, Memorandum for Cabinet Social and Family Policy Committee, The Introduction of Contestability into the Prison System, Office of the Minister of Justice, Department of Justice, New Zealand.

Part I

Setting the boundaries

1

Private contract management of corrections in Victoria: some pressing issues that will challenge policy makers

Paul Moyle*

With the introduction of the *Contract Management Act 1993* (Vic), Victoria joins Queensland and New South Wales which have operational private prisons. New Zealand has also announced its intention to privatise the financing, design and operation of a 250 bed remand centre in Auckland and a 350 bed medium and minimum correctional centre in South Auckland. Victoria is in a unique position to learn from the positive and negative consequences of the implementation of this policy in Queensland at the Borallon and Arthur Gorrie correctional centres.

To learn from this experience, it is necessary to draw from a much broader information base than government sources alone. Evidence suggests that the Queensland Corrective Services Commission (QCSC) has developed a vested financial interest in the success of privatisation. It gains profits through consultancies with other states, such as Victoria, which is planning this move.

Private contract management of prisons has traditionally been associated with improvements in the operation and efficiency of correctional centres. Often, advocates of private sector involvement, ignore the complex and competing interests within different agencies of the criminal justice system. The approach in Queensland has revealed an agenda by the QCSC to change public custodial officers' work practices, which resulted in a high incidence of industrial conflict. The QCSC has attempted to force custodial officers to change their work practices, yet often the type of changes that are required are vague. Regulatory agencies must define what is involved in improving corrections if they expect other groups to satisfy this criteria. Perhaps a good starting point for improvement would be to achieve a reduction in violence in correctional centres; to provide meaningful employment for inmates that gives them skills that are appropriate for employment upon release; to provide education services for inmates, including basic literacy and numeracy skills; and to encourage custodial staff to become more multi-skilled by providing proper financial and administrative support and periods of leave necessary for them to upgrade their skills.

In the second reading of the Corrections (Management) Bill 1993 (Vic) the Minister for Corrective Services, Mr McNamara identified principles which applied to the contracting out of services: 'Standards of correctional service delivery will be maintained or improved. Prisoners and offenders will legally remain in the custody or supervision of the state. There will be strict auditing and monitoring of financial and program standards to ensure a system of public accountability is put in place for all correctional services.'

These objectives overlook something important. Where is a reference to the people who will be subjected to this change? To implement change, it is necessary to empower and involve groups that will be required to change their practices within the corrections system. Public correctional officers will be asked to become involved to a significant extent in award restructuring and changes in work practices. They must be involved in discussion and their views incorporated into a framework for the future. Empowerment will ensure cooperation in the restructuring process. Unless governments are planning to privatise the whole corrections system, it would seem irrational to exclude groups which will be asked to bear a significant portion of restructuring.

A weakness of the Queensland approach to private sector involvement in corrections has been the use of this policy as an industrial strategy heightening confrontation. The QCSC has come to be seen, whether rightly or wrongly, as naive and pro-private sector involvement to the exclusion of other perspectives. The QCSC has run two parallel campaigns. The first is an adoption of private sector involvement in corrections. The second is that this campaign has occurred within the context of staff reductions, elimination of overtime and the disciplining of individual public correction centres which do not meet the QCSC's expenditure guidelines. In some cases this approach has been applied randomly. The Commission has threatened Lotus Glen Correctional Centre with privatisation. This centre had been awarded an inaugural corporate human rights prize for its humane treatment of offenders. The nominating body was the Aboriginal-run Tharpuntoo Legal Service of Cairns which praised Lotus Glen for improving service delivery in both the private and public sectors.

A confrontationist approach is often counter-productive. Add to this confusion about the justification for the change and you have the potential for wide scale industrial conflict. The QCSC really has not considered how to transfer improvements between the private and public sectors. Surely it would have been beneficial to explore the selective use of private sector involvement in providing services that complement the existing strengths, talents and expertise of public sector employees. If lasting reform is to occur, custodial officers at the grass roots level need to be empowered as part of the process and be given proper incentives to engage in change. The selective use of privatisation would also allow policy makers to more rigorously identify if and what improvements in quality and efficiency are achievable. The current strategy of privately managing individual centres has brought few if any improvements in the efficiency and quality of corrective services across the Queensland system.

In Victoria the government needs to identify what improvements it hopes to gain by introducing private sector involvement in corrections. Criteria and outcomes need to be linked to contract payments. Monitoring techniques should identify and measure specific outcomes rather than relying on vague claims of the inherent superiority of private sector performance. The Victorian government needs to conduct proper preliminary research in the planning phase (when its bargaining position is highest) as there is little point trying to re-negotiate conditions of the agreement after private companies are entrenched in the market.

Borallon Correctional Centre, Australia's first private prison, has a special place in Australia's experimentation with privatisation. Built by the Queensland government, it was initially intended to be a maximum, medium and low security centre with an emphasis on inmate programs. Early evidence (1991—see chapter 7) suggested that Borallon was a well run centre and was popular among inmates. In part this popularity was attributable to a genuine desire by management, program staff and custodial staff to consult with inmates thereby allowing them genuine input into the management of the centre. The introduction of an inmate needs committee was an innovative technique and should be commended. It is difficult to quantify how many disturbances and escapes this type of committee has quelled because inmates have had a forum to air grievances. The centre has an open campus style which means that inmates can move freely around to attend various activities during the day but are always kept within a secure perimeter.

It is interesting to note that similar consultative processes occurred at Lotus Glen Correctional Centre, a public centre used as a comparison with Borallon in the 1991 study (see above). But is private sector involvement necessary as the precursor for reforming prisons? At both Borallon and Lotus Glen, other factors seemed responsible for improvements on existing models. Both centres had managers who openly encouraged a more humane and conciliatory correctional environment therefore reproducing these attitudes throughout the centre. The general manager at Borallon had 28 years experience in the public sector serving at all levels within custodial ranks, including management levels. It is unlikely that the behaviour of the general manager of Borallon differed markedly when he was in the public sector. At Lotus Glen (where a similar environment existed) there was no fanfare or claim that these management techniques were a result of public sector involvement.

Rather than focus on whether a centre is privately or publicly managed, it is perhaps more appropriate to recognise quality centres and promote the approaches taken within them. Lotus Glen shows us that the public sector is just as able to introduce management initiatives and improve operational efficiency. One of the main sources of this improvement had been the Prison Officers Union which has established local review groups to reduce overtime, improve roster arrangements and introduce case management approaches.

An unexplored question about Queensland developments is the effect upon the public sector of the special treatment received by Borallon. From 1990 to 1992 Borallon had more exclusions (under its contract grounds to refuse to accept inmates) than any other correctional centre in Queensland. Many of the grounds to exclude related to inmates with behavioural and management problems. It is really not a matter of dispute (although some members of the Commission will still deny this) that Borallon received selected inmates who were, on the whole, well adjusted. Borallon had extensive grounds to reject inmates under its contract and received a high amount of administrative support from the Commission, especially when there were difficulties with the management of inmates. Has this special treatment been a significant factor in Borallon's success? How would the private sector perform if it were given mainstream inmates across a full range of security classifications? We can test these hypotheses against developments at the Arthur Gorrie Correctional Centre.

Arthur Gorrie Correctional Centre is Brisbane's remand and reception centre and is operated by Australasian Corrections Management (ACM). Commencing operations in June 1992 it took many of its inmates from the notorious Boggo Road Prison which was closed. ACM's management of Arthur Gorrie has been poor. Inmates have reported they have spent up to 20 hours in their cells, have nominal exercise regimes, poor quality programs, delays in getting access to books from the library, inadequate basic facilities and a high incidence of assaults within the centre. The QCSC has conceded that there have been 'teething problems' which in view of the information available is an understatement. Within 14 months of operation there had been two riots, one of them leading to hundreds of thousands of dollars worth of damage when a unit was set alight, and three suicides, including one by an Aboriginal inmate who was experiencing a gender identity crisis. This inmate clearly needed specialist counselling services. It was alleged he did not receive adequate treatment. The Prisoners Legal Service indicated that it was very difficult to gain regular access to the centre to take instructions from clients. It would not be prudent to draw final conclusions from these difficulties so early in Arthur Gorrie's operations but they do not make a promising start.

The difference in the performance of Borallon and Arthur Gorrie Correctional Centres indicate that it is a mistake to rely primarily on economic justifications to privatise. Such a narrow approach is simplistic and ignores the diverse needs of inmate populations for specific types of intervention.

The difference in the performance by the companies running Arthur Gorrie and Borallon has implications for policy development. ACM made errors which were easy to identify in retrospect. It appointed a general manager who had no experience in Australian corrections and had a confrontationist management style. Its inmate population consisted of some of the most difficult inmates from the state system, who had been transferred to Arthur Gorrie. These prisoners were very tense because they were awaiting trial or classification. Many custodial staff at Arthur Gorrie had no prior custodial security experience and there were too few staff for the number of inmates at the centre.

Given the high security classification of inmates at the centre, and given that it was a remand and reception centre, the QCSC would have been better advised to use the expertise of the public sector, especially in the custodial area. ACM could have provided ancillary services such as perimeter security, educational and work programs catering and cleaning. The establishment of Arthur Gorrie was linked with industrial threats by the QCSC vis-à-vis the public sector unions. It was commonly understood that Arthur Gorrie was privatised because the Queensland State Service Union and the QCSC failed to agree on staffing and industrial conditions.

We now have a private company performing a remand and reception function which involves classifying inmates in the corrections system. It is arguable that the remand and reception function involves allocating punishment. There should be public discussion about whether private companies should perform this important role. A breakdown in industrial negotiations cannot be used to justify such a transfer of responsibility. Policy needs to be developed in a coherent and structured way where industrial concerns become part of the process rather than dominate it.

The QCSC made the decision to allow ACM to manage Arthur Gorrie without having an appreciation of the state's responsibility to allocate punishment. The state has an obligation to citizens within a democracy to administer those things which affect the length of sentence. Governments do not have unlimited power to divest coercive functions within the criminal justice system. The distinction between allocating and administering punishment exists to protect citizens from the capricious exercise of force by non-government entities. The QCSC has either failed to recognise this important distinction, or worse, rejected it. It is difficult to know which is the case because many senior bureaucrats within the QCSC do not understand the legal and constitutional issues that require a distinction between the allocation and administration of punishment.

Given the importance of this distinction it is incumbent upon citizens to indicate they require policy makers to have the skills to appreciate fundamental constitutional safeguards. The remand and reception function, parole, disciplinary breaches and reviews, transfers and remissions are the state's responsibility, not because it would be nice for them to be so, but because in a democracy citizens vote for governments which define the criminal law through political consent. The power to allocate punishment is non-delegatable within Australian society because governments exercise their power through the authority given to them by suffrage. Private companies do not have the same authority as governments to exercise these processes. Within a mixed economy, private companies represent their own proprietary interests which should not be confused with the exercise of political power based on authority given to governments by citizens.

Once you cross the boundary between allocating and administering punishment, it is theoretically possible to privatise everything, including judges and politicians. We do not mix these functions because of the limitations identified. It is not acceptable for private companies to have direct input into determining issues that affect a citizen's liberty in such a direct and obvious way as performing a remand and reception function.

There has been a difference between the QCSC's perception of its effectiveness in its monitoring role, and reality. It is problematic to rely solely on the QCSC's annual reports, which give the impression that contract monitoring is functioning effectively. In its 1991 Annual Report under the contracts auditing section, the Commission noted: 'The performance of the company or organisation in meeting mandatory standards, as specified by contract conditions and legislative requirements, is audited on a regular but random basis. The audit process involves a program of observation and testing of performance against each contracted service standard' (p. 24).

It is a matter of history that these claims were misleading. After careful checking of the published QCSC literature against data collected whilst on field research at Borallon in 1991 it became obvious that it was unsafe to rely on official sources. For example, the Deed of Agreement to manage Borallon was poorly drafted. It was easy for the managers of Borallon to satisfy their legal requirements because the deed contained no real innovations such as qualitative improvement in program delivery, no specific requirements for industrial and trade training of inmates and staff, no requirements to ensure that inmates were employed upon release, and finally, no specific targets that would lead to a reduction in re-offending.

It is puzzling why reducing re-offending has not been linked to private sector involvement in the provision of corrective services. The QCSC has not attempted to make such a link. Perhaps this is because such an approach would have required emphasis on the adequacy of the policy research and analysis function of the Commission.

The QCSC could have taken comprehensive steps to link private sector involvement to program outcomes that would impact on recidivism rates. There is little point embarking on a privatisation program if the directorate of the monitoring agency is dominated by the dictates of economic rationalism. A policy which focuses on cost savings will challenge service providers to find methods to reduce the levels of custodial staff without necessarily changing the corrections environment so that it is a more rehabilitative one.

In the popular media, private contract management has been justified as part of a broader process of reform. The QCSC has never stated that the policy was intended solely to save costs. If it did, a response would be that it is inappropriate to replace public correction centres with private ones primarily because it saves money. The adoption of a replacement model would belie the argument of proponents of privatisation who link private contract management with a strategy to fundamentally change the corrections system.

It is not sufficient justification for private sector involvement that the standards of service delivery be maintained at their existing levels. The objectives for the introduction of private sector involvement in corrections must be that the standards of corrective service delivery *be substantially improved in real and measurable ways*. If it wishes to improve upon the Queensland model the Victorian government must outline how it intends to improve the standard of delivery of correction services. This should include the criteria it proposes to use to identify improvements and how private sector involvement will be linked to this process. There must be a justification for the policy move.

The government must define what it means by declaring that offenders will legally remain 'in the custody *or* supervision of the state'. The Queensland experience indicates that when policy makers have little legal or constitutional training their understanding of the allocation and administration of punishment is distorted. For private sector involvement to be acceptable both legally and politically, private companies and their employees should not be placed where they can directly affect remission, parole, disciplinary decisions or any other issues which potentially increase the length of sentence of an inmate. The distinction between the allocation and administration of punishment is clear. It is important both symbolically and legally for the Victorian government to indicate that it understands this distinction before it embarks on privatisation.

The Victorian Government needs to be specific about how 'strict auditing and monitoring of financial and program standards' will occur. Mr McNamara outlines that the 'objectives and performance standards in relation to the provision of the contracted service and the indemnity by the contractor of the Crown' will be included in the process. He states, 'an independent monitoring process of contracted services whereby monitors will be appointed to assess and review the provision of services against minimum standards will be prescribed in the management agreement'. Objectives and performance standards should be clearly defined in the legislation to avoid the possibility of misunderstanding. There are specific questions we need to ask about these issues. Why has the Minister only used maintaining standards as a justification for private sector involvement? What does the Minister mean by 'offenders will legally remain in the custody '*or*' supervision of the state? Which standards will be monitored and audited?

How does one identify objectives and performance standards? If it depends upon a diversity of sources then this is a positive approach and unless the public is given an opportunity to participate in the process of identifying objectives and performance standards, then the potential for reform is limited. It is obvious that if a select group of people with a narrow viewpoint is given responsibility for defining the objectives and performance standards, then the results will demonstrate the same deficiencies as the Queensland experience. It is not acceptable to ignore the important role that genuine community consultation, including the submission of comments from the public, plays in corrections policy.

It is important to identify the objectives of the privatisation process and put into place a multi-faceted approach to monitoring. Monitoring should not be seen purely as an internal process. Citizens should resist the secretive and narrow interpretation of the monitoring process which unfortunately has been the approach adopted in Queensland. Governments face challenges in correction reform and they need to move into evaluating qualitative aspects of the operations of corrections. The perceptions of officers and inmates of job satisfaction, the quality of the environment, staff-inmate relations, and the inter-subjective perceptions of people working within the corrections environment are valid indicators of success in a corrections system. These should be included in the monitoring process and we must reject the positivistic and quantitative obsessions of career bureaucrats. Evaluation is much more complex than they would have us believe.

The state needs to control the privatisation process and not be controlled by it. Private sector involvement in corrections should not mean a lack of availability of information to citizens. Evaluations performed by the Director General, including periodic reports, should be placed on the public record for examination. If the justification for private sector involvement in corrections is to provide superior services, then there is no reason for secrecy. Secrecy only leads to suspicion and unnecessary speculation.

It is necessary to strengthen Freedom of Information legislation and governments should make it clear to private companies that confidential information exclusions based on 'commercially sensitive information' are not appropriate. The public interest in ensuring an open and accountable corrections system needs to be stressed. To date it is unfortunate that commercial confidentiality has become a justification to exclude far too much information from the public record. Clear standards need to be set for access to information held by private companies that perform incarceration. Where there is an inter-meshing of public functions such as private companies performing incarceration, it is fundamentally undemocratic to interpret com-mercial information exclusions in a broad way. Private companies should not be exempt from modern trends in public administration which require greater access to information held by governments.

It is important that the Victorian government admit and deal with all the complexities that private sector involvement in corrections raises.

---

* This is a revised version of a paper presented to a public seminar at the State Film Centre, Melbourne, August 18, 1993. At the time of this presentation, the state government of Victoria was preparing to call for expressions of interest to finance, design, construct and manage three private prisons.

2

The privatisation of punishment: a review of the key issues

Janet B. L. Chan*

Abstract: Both the New South Wales and the Queensland governments have opened the door to the privatisation of prisons in Australia. The term 'privatisation' refers to a range of processes in the financing and provision of corrective 'services' to criminal offenders. This chapter canvasses the theoretical and policy issues related to the privatisation of prisons. Through a review of the international literature, the author suggests key areas of concern for future policy development and evaluation. The paper concludes with a comparison between the privatisation and the deinstitutionalisation of punishment and outlines the theoretical implications of such a comparison.

If 'deinstitutionalisation' was the catchword of the 1960s and 1970s among corrective services administrators, then 'privatisation' must be its equivalent in the '80s and '90s. Whereas the former had always carried the progressive, if somewhat romantic, connotation of 'returning' the deviants to the 'community', the latter is often associated with the morally ambiguous and slightly offensive enterprise of making profits from the infliction of punishment. There is, in fact, a great deal of overlap in the two policies: many of the community-based correctional facilities in the United States, for example, are run by the private sector (Curran 1988). Moreover, the privatised punishment industry is not the exclusive domain of for-profit corporations: most of the privatisation which has taken place in Canada, for example, has been in the form of contracting out correctional services to non-profit organisations (McKenzie 1986). Just as there are dangers in treating the diversity of policies, programs and innovations using the deinstitutionalisation label as a unitary phenomenon, it is important to differentiate the variety of initiatives which are often lumped together in the name of privatisation. A review of the key issues in relation to privatisation, therefore, must begin with the problem of definition.

The problem of definition may be seen as technical, but more often than not it is also political. The term 'privatisation' is said to be 'lamentably imprecise': 'The word can signify something as broad as shrinking the welfare state while promoting self-help and voluntarism, or something as narrow as substituting a team of private workers for an all-but-identical team of civil servants to carry out a particular task' (Donahue 1989, pp. 5-6).

The broad meaning of privatisation appears to embody popular enthusiasm for private enterprise, hostility to politicians, and contempt for bureaucracy (Donahue 1989, p. 3). Consequently, privatisation in that sense is typically seen as part of the agenda of the New Right, the fiscal conservatives and the law-and-order lobby. An important point to note is that privatisation in the US is qualitatively different from privatisation in many other parts of the world. While for other countries privatisation has meant a massive sale of public assets, American governments' privatisation efforts have mainly involved the use of private means to improve the performance of public tasks (Donahue 1989, pp. 6-7).

In the United Kingdom, for example, the initial response to private prisons was 'predictable on party political lines', with organised labour opposing all forms of privatisation, including prisons (Taylor and Pease 1989, p. 180). A more dispassionate approach to the study of privatisation suggests that the ideological and political lines are not as clearly drawn as opponents (or proponents) of privatisation may suggest.

Privatisation theoretically involves choices along two dimensions: *financing*, i.e. whether collective (taxes) or individual (fees) resources are to be used, and *provision*, i.e. whether the service is to be delivered by a government or non-government organisation (Donahue 1989, p. 7). To use prisons as an example, the above typology implies that there could be four types of prisons: publicly run prisons financed through taxes (i.e. the existing model), publicly run prisons financed through private fees (as in 18th century debtors prisons), privately run prisons financed through taxes, and, finally, privately run prisons financed through private funds. In practice, the distinction between collective and individual sources of financing may not be as clear cut as it appears, and the 'publicness' and 'privateness' of organisations may be a matter of degree (Donahue 1989, p. 9). Moreover, as mentioned earlier, private organisations are not all profit-seeking corporations. In the correctional sector, the use of voluntary, non-profit or religious organisations has been a historical reality. In fact, the growing dependence of some of these non-profit organisations on government contracts as a result of privatisation has led some analysts to conclude that what is going on may be more accurately described as the 'publicisation' (Ericson, McMahon and Evans 1987) or 'governmentization' (John Howard Society of Ontario 1986) of private agencies.

When one takes into account the variety of goods and services which can be privatised in the correctional sector, together with the choices in relation to financing and service delivery outlined above, it is patently obvious that privatisation of corrective services cannot be taken as a unitary phenomenon. The advantages and disadvantages, risks and benefits, of privatisation will not be identical in all instances.

THE TREND TOWARDS PRIVATISATION

Historians of ideas would no doubt delight in analysing the origins and development of the concept of privatisation as it swept like wild-fire from Thatcher's Britain to other parts of Europe and to North America. Such a history would probably examine the complex currents of political ideologies, economic theories, and managerial cultures crossing and converging in the corporatist world of politicians, industrialists and unionists.

Compared with the privatisation of other state enterprises, however, the idea of *privatising criminal justice* is at once much less ambitious in scope and much more potent in symbolism. After all, it is one thing to sell off British Airways or privatise garbage collection, but the prospects of 'dial-a-cop', 'rent-a-judge' or 'punish for profit' seem deeply antithetical to the justice traditions of most of the countries which are now contemplating privatisation. Why, then, has privatisation of punishment become, within a relatively short period of time, not just a remote possibility but a reality in many jurisdictions?

The truth is, of course, privatisation is not a new concept. Punishment of criminal offenders was never a monopolised function of the state. The involvement of religious and other non-profit agencies in corrections also has had long historical roots. Some call the present drive a mere effort to *re-privatise* punishment (Matthews 1989; Weiss 1989). The revival of the concept appears to have come at the right time in the right place.

The growing acceptance of privatisation is a development which — if official accounts are to be believed — seems to follow a similar path everywhere. Prisons are overcrowded. It does not matter whether overcrowding is the result of more criminal behaviour, more law enforcement activities, or a more punitive sentencing policy. The fact remains that there are not enough jails to hold all the prisoners sent there by the courts. Prison conditions therefore deteriorate. Governments, deep in fiscal crisis, are faced with hard choices: to continue building more prisons and blow out the correctional budget, to allow prison conditions to deteriorate, or to look for alternative ways of financing and running penal institutions. In most cases, deinstitutionalisation is simply not a viable solution, not only because it is not always successful in reducing overcrowding, but also because governments cannot afford not to 'get tough' on criminals in a climate of punitive public opinion. (See Cohen (1985) for a review of the evidence of 'net-widening'. Although some researchers disagreed with Cohen's interpretation, there is considerable empirical evidence that sentencing options intended to be used as alternatives to imprisonment have been used as alternatives to fines and recognizance (probation) by sentencers. For evidence in New South Wales, see Bray (1990) and Bray and Chan (1991)).

This 'natural history' of the development of privatisation of punishment, however, masks important distinctions between the circumstances under which different jurisdictions chose the privatisation option. The movement towards privatisation in the US penal system, for example, emerged from a relatively unique set of circumstances. (See Cody and Bennett (1987) for a detailed account of the origin of privatisation in Tennessee.)

Privatisation of prisons first became popular in the US in the 1980s. The United States has the world's highest rate of incarceration, at 426 prisoners per 100,000 population. There are one million Americans in state or federal prisons and local jails, costing approximately $16 billion a year (Maurer 1991). Overcrowding in American prisons reached crisis proportions in the last few years, with no relief in sight. State prisons were estimated to be operating at between 107 and 124 per cent capacity (Weiss 1989, p. 26).

While prisons and jails were bursting at the seams, opinion polls reported overwhelming public support for tougher penal policy.

Tougher policies in turn put additional pressure on the overcrowded institutions. In the US, the building of new prisons is financed either with the State or local government's *current operating revenues* or with *general obligation bonds*. The former has several major limitations, including the heavy burden it puts on current budgets. The selling of general obligation bonds on the open market, however, usually involves voter approval as well as various tax and debt limitations. Referendums to authorise the issuance of bonds to finance the building of prisons have frequently been defeated by the same taxpayers who would like to lock up more offenders. (The use of current operating revenues is a pay-as-you-go method which involves appropriating funds from the budgets over two or more years without borrowing. General obligation bonds are referred to as 'full-faith-and-credit' bonds which are based on the government's unconditional commitment to pay the principal and interest at a specified future date. A survey of 50 states conducted in 1984 indicated that about 40 per cent of the states relied exclusively on current revenues, about 50 per cent on bonds, and the remaining 10 per cent used both methods of financing for prison and jail construction (Mullen et al 1985, pp. 33-37)).

Overcrowded prisons are not merely breeding grounds for violence, tension and communicable diseases, they also breed a great number of lawsuits: 'Between .June 1983 and June 1984, there were some nineteen thousand lawsuits filed by prisoners claiming violation of their civil rights. Most of these complaints were directly or in-directly related to overcrowding, and virtually all of them were beyond remedy without a major infusion of new funds' (Donahue 1989, p. 153).

A fair number of these complaints have been successful and prison authorities are under court orders to improve conditions:

> . . . prisons in two-thirds of the nations' (sic) states are under court order to correct conditions which violate the United States Constitution's prohibition against cruel and unusual punish-ment. . . . Corrections officials who fail to comply with court-established deadlines are threatened with contempt. Several state corrections systems have been ordered to stop new admissions, under penalty of heavy fines, until they fall below their rated capacities. (Weiss 1989, p. 26)

Yet these authorities have virtually no financial resources to comply with the court orders. Consequently, straight lease or lease/purchase agreements have become a welcome alternative to current revenues and general obligation bonds as methods of financing prison construction:

> [In straight leasing] brokerage houses and investment banks . . . earn commissions by getting their clients to invest in property that other private firms, such as real estate agencies and leasing companies, can then market to potential government lessors. In lease/purchase arrangements, investment banks have often helped governments to create legal entities, such as nonprofit corporations [The use of non-profit corporations is primarily to take advantage of tax exemptions.] that can issue the revenue bonds needed to finance construction, hold title to the completed facility, and receive lease payments . . . Governments remain responsible for financing the lease payments, and ultimately the bonds, with tax dollars. (Mullen et al 1985, p. 38)

Such arrangements have the advantage of not being limited by debt ceilings and not subject to referenda requirements; they are becoming a popular method of financing prison construction in the US. Straight leases were being used by 18 states and lease/purchase financing was used by only one state in the 1984 survey, although many other states were considering the latter option (Mullen et al 1985, pp. 41-43).

This brief account of the background to the privatisation of punishment in the US raises an important point. Private sector involvement in the US correctional system is not new. The contracting of auxiliary correctional services such as food preparation, building maintenance, social services and so on to private companies has been happening for many years. The new privatisation initiatives, of course, are intended to go much further, including the financing, design, construction, and management of prison facilities, as well as the operation of prison industries. However, as the earlier discussion about the financing of prison construction shows, the move towards accelerated privatisation has been driven by rather desperate circumstances. The new privatisation, therefore, offers governments a way out of their immediate problems. Besides, if the costs of punishment can be reduced or contained through the involvement of the private sector, then governments can maintain their tough stance on law and order without facing the peril of prison riots or court challenges over prison conditions.

It should be pointed out, however, that in terms of actually operating prisons, the number of entrepreneurs is still quite small despite their high profile in the media. By the late 1980s, there were only around 20 or 30 privately run prisons among the 5000 or so adult correctional institutions in America, although there were hundreds of juvenile detention centres run by private bodies, including profit-seeking firms (Donahue 1989, p. 151).

Another important point which emerges from a reading of the US experience is the unevenness of development among the different jurisdictions. It would be misleading to assume that privatisation is happening in all American jurisdictions or that it is universally accepted by Americans:

> . . . the advocates of privatization tend to play down the variety of jurisdictions, for the very good reason that doing so allows talk about what is 'happening in Tennessee' to be loosely translated into what is 'happening in America.' The truth is, of course, that there is no state which is 'typically American', and the idea of private prisons is favored — though only a handful are actually in place — in just a few states where fiscal conservatism is strong and public sector unions weak. In some states, such as Pennsylvania, opposition to privatization has been intense, and the Federal Bureau of Prisons is openly skeptical . . . (Ryan and Ward 1989a, p. 7)

Though the situation in the US may have been quite unique, the concept of privatising prisons is being sold elsewhere with great success. In Britain and in other European countries the privatisation of prisons and other correctional services has been hotly debated and more or less accepted as inevitable in the near future (see Ryan and Ward 1989a, 1989b; Porter 1990; Council of Europe 1990; Robert 1989). In Canada, privatisation has mainly occurred in the non-custodial services such as probation, community service orders, victim-offender reconciliation programs and restitution services (McKenzie 1986, p. 9). The British Columbian government excluded from consideration the contracting out of any services with staff designated as 'peace officers' or 'officers of the court', which effectively meant that the operation of adult and juvenile custodial facilities would not be privatised (Harrison and Gosse 1986).

In Australia, privatisation of prisons is no longer simply a point of debate. Queensland has opened the door to privatisation by having Australia's first privately operated maximum security prison: Borallon Correctional Centre. The centre is being managed by Corrections Corporation of Australia, a consortium of Australian companies, Wormald Security Australia and John Holland Holdings, and the US company Corrections Corporation of America. The Borallon contract is for three years with a two-year option. Queensland's Corrective Services Commission allocates $100 a day for each of the jail's 240 prisoners (Jarratt 1990).

In NSW, where the daily average prison population has increased dramatically in the past few years, the privatisation of prisons was adopted on the basis of a consultant's report (Kleinwort Benson Report 1989). (The daily average prison population has risen from 4124 in 1988 to 5002 in 1990 (NSW Department of Corrective Services 1990). More recent figures suggest that the daily average for 1991 may be well above 5500 (Gorta 1991)). With enabling legislation in place by 1990, the NSW government has approved the tender from Australasian Correctional Services (ACS) to design, build, and operate a 600-cell medium and minimum security jail in Junee. The ACS consortium is made up of Thiess Contractors, ADT Security, and Wackenhut Corrections Corporation (*Sydney Morning Herald*, 26 June 1991).

Developments in NSW would constitute an interesting case study of how privatisation of punishment was adopted under circumstances substantially different from those in the US. For example, although overcrowding is a problem in NSW prisons, there have been no court orders to improve prison conditions or to close down prisons. Unlike the US, there is no need to go to the voters for approval to raise money for prison construction. In fact, the budget for building new prisons has increased in the past few years. Total capital works expenditure was $27 million in 1987-88, $47 million in 1988-89, and $72 million in 1989-90. This partly reflects the major ten-year prison construction program approved in 1990. The new prisons include a 300-cell maximum security jail in Lithgow (total cost, $59 million), a 250-cell maximum security jail in Windsor (total estimated cost, $60 million), and various extensions of existing institutions. (See NSW Department of Corrective Services 1990). The Kleinwort Benson Report gave little evidence to support the claim that private prisons would solve the existing problems in the prison system: inadequate facilities, staff shortages, lack of staff training, and inappropriate management practices. The consultants cite the success of overseas experience as the justification for pressing ahead with privatisation. Yet, when one looks at the overseas literature, the verdict is by no means clear.

THE PROMISES OF PRIVATISATION

The entrance of private contractors into the punishment industry is heralded by a host of attractive promises: 'good housekeeping with special emphasis on accountability and sound financial management', competition, full-time employment on award wages for prisoners, professional conselling and educational services, motivated prison staff, and better value for the tax dollar (Dayton 1989). With correctional budgets in the US and Britain involving billions of dollars, the prospect of any improvement in cost-effectiveness is bound to be an attractive proposition to prison authorities and governments. (Financial statements for the year ended 30 June 1990 show that the NSW Department of Corrective Services spent approximately $267 million (excess of payments over receipts). See NSW Department of Corrective Services (1990, pp. 74-75)).

It is, as will be discussed later, not always easy to assess the cost-effectiveness of privatisation in the correctional sphere. Advocates of privatisation sometimes offer what Matthews called 'a shifting series of justifications . . . with various objectives being substituted for those which are discarded':

> The uncertainty of the cost-effectiveness of privatization has forced its advocates to stress other possible advantages. They have come increasingly to suggest that its real advantage may lie in its increased flexibility, its ability to realize objectives that might be difficult or impossible to achieve in the public sector and its ability to quickly mobilize facilities to meet pressing needs; or that it might encourage experimentation and the introduction of innovative practices. Further, the advocates of privatization have argued that it increases competition, reduces the power of the unions and opens up new managerial possibilities, as well as generating new forms of public participation. (Matthews 1989, p. 5)

Occasionally, the sales pitch may reach some high notes that penologists would find oddly disconcerting:

> . . . correctional entrepreneurs have argued that, free of bureaucratic red tape and restrictions, they can also deliver a better, more innovative service. Ted Nissen, the head of Behavioral Systems Southwest, promised that he could outperform governmental competitors on rehabilitation, that once-central but currently distant goal of corrections policy: 'We have a national recidivism rate of 50 percent. I offer to forfeit my contracts if the recidivism rate is more than 40 percent.' (Donahue 1989, p. 154)

Academic penologists may well point out the hazards of comparing recidivism rates where private prisons only admit less 'recidivism-prone' prisoners, but the promise of lower recidivism rates nevertheless holds enormous political currency among policy makers. For many people, however, the prison system has been such a dismal failure for so many years that even if the private prison operators were half as good as promised, they could hardly do worse than the present prison system run by the public sector (Donahue 1989, p. 154; Matthews 1989, p. 4).

KEY ISSUES IN ASSESSING THE PRIVATISATION OF CORRECTIONS

The major issues which arise from the privatisation experience in the US have been canvassed by a number of authors (e.g. Mullen et al. 1985, Donahue 1989, Robbins 1987). The following discussion is primarily based on Donahue's excellent analysis.

At the heart of the assessment is the *theory* of why private enterprises should be superior to public ones:

> The chief virtues of delegating public tasks to the private sector are the cost discipline inspired by competition, and an institutional setting that affords superior motivation to discover better, cheaper ways to deliver value. The more the technical nature of a public task allows for innovation to improve quality or to lower cost, the greater the potential benefits of contracting out — provided, of course, it is possible to forge a firm contractual link between creating value and collecting profits. This link depends, in turn, on the existence of realistic competition, on how carefully and completely the product can be specified; on the degree to which quality can be monitored; and, finally, on the purchaser's ability and inclination to reward, penalize, or replace contractors on the basis of performance. (Donahue 1989, p. 159)

Three key areas of concern immediately arise from this line of reasoning. First, *to what extent is innovation and efficiency improvement possible in correctional services?* Some services may have more scope for innovation than others, and some institutional costs cannot be reduced without substantially changing the nature of the service. The second concern is: *how can the quality of service be measured and guaranteed?* Quality is always difficult to measure, but privatisation means that not only must appropriate measures be developed, the anticipated level of performance must also be specified, monitored and written into contractual agreements. Finally, *who defines what the appropriate level of demand for service should be?* The public's demand for law and order and tougher penalties is difficult enough to satisfy by an elected government concerned with political support. The problem is doubly complex when such a demand can be tied to some correctional entrepreneur's profit level. The danger of self-interested manipulation of public fear of crime and hence demand for correctional services cannot be ignored.

If privatisation is to be more than an empty promise, these questions must be adequately investigated and addressed in any policy to privatise.

Scope for Efficiency

Proponents of privatisation would argue that private correctional services can be more efficient because there will be less 'red tape', more incentives and motivation to control costs. Naturally, some services have more scope for efficiency improvement than others. With imprisonment, as one analyst points out, there are only two ways of cutting costs without sacrificing quality: 'using *fewer* resources, or *paying less* for the resources used' (Donahue 1989, p. 161). Donahue does not see much scope for savings through innovations when the task being privatised is imprisonment, i.e. the sheltering, feeding, caring (in case of sickness), protection (from each other), and security (from escape) of prisoners:

> Private firms almost surely are better than corrections bureaucracies at economizing on resources. Behavioral Systems Southwest detains illegal aliens in converted motels; the Corrections Corporation of America alien detention center in Houston was designed to be used as a warehouse if the detention business hit a slump. Using such structures — when they do the job — represents a real efficiency gain over specialized detention buildings that must stand empty when they are not needed to hold prisoners. Better food service practices, such as portion control, can limit waste. There are also opportunities for cutting labor costs through automation. Carefully designed and installed surveillance cameras and electronic security systems can substitute, to some extent, for human guards. (Donahue 1989, p. 162)

The limited scope for cost cutting through innovation means that savings will have to be achieved by 'driving harder bargains' with suppliers of goods and services, including labour. The scope for saving in labour costs, argues Donahue, is equally limited unless a lower quality workforce is resorted to, since state institutions often have trouble filling prison officer posts in spite of the relatively favourable wages and benefits in the public sector.

There are very few published research studies on cost comparisons. The available evidence is either based on juvenile institutions or on a small number of cases. Using figures in 1985 for the US, Donahue compares the costs per resident between 1996 private and 1040 public custodial centres for juveniles. He finds that the cost differences are very small, with total cost per resident of private facilities one per cent higher than that of public centres, while operating costs are lower for private centres, by only three per cent (Donahue 1989, pp. 160-161). Using similar data, Curran (1988) finds that the per capita operating cost of private facilities rose from 83 per cent of public outlays in 1974 to 97 per cent in 1983, even though nine out of ten private facilities were 'open' facilities (which should be cheaper to run) while only four out of ten public facilities were open.

There are, of course, success stories such as Corrections Corporation of America's management of a Florida prison:

> In October 1985, when the Bay County, Florida, gaol was faced with two lawsuits charging overcrowding, fire safety violations and inadequate medical care and staffing, county commissioners decided to take control of the gaol away from the sheriff. They turned its operation over to the CCA, and it became the first large maximum-security gaol to be given to a private company. Within eight months of assuming operation of the gaol, the state dropped its lawsuit . . .; overcrowding was reduced, major building renovations conducted, extra staff was added, inmates were provided with numerous amenities, and CCA saved the county an estimated $700,000. And all this was accomplished using most of the sheriff's original staff, who received pay rises. (Weiss 1989, p. 32)

Such a spectacular success is not always achievable, as Weiss points out. The $200,000 cost overrun in the first seven months of CCA's contract with Silverdale Detention Centre, Tennessee, is an example of privatisation not living up to expectations.

Sellers (1989) offers some stronger evidence in support of the privatisation claims. His study compares three privately operated prisons (including Tennessee's Silverdale Detention Centre) with three publicly operated ones. The institutions were selected so that they were similar in size, location, structure, age, type, capacity, and average daily occupancy. The results show that the three private prisons were operated at lower costs per prisoner than the public ones. After adjusting for the number of services in each institution, Sellers finds that the daily costs per inmate were $91, $29, and $19 in the private prisons, compared with $141, $32, and $48 in the corresponding public facilities. Moreover, the private facilities appeared to offer more programs than the public ones, and two of the three private prisons were in better overall condition than the public ones. Sellers concludes that governments should contract private firms to operate prisons and 'allow tax payers to benefit from the cost-savings contracting will provide' (Sellers 1989, p. 254).

Donahue has argued, however, that even if private operators are able to reduce costs, it does not automatically follow that these savings will be passed on to the government, since the efficiency of private prison operators depends on the nature and degree of *competition* in the industry:

> Without competition or tightly drawn contracts, savings on wages and other inputs increase profits instead of shrinking public spending . . . Even if the number of corrections firms eventually exceeds the current handful, it is unlikely that there will ever be more than a few serious contenders in any given region at any given time. Firms are likely to face substantial costs of entering the incarceration industry, as well as potential *exit* costs [particularly if any entrant must invest in specialized buildings] high enough to deter many firms from experimenting with the business . . . Nobody expects the prison industry to be competitive in the way that the fast-food industry is competitive. But there is some reason to fear that, instead of being competitive like the trash collection industry, it will be competitive like the nuclear submarine industry—which is to say, not at all. Thus, even if private management does result in greater efficiency, the cost savings may not be passed on to governmental clients. (Donahue 1989, p. 165)

The experience in NSW—in one area of privatisation at least— appeared to fit with Donahue's prediction. It was reported that there had been no interest from private companies in tendering for the running of prison industries nearly six months after the Department of Corrective Services advertised for such applications (*Sydney Morning Herald*, 5 October 1990).

Problems of Evaluation

If the privatisation of punishment is justified on the basis of cost-efficiency, then methods of measuring outcomes must be devised. A

major consideration, of course, is the *cost* of private services compared
with public services, assuming that the *quality* of service remains
unchanged. Yet this apparently simple indicator is not always simple to
use:

> Comparisons between the costs of public and private institutions
> are extremely difficult to evaluate. The division of labour
> between public and private agencies, and the differences in roles,
> level of training and range of functions, make direct comparisons
> difficult. Also, there may be critical functions which are not
> amenable to quantification (for example, of rehabilitation, or
> crime prevention). There are also problems of evaluating short-
> term and long-term costs as well as the hidden costs of monitoring
> private providers. (Matthews 1989, p. 4-5)

Meaningful comparisons can only be made if such comparisons are
based on the performances of private and public jails with similar
profiles of prisoners, levels of security operation and types of facilities.
If private prisons are predominantly low security operations, then their
performance must be compared with government-run low security
operations alone, not with public prisons as a whole. Sellers' (1989)
study mentioned earlier seems to have taken these factors into account,
but some factors may not be as obvious:

> Cost comparisons may be still more distorted if private prisons
> differ systematically in the characteristics of their inmate popula-
> tions. For example, the Marion Adjustment Center, run by the
> U.S. Corrections Corporation, costs Kentucky $25 per inmate
> per day, or roughly in the middle of the $18 to $31 dollar (sic)
> range of publicly run prisons. But inmates are screened for
> medical and behavioral problems before they are assigned to
> Marion. 'We don't want to overload them with problem cases,' the
> administrative director of the Kentucky corrections system has
> explained. 'We tend to send them the best in the bunch.' Similarly,
> the Immigration and Naturalization Service rates deportation-
> bound aliens by the probability of escape attempts, saves its own
> facilities for the tougher cases, and assigns the more docile aliens
> to the contract detention centers. Such practices ensure that the
> evidence yielded by such experiments will remain inconclusive.
> (Donhaue 1989, p. 158)

As pointed out by Durham (1988), a number of obstacles exist to the
effective assessment of privatisation. The novelty of the privatisation

experience means that evaluation will not be a straightforward or predictable task. Yet the expense of acquiring competent analysts and setting up sophisticated mechanisms for evaluation is not likely to be a high priority for private companies nor for governments anxious to reduce costs. Similarly, proper evaluation efforts may require a much longer time-frame than politicians or entrepreneurs would be willing to put up with. Finally, it may be difficult to obtain the necessary data for evaluation if a negative assessment could threaten future contracts or renewal of the present contract, or place employees at risk of losing their jobs.

Accountability

Opponents of privatisation of punishment often object in principle to the delegation of the state's power to punish to private, profit-seeking corporations:

> . . . questions concerning people's freedom should not be contracted out to the lowest bidder. In short, the private sector is more interested in doing well than in doing good. This idea was succinctly expressed recently by the director of program development of Triad America Corporation, a million-dollar Utah-based company that has been considering proposing a privately run county jail in Missoula, Montana: 'We'll hopefully make a buck at it. I'm not going to kid any of you and say we are in this for humanitarian reasons.' (Robbins 1987, p. 816)

Others are less concerned with the ideological or symbolic dimensions of privatisation than with the *ethical consequences* of privatising punishment. Obviously a structure of accountability must be established in conjunction with any privatisation initiative. Accountability in the use of public funds, the maintenance of discipline, the use of force, and other conditions of confinement, may be established through constitutional provisions, special legislation or specific contracts. An appropriate structure of accountability should include the setting of clear standards, as well as the establishment of monitoring and enforcement mechanisms.

In the US, the courts have ruled that private operators of detention centres are acting 'under the colour of state law' and are thus liable for any deprivation of life and liberty prohibited by the US constitution (Robbins 1987, pp. 818-822). Prisoners may also sue a private prison guard and sometimes even the corporation itself for excessive use of force (Spurlock 1987).

In Australia, as in Britain, prisoners are not protected by constitutional safeguards, and there is no provision for prisoners or members of the public to sue private prison operators over contractual breaches, since the contracts are between the operator and the government (Ryan and Ward 1989a; Zdenkowski 1989). In NSW, sections 31G and 31H of the *Prisons (Contract Management) Amendment Act 1990* provide for the Independent Commission Against Corruption and the Ombudsman to investigate corruption and complaints against private prisons and private prison employees. The effectiveness of these provisions in making private prison operators accountable remains to be seen.

Contractual agreements for private prisons present a challenge and an opportunity for establishing standards and spelling out rights and obligations. The issues to be addressed are numerous:

> Compared with payroll processing, parking maintenance, waste disposal, and other tasks that a city or state might entrust to a private firm, incarceration is a complicated undertaking. The contract regulating the relationship between the jurisdiction and the corrections firm is likely to be correspondingly lengthy, detailed and tricky to write . . . Who pays the medical bills when an inmate in a private prison contracts AIDS? Who is liable if he sues, claiming that he was wrongfully exposed to the disease while imprisoned? How are changes in incarceration costs to be shared if the number of convicts rises or falls sharply from year to year? If facilities are destroyed in a riot, who pays to rebuild them? (Donahue 1989, p. 166)

Robbins (1987, pp. 825-826) gives an even longer list of questions which must be unambiguously spelt out in statutes or in contracts. These include standards of operation, monitoring mechanisms, public access, responsibility for security and use of force, responsibility for disciplinary procedures, variation of fees, safeguard against low initial bid and subsequent raising of prices, safeguard against bankruptcy and manipulation of public opinion to further business (see also Thomas et al. 1988).

Sellers (1989) suggests that there should be an occupancy limit in the contract, since existing contracts had no provisions for applying sanctions for prison overcrowding. However, even with a comprehensive contract, if a company's performance is not up to standards, the state's ability to switch contractors is extremely limited. Private prison operators usually demand multiyear contracts or require compensation for cancellation (Donahue 1989, p. 165). The 'flexibility' that is often accorded the privatised system is in practice fairly constrained.

Profiting from the Fear of Crime

Finally, the assessment of privatisation must not lose sight of the aims of punishment in over-focusing on cost-efficiency. The profit motive provides no incentive to reduce overcrowding or to increase the use of non-custodial penalties. Instead, it encourages the filling of prison cells and the building of more prisons (Robbins 1987, p. 815). Donahue (1989) describes three major problems brought about by privatisation:

i. Obscuring Information about the Cost of Incarceration

In the US at least, privatisation of corrections started out in fact as a 'fiscal sleight-of-hand', a 'budgetary gimmickry'—a way around the taxpayers' refusal to pay for increased expenditure on corrections (Donahue 1989, p. 175; Robbins 1987, p. 816). This bypassing of democratic processes also serves to hide the real cost of imprisonment from the public, removing them from the difficult choices they need to make between spending more public money and escalating the level of punishment. There is, however, no reason why privatisation could not result in *better* access to information. Costing details and con-tractual conditions, if made available to the public, may provide higher visibility and scrutiny of both the performance of the private operators and that of the public correctional system. Such scrutiny may even result in applying pressure for the public prisons to be equally cost effective. Donahue argues, however, that since it is difficult to project accurately the long-term demand for prison capacity, privatisation may create a situation where the decision to commit public resources without public endorsement results in an inferior public choice:

> [U]nlike detention centers for aliens or juveniles, secure adult prisons require special structures with few alternative uses. If new prisons are built and the need for them subsequently drops, *somebody* gets stuck with the extra cell space. Corrections entrepreneurs — unless they are improbably short-sighted — will accept this risk only for a price, or will ensure that jurisdictions are effectively bound to renew what are technically short-run contracts. It seems unlikely that private firms have any special advantage in bearing the risk of overcapacity, and thus it is equally unlikely that a jurisdiction is better off contracting out for

peak capacity than it is building its own facilities. (Donahue 1989, p. 175)

ii.   Financial Temptation to Manipulate Prison Population

Where private operators are doing more than simply managing the physical plant and basic services of prisons, but are given the power to establish prison rules, discipline prisoners and make recommendations regarding the suitability of parole, an untested dimension of privatised justice arises. Since prison operators are paid according to the number of prisoners being institutionalised, a figure obviously affected by the length of sentence served, it is simple arithmetic to demonstrate that private jails could increase profit by refusing parole or taking away remissions (where they still apply).

> The chief of one private detention center, in an effort to reassure critics raising fears of guards' arbitrary authority, said, 'I review every disciplinary action. I'm the Supreme Court.' This should make us nervous. Will profit-seeking prisons multiply rules during slow periods in order to ensure enough infractions to deny parole to existing inmates until new convicts come to fill the cells? Not necessarily, perhaps not even probably, but it could happen. It is even conceivable that an unscrupulous corrections entre-preneur would perversely rig parole recommendations to release prisoners who are troublesome, dangerous, sickly, or otherwise expensive to detain, while holding on to the more profitable inmates . . . Public prison officials are at least free of any direct financial temptation to manipulate the prison population. (Donahue 1989, p. 176)

These problems, of course, can be remedied by changing the pro-cedures for parole recommendation and imposing a 'public' component to oversee disciplinary procedures, but this requires careful planning and additional costs.

iii.   Ability to Influence Officials and Shape Public Opinion

Constitutional protection can lessen the potential for violation of prisoners' rights in private prisons. Better contractual agreements can improve the chances of private jails providing the required quality of service. Statutes can impose a structure of accountability regarding corruption or excessive use of force. None of these mechanisms, however, protect the public against a subtler form of potential abuse: the shaping and manipulation of official and public opinion on crime and punishment. The danger of abuse is real and difficult to avoid:

> Since public enthusiasm for imprisoning criminals is demonstrably variable, might it not vary in response to publicity compaigns orchestrated and paid for by firms with a financial interest in locking more people up? 'With a 99-year lease, they're going to see to it that people are sentenced', warned an Illinois sheriff, 'They're going to lobby against alternative programs including probationary programs.' . . . the prospect of profit-motivated groups fanning the flames of popular vindictiveness is repulsive enough to make objectionable even a small chance that such lobbying would succeed. (Donahue 1989, pp. 176-177)

Studies of public attitudes to crime and punishment have consistently shown the powerful influence of stereotypes perpetuated by the media (Walker and Hough 1988). Politicians are also more than willing to take advantage of law-and-order panics for political gains. The existence of a well-funded and motivated force behind a push for tougher policies will pose additional problems in any effort to arrive at more rational and humane penal policies.

THEORETICAL ISSUES: PRIVATISATION VS DECARCERATION

With privatisation of prisons still a relatively new development in Australia and other countries, it remains to be seen how each country adopts privatisation strategies and what types of outcomes emerge. For those interested in understanding the causes and consequences of change in penal strategies, the move towards privatisation raises some fundamental issues about the punishment enterprise: 'At issue is the locus of the power to punish; the nature of the penal reform process; the relationship between the state and civil society regarding both punishment and reform; and the role of the political economy in both punishment and reform' (Ericson et al. 1987).

Recent works on the history of punishment have recognised the limitations of general theories and simplistic models which have proved inadequate for explaining changes in penal discourse and penal practice (see Garland 1990; Cohen 1985; Garland and Young 1983). The study of decarceration, for example, has moved from a narrow economistic model to models which allow for the interplay of fiscal, ideological and political factors in specific contexts in order to account for widely different forms and consequences of decarceration (Chan

1990). The development of privatisation policies in the penal sphere must likewise be studied as a complex phenomenon which displays similarities as well as peculiarities over time and geographical regions.

A number of relevant theoretical issues can be explored by comparing the movement to privatise with the earlier movement to deinstitutionalise punishment. In spite of their apparent origins in diametrically opposed ideological positions, the two movements share some striking similarities as well as interesting differences when analysed at the level of policy development.

The Rhetoric of Reform

First, there are many similarities in the way the two policy initiatives have typically been 'sold', i.e. the rhetoric of reform is very similar in each case. The focal point has been the failure of imprisonment as it exists: its cost and its ineffectiveness. Deinstitutionalisation provides the solution by reducing or limiting the use of imprisonment, especially for cases which could be dealt with by alternative means. Privatisation is less concerned with this reductive aim, but provides the solution by finding ways of rationalising costs. For correctional administrators constantly struggling to control the costs of punishment, both movements point in the same direction: some degree of control over state expenditure on corrections.

Both movements share an idealised vision of the minimal state: decarceration wants less state intervention in the control of deviants because the 'community' can do a better job; privatisation wants less state involvement in the running of the control apparatus because the private sector can do a better job. In both cases the critique is aimed at the inefficient, costly and uncaring public bureaucracy. The locus of punishment is seen to be more properly shifted back from the centralised state to civil society.

The rhetoric of deinstitutionalisation was pursuasive in the political climate of the '60s and '70s in the wake of civil rights movements and prison riots. In the political climate of the '80s and '90s, the appeal of deinstitutionalisation is extremely limited, but privatisation captures the imagination of policy makers because it accords with the predominant ethos of public sector economic rationalism, and public disillusionment with the welfare state. I have argued elsewhere (Chan 1991) that correctional authorities often capitalise on the popular reform rhetoric at a given time to introduce programs which solve their recurrent problems of implementing penal policy with little scope for the prediction of future demands and increase in resources. Privatisation is simply a product that has excellent chances of being sold in the present economic and political climate. As Donahue (1989, p. 5) observes in the US context, the rhetoric of privatisation is a valuable resource: '(b)y the second Reagan term, officials took to joking that virtually any proposal could become administration policy if it carried the label privatization'. Ironically, most of what has happened in the US in the privatisation of punishment has been in the care and custody of deinstitutionalised juveniles.

Contests of Legitimacy

A second area of theoretical interest is the way in which the legitimacy of the two policies is established or destroyed. I have noted (Chan 1990) that with penal policy, the contest of legitimacy can be especially fierce when certain powers are taken away from authorities or certain traditions are overthrown. Both deinstitutionalisation and privatisation appear to have the effect of weakening public sector unions, especially prison officers' unions. Consequently, opposition from organised labour would be anticipated. Yet, the contest of legitimacy has taken on quite different forms in the two movements.

Deinstitutionalisation of punishment has never been an easy policy to sell on humanitarian grounds and thus advocates often resorted to marketing it as a cost-saving innovation as well as one that involves the 'community'. Yet the introduction of community based alternatives to custodial sanctions has not been very successful in reducing the use of imprisonment or the cost of punishment. One of the most successful decarceration initiatives in NSW, the release on licence program, met an early demise when its legitimacy was successfully challenged (Chan 1992). Opponents of deinstitutionalisation see alternatives to imprisonment and especially the early release of prisoners as weakening the deterrent effect of the law, being soft on criminals and putting the community at risk. Justifications of decarceration on efficiency grounds simply fail to win over the hardline opponents.

Privatisation raises a different set of legitimacy problems. In the US the constitutionality of delegating the state's penal function to private corporations is still unclear (Robbins 1987). Members of the National Sheriffs Association opposed the policy strenuously (Donahue 1989, p. 155). The American Bar Association urged that prisons not be privatised until constitutional, statutory and contractual issues are resolved. The American Civil Liberties Union also opposed the concept of prisons for profit (Donahue 1989, p. 155). The powerful American Federation of State County and Municipal Employees, representing over 50,000 corrections employees, were also vehemently opposed to privatisation on a variety of grounds, including the deterioration of wages, benefits and training for correctional employees. In Britain opponents of privatisation came from some Labour members, the Prison Officers Association, and various prison reform groups (Ryan and Ward 1989b). In Australia, where the federal Labor government has been following a policy of privatisation and deregulation, privatisation of prisons has not been a controversial issue. The Queensland and NSW prison systems have had such adverse publicity about their poor conditions that, ironically, it has been the superior conditions of the private jail rather than its cost-efficiency that have won over its opponents. This has meant that there has been surprisingly little activity in contesting the legitimacy of privatisation (see, for example, *Sydney Morning Herald*, 14 December 1990).

The Discourse of Success

The concept of success in policy discourse is almost always imprecise and often deliberately left as such. When policy goals are vague or can be shifted, success can be likewise difficult to measure or ascertain. With deinstitutionalisation, the original goal of reducing the use of imprisonment has often been translated into the administrative goal of reducing the prison population (see Chan 1992). Success may be measured in terms of reduction in prison population, better allocation of correctional resources, or even the expansion of alternatives to imprisonment. Although a crucial measure of success must also be the policy's long-term acceptance by the community, proponents of deinstitutionalisation rarely see securing public support as one of the goals. Instead, reforms are typically 'smuggled' in quietly through the backdoor, sometimes even without consulting those involved in implementing the policy. The results of such efforts have often been counterproductive.

With privatisation, success can be measured in terms of cost-effectiveness for the government, and profitability for the private operators. Some operators also claim success in terms of lower recidivism and higher productivity among prisoners engaged in prison industries. Because of the necessity of drawing up contracts which specify standards of performance, obligations and safeguards against abuse, privatisation could well result in a more accountable operation than the publicly run prison system allows. Because it is a potentially controversial policy, privatisation of punishment has proceeded rather more slowly and under more public scrutiny than most other correctional initiatives. Despite the narrow economic justification of privatisation, there is room for a discourse of success which includes important aspects such as public support, accountability, monitoring and legal protection which proponents of deinstitutionalisation tend to ignore.

CONCLUSION

In this review I have focused on the more controversial aspects of privatising punishment, i.e. the privatisation of prisons, although a comprehensive analysis of privatisation of punishment should also examine the privatisation of non-prison services, such as the contracting out of probation and parole service, community service order supervision, and other counselling, treatment and supervision services (cf Ericson et al. 1987, pp. 364-365). It is also important to recognise the growing role of the non-profit or voluntary sector in the privatisation of punishment (see Gandy 1985, Scott 1990, John Howard Society 1986). I have, nevertheless, chosen to focus on the role of profit-seeking corporations in the running of private prisons, recognising the latter as a much more contentious policy which represents a significant departure from penal practices in the past hundred years.

Privatisation of prisons is still at a very early stage of development and there has been little systematic evaluation of these initiatives. As this paper points out, there are many unresolved issues to be addressed, including the problem of evaluation, the scope for efficiency savings, the effectiveness of structures of accountability and the potential for manipulating public opinion.

I have chosen to leave open the possibility that progressive changes may result from the privatisation of punishment, while insisting on a scrupulous examination of each privatisation initiative. To describe the privatisation of prisons in the 1990s as no different from the early colonial practice of assigning convicts to work for private masters (Shaw 1977) is to misunderstand the penal reform process and ignore the historical specificity of the present conditions. To dismiss private prisons as simply another product of the crisis-ridden welfare state and its culture of economic rationalism is to fail to recognise the duality of social and ideological structures (Giddens 1984): economic rationalism can be as much a *resource* as a constraint in penal reform. (See Chan (1992) for an elaboration of this argument.) Finally, to reject the privatisation of punishment on political or ideological grounds is to underestimate the role of legitimacy contests in influencing the outcomes of policy implementation. Specific instances of privatisation must be judged on their own merits and, if necessary, contested within their own institutional and legal contexts. This paper has offered some pointers for doing so.

References

Bray, R. 1990, _The Use of Custodial Sentences and Alternatives to Custody by NSW Magistrates_, Judicial Commission of New South Wales, Sydney.

Bray, R. and Chan, J. 1991, _Community Service Orders and Periodic Detention as Sentencing Options: A Survey of Judicial Officers in New South Wales_, Judicial Commission of New South Wales, Sydney.

Chan, J. 1990, 'Decarceration: A Case for Theory Building Through Empirical Research', _Law in Context_, vol. 8, no. 1, pp. 32-77.

— 1991, 'Decarceration and Imprisonment in New South Wales: A Historical Analysis of Early Release', _University of New South Wales Law Journal_, vol. 13, no. 2, pp. 393-416.

— 1992, _Doing Less Time: Penal Reform in Crisis_, Institute of Criminology, University of Sydney, Sydney.

Cody, W. J. M. and Bennett, A. D. 1987, 'The Privatization of Correctional Institutions: The Tennessee Experience', _Vanderbilt Law Review_, vol. 40, no. 4, pp. 829-850.

Cohen, S. 1985, _Visions of Social Control_, Polity Press, Cambridge.

Council of Europe 1990, _Privatisation of Crime Control_. Reports presented to the 18th Criminological Research Conference (1988), Council of Europe, Strasbourg.

Curran, D. 1988, 'Destructuring, Privatization, and the Promise of Juvenile Diversion: Compromising Community-Based Corrections', _Crime and Delinquency_, vol. 34, no. 4, pp. 363-378.

Dayton, M. 1989, 'The Case for Private Prisons', _The Bridge_, vol. 12, no. 3, p. 3.

Donahue, J. 1989, _The Privatisation Decision: Public Ends, Private Means_, Basic Books, New York.

Durham III, A.M. 1988, 'Evaluating Privatized Correctional Institutions: Obstacles to Effective Assessment', _Federal Probation_, vol. 52, no. 2, pp. 65-71.

Ericson, R. et al. 1987, 'Punishing for Profit: Reflections on the Revival of Privatization in Corrections', _Canadian Journal of Criminology_, vol. 29, no. 4, pp. 355-387.

Gandy, J. 1985, _Privatization of Correctional Services for Adults_, Ottawa.

Garland, D. 1990, _Punishment and Modern Society: A Study in Social Theory_, University of Chicago Press, Chicago.

Garland, D. and Young, P. (eds) 1983, _The Power to Punish: Contemporary Penality and Social Analysis_, Heinemann, London.

Giddens, A. 1984, _The Constitution of Society_, Polity, Cambridge.

Gorta, A. 1991, Impact of the Sentencing Act, 1989 on the NSW Prison Population, Paper presented at the Institute of Criminology Professional Seminar, The Sentencing Act 1989: A Review and Reappraisal, 8 August 1991, Sydney.

Harrison, e. W. and Gosse, M. G. 1986, 'Privatization: A Restraint Initiative', _Canadian Journal of Criminology_, vol. 28, pp. 185-193.

Jarratt, P. 1990, 'Not a warehouse for crims', _The Bulletin_, 3 July 1990.

John Howard Society of Ontario 1986, _Policy Position on Privatization and Commercialization of Correctional Services_, unpublished.

Kay, S. 1987, 'The Implications of Prison Privatization on the Conduct of Prisoner

Litigation Under 42 U.S.C. Section 1983', *Vanderbilt Law Review*, vol. 40, no. 4, pp. 867-888.

Kleinwort Benson Australia Ltd. 1989, *Investigation into Private Sector Involvement in the New South Wales Corrective Services System*. Stage 1 Report, Sydney.

Matthews, R. (ed) 1989, *Privatizing Criminal Justice*, Sage, London.

Maurer, M. 1991, *American Behind Bars*. The Sentencing Project.

Mawby, R. 1989, 'The Voluntary Sector's Role in a Mixed Economy of Criminal Justice' in *Privatizing Criminal Justice*, (ed) R. Matthews, Sage, London.

McAfee, W. 1987, 'Tennessee's Private Prison Act of 1986: An Historical Perspective With Special Attention to California's Experience', *Vanderbilt Law Review*, vol. 40, no. 4, pp. 851-866.

McKenzie, H. 1986, *The Privatization of Prisons*, Backgrounder BP145-E, Library of Parliament, Ottawa.

Mullen, J. et al. 1985, *The Privatization of Corrections*, U.S. Department of Justice, National Institute of Justice, Washington, D.C.

New South Wales (NSW) Department of Corrective Services 1990, *Annual Report 89/90*, Sydney.

Porter, R. G. 1990, 'The Privatisation of Prisons in the United States: A Policy That Britain Should Not Emulate', *The Howard Journal of Criminal Justice*, vol. 29, no. 2, pp. 65-81.

Robbins, I. 1987, 'Privatization of Corrections: Defining the Issues', *Vanderbilt Law Review*, vol. 40, no. 4, pp. 813-828.

Robert, P. P. 1989, 'The Privatization of Social Control' in *Crime and Criminal Policy in Europe: Proceedings of a European Colloquium 3-6 July 1988*, (ed) R Hood, Centre for Criminological Research, University of Oxford, Oxford.

Ryan, M. and Ward, T. 1989a, 'Privatization and the Penal System: Britain Misinterprets the American Experience', *Criminal Justice Review*, vol. 14, no. 1, pp. 1-12.

— 1989b, 'Privatization and Penal Politics' in *Privatizing Criminal Justice*, (ed) R. Matthews, Sage, London, pp. 52-73.

Savas, e. 1987, 'Privatization and Prisons', *Vanderbilt Law Review*, vol. 40, no. 4, pp. 889-902.

Scott, D. 1990, The Politics of Voluntary Sector Involvement in Community Corrections: Privatization in Ontario, M.A. Research Paper, Centre of Criminology, University of Toronto, Toronto (unpublished).

Sellers, M. P. 1989, 'Private and Public Prisons: A Comparison of Costs, Programs And Facilities', *International Journal of Offender Therapy and Comparative Criminology*, vol. 33, no. 3, pp. 241-256.

Shaw, A. G. L. 1977, *Convicts and the Colonies*, Melbourne University Press, Melbourne.

Spurlock, D. 1987, 'Liability of State Officials and Prison Corporations for Excessive Use of Force Against Inmates of Private Prisons', *Vanderbilt Law Review*, vol. 40, no. 4, pp. 983-1021.

Sydney Morning Herald, 'Prison Inc appeal falls on deaf ears', 5 October 1990 .

— 'A prison where time is money', 14 December 1990.

—— 'US-style system for first private jail', 26 June 1991.

Taylor, M. and Pease, K. 1989, 'Private Prisons and Penal Purpose' in *Privatizing Criminal Justice*, (ed) R. Matthews, Sage, London, pp. 178-194.

Thomas, C., Lanza-Kaduce, L., Hanson, L. and Duffy, K. 1988, *The Privatization of American Corrections: An Assessment of its Legal Implications*, Centre for Studies in Criminology and Law, University of Florida, Florida.

Walker, N. and Hough, M. (eds) 1988, *Public Attitudes to Sentencing*, Gower, Aldershot.

Weiss, R. 1989, 'Private Prisons and the State' in *Privatizing Criminal Justice*, (ed) R. Matthews, Sage, London, pp. 24-51.

Zdenkowski, G. 1989, 'Privatising Punishment', *The Bulletin*, 15 August 1989.

* A version of this paper appears in Australian Journal of Social Issues, vol. 27, no. 4, November, 1992, pp. 223-247. I would like to thank Michael Johnson for his support for this research and Peter Saunders for comments on the initial draft of this paper. I am also grateful for funding support from the Faculty of Arts and Social Sciences, University of New South Wales.

3

Models of accountability for the contract management of prisons

Richard Harding*

Abstract: The pragmatic justification for permitting some degree of contract management of prisons by the private sector lies in the historically entrenched negativism of the publicly operated custodial environment. From the point of view both of prisoners and of the public interest in getting value for money out of the penal system, private sector contract management could stimulate beneficial change across the whole system. To believe that this may happen simply through internal renewal of the public system is to allow hope to triumph over experience. That being so, accountability becomes the key issue. There are two main elements to this: contractor-focused *elements and* public interest *elements.*

The models of accountability so far encountered in the United Kingdom, the United States and Australasia have been contractor-focused. This has arisen out of the fact that the public authorities have been responsible for deciding to put a prison out to contract management so that, in effect, the contract managers have become agents to carry out a function which would otherwise have been carried out by the public authorities as principal. Such an arrangement is ripe for capture — *a situation where, over time, 'regulators come to be more concerned to serve the interests of the industry with which they are in regular contact than the more remote and abstract public interest'. The paper illustrates in detail aspects of capture.*

*This danger is likewise prominent with the public interest elements of account-
ability. The main issues under this head come down to ensuring that the overall
performance of the whole, or dual-element, system is enhanced by the decision to
permit private sector involvement, so that for example the initial contract is properly
drawn up in terms of measurable outputs, there is proper monitoring and
evaluation, and cross-fertilisation is productive. None of the existing or officially
proposed models of accountability quite meets the suggested needs or completely
avoids the dangers of capture. Aspects of the British system approach desirable
standards, however.*

*The chapter concludes by suggesting a model which would facilitate productive
competition and interaction between the parts of the dual system, avoid capture, and
achieve a flexibility across the whole system. Contract management by the private
sector poses real hazards. The suggested model of accountability provides a
framework within which the performance not only of the newly emerging private
sector but also the traditional public sector may be fundamentally improved, in the
interest of prisoners and of effective penal practice.*

In the debate about contract management of prisons, it is crucial to
clarify where one is coming from.[1] My own starting-point is concern
about the historically entrenched negativism of the custodial environment and the impoverishment of the services which have been delivered
in that environment. With this is coupled a belief that we can still do a
lot less badly than has so far been the case in making prisons places
where not only can deterioration be forestalled (Cross 1971) but also
opportunity for change may actually be facilitated (Morris 1974).
These modest objectives should be attainable at reasonable cost to the
community.

In most English-speaking western nations, a plethora of crises have
highlighted the moral and managerial bankruptcy of significant
components of the publicly-operated prison system: for example, in the
US, Attica (Weiss 1991) and Santa Fe (Dinitz 1981); in Britain, the
April 1986 riots (HM Inspector of Prisons 1987) and the violence at
Strangeways (Woolf 1991); and in Australia the near-collapse of the
New South Wales prison system (Nagle 1978), the 1987 fire and deaths
at Pentridge Prison, Victoria (Hallenstein 1989), the 1988 riots at
Fremantle Prison (McGivern 1988), and generally the Final Report of
the Royal Commission into Aboriginal Deaths in Custody (Johnston
1991). Less dramatically, those of us who regularly visit prisons do not
need to be reminded of the stultifying restrictions which strip inmates
of their individuality, self-esteem and optimism, contributing to
excessively high return-to-prison rates (Broadhurst and Maller 1990).
These repetitive failures have occurred against a background of

steadily rising costs of imprisonment — both recurrent and capital, individual and systemic — to the point where they are now a legitimate source of community and political frustration and puzzlement.

Acknowledging the validity of such concerns, Shaw (1989), an opponent of privatisation, has said: 'I think, however, the case against privatisation would be that much stronger *if there were not substantial evidence that the public system is either squalid or ludicrously wasteful of resources. The opponents of privatisation have to be careful not to be defenders of public squalor.*' (Emphasis supplied) In the context of Australian imprisonment (Harding 1992) put the flip-side of Shaw's point: 'Properly scrutinised and regularly evaluated, private prisons can stimulate improvement across the whole of Australia's prison system — a system which during its first two centuries' wholly public existence has been no less squalid, oppressive, inequitable, degenerate and demoralising than the English system upon which it was modelled.'

In other words, at this moment in the history of western penology, the main question about contract management is not whether it should be tried in relation to prisons but to what extent it should take place, in relation to which types of custodial regime, whether for new or also existing institutions, on what costing basis, and so on. All such questions are subject to a single over-arching issue: how best to avoid the hazards which such a form of service delivery potentially opens up. *Accountability thus becomes the crucial issue.*

THE ELEMENTS OF ACCOUNTABILITY

If accountability is to be effective, there seem to be at least six matters which need to be carefully scrutinised and in relation to which control mechanisms may be required. They are:

- the continuing applicability of the standard accountability mechanisms which apply in the public prison system — e.g. official visitors' schemes, ombudsman access, parliamentary scrutiny, FOI where applicable, right to sue for actionable breaches, due process in relation to disciplinary proceedings, and so on;
- ensuring that the contractor's role is limited to administering punishment, not allocating it — a concern which spills over into filtering disciplinary proceedings, parole decisions, and key aspects of sentence planning away from the contractor's control;
- specific monitoring of performance under the terms of the management contract — a notion which in turn hinges on the scope and detail of contractual arrangements;

- appointment of suitable staff;
- financial accountability so as to ensure that services contracted for are actually provided; and
- political accountability so as to ensure that the contractor remains merely a provider of services, and does not become a lobbyist for the expansion of those services by way of more oppressive incarceration policies or the like.

These elements of accountability are all *contractor-focused*. To this point, that has been the conventional wisdom — it is the contractor who must be conscientiously scrutinised if non-government sector involvement in prisons is to be productive. However, the emerging experience, particularly in Australia and Britain, strongly suggests that *it is no less important to find ways to make the public system accountable for the proper functioning, or accountability, of non-government contractors*. In the area of contract management, then, we have to confront that age-old question: *Quis custodiet ipsos custodes?*

The way this problem arises is as follows. Conceptually, the late 20th century examples of contract management of prisons have involved the private contractor acting as *agent for the public system authorities* in the discharge of their statutory responsibilities. The Commission or department running the public system thus becomes also a regulatory body; it is both principal and supervisor. That is the sort of arrangement whereby the regulatory authority is ripe for what literature pertaining to business regulation and organisational theory describes as *capture*. The skeletal model is set out in Figure 1.

This concept describes a situation where, over time, 'regulators come to be more concerned to serve the interests of the industry with which they are in regular contact than the more remote and abstract public interest' (Grabosky and Braithwaite 1986, p. 198). Contract management of prisons is not an archetypal capture situation; but, as will be explained in more detail later, the particular process which seems to be occurring certainly fits into this broad theoretical structure.

The 'remote and abstract public interest' matters which are of relevance in this context include the following:

- ensuring that the initial contract suitably reflects modern penological needs and incorporates measurable performance criteria;
- ensuring that suitable mechanisms for monitoring contract performance are put in place and are actually utilised, not only during the contract period but also as contract renewal decisions have to be made;

Figure 1

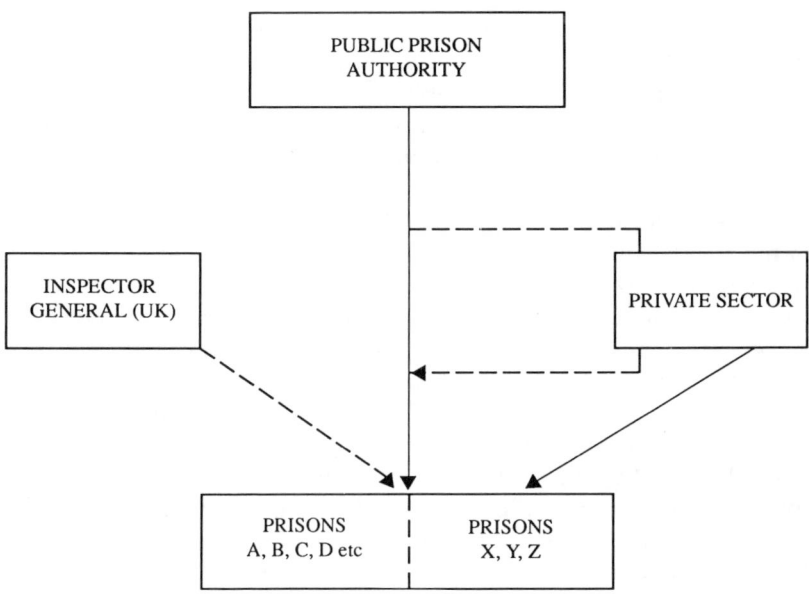

- ensuring that the community receives value for money as a result of the contractual arrangements, though this is not necessarily the same as saying that there should invariably be a lower level of expenditure;
- ensuring that the public system is stimulated and gingered up by the experience of the privately managed part of the system, a requirement which in turn involves addressing such matters as the question of the mix of the two aspects of the system, the development of innovative ideas and approaches, the means for achieving cross-fertilisation between the two aspects of the system, and the role of staff; and
- generally, that a practice/evaluation/modification loop is created and functions effectively across the whole organisation.

At this early stage in the development of the contract management of prisons, it is already apparent that there are some significant hiatuses in accountability, with regard both to contractor-focused standards and also to remote and abstract public interest matters. This observation will be illustrated and alternative models for accountability explored.

ACCOUNTABILITY IN PRACTICE

Standard public system mechanisms

The basic statutory and administrative structures in each of the principal jurisdictions where contract management of prisons has already occurred proceed on the basis that the normal account-ability structures within the public system remain in place.[2] Cases apparently to the contrary may turn out merely to be a replication within the private system of previously concealed defects in that public system.

An example identified by Moyle (1992) was the somewhat pre-emptory procedural disposition of a disciplinary charge against a prisoner in Borallon Prison, Queensland, resulting in seven days' solitary confinement.[3] Further probing, however, revealed that *all* such charges are dealt with in ways where due process is not fully met; the problem was one of legal regimes within Queensland prisons generally, rather than a specific function of the way a prison under contract management was run (Harding 1992).

McDonald (1992, pp. 409-10) has suggested that in the US system the normal line of accountability may be fragmented. This is particularly at the local jail level, where the elected sheriff is often responsible for day-to-day management whilst county officials bear the political responsibility. He argues that, 'in such circumstances, contracting may increase a county board's control of a jail' and, indeed, that 'in some cases contracting has been chosen by county commissioners for this explicit purpose'.

With regard to parliamentary scrutiny, Vinson and Baldry (1993) have shown, in the context of NSW (Australia) and the privately managed prison at Junee, that it has not afforded anything in the way of safeguards. There have only been two parliamentary questions in five years, each of them contemptuously dismissed by the responsible Minister. Unfortunately, it must also be said that the general level of parliamentary interest in the conditions of prisoners, as opposed to the supposed safety of the public if something goes awry, is likewise lamentably low.

In summary, accountability is no worse and may exceptionally be a little better in this area than in relation to the public part of the system.

The administration of punishment, not its allocation

At the heart of many fervent objections to contract management as such is the view (Radzinowicz 1988) that 'in a democracy grounded on the rule of law and public accountability, the enforcement of penal legislation . . . should be the undiluted responsibility of the State'. Shaw (1992, p. 32) comments: 'Surely this is the crux of the matter. Privatising prisons is not like any other privatisation. The question of who runs the prisons is on an entirely different scale from that of who runs the telephone service or empties your dustbins.'

This is stirring stuff. However, the familiar distinction between *allocating* punishment to citizens for breach of the generally applicable law (the archetypal, non-delegatable, duty of the state) and *administering* that punishment is conceptually clear-cut. Historically, it may not always have been strictly maintained (Moyle 1993, pp. 232-33). Nevertheless, delegated administration of criminal punishment, as well as other involuntary forms of institutionalisation (McDonald 1992, pp. 362-3), is commonplace. As long as there are effective procedures in place to ensure that administration does not imperceptibly merge into allocation, that the delegate in other words does not exceed its authorisation, it is difficult to accept that there is a fundamental objection of principle.

There are two areas where the distinction may become blurred and which should, accordingly, be subject to particular scrutiny. These are: release decisions, such as parole or work release; and disciplinary decisions, which may either extend the length of incarceration or cause it to be more onerous than normal. Related to these is the issue of sentence planning.

In Britain the importance of imposing disciplinary sanctions in contract managed prisons directly by and in the name of the state has been recognised and enshrined in the empowering legislation. Section 85 of the Criminal Justice Act 1991 provides that the 'director' (the name given to the private contractor's prison governor) shall not:

> (a)   inquire into a disciplinary charge laid against a prisoner, conduct the hearing of such a charge or make, remit or mitigate an award in respect of such a charge; or
> (b)   except in cases of urgency, order the removal of a prisoner from association with other prisoners, the temporary confinement of a prisoner in a special cell or the application to a prisoner of any other special control or restraint.

All such functions are the responsibility of the 'controller', who is the on-site representative of the public system authorities.[4]

In practice, this function has been a significant one. At the time of the inspection of The Wolds by HM Inspector General of Prisons (Tumim 1993, pp. 59-60), 'adjudications' by the controller had been running consistently at about 20 a week. This is higher than would be the case at a comparable publicly managed prison, an observation which was likewise the case at Blakenhurst Prison in late September 1993 (author's own visit and discussions). Tumim (1993, pp. 59) unambiguously rejected calls for adjudications to be carried out by the director as part of his responsibility for controlling inmate behaviour, simply stating: 'We preferred the safeguards offered within the present arrangements'.

In both Australia and the US, the disciplinary function resides with the private operator and its staff. Whilst, technically, sanctions for misconduct within prisons may not be allocation of punishment *for crimes against the criminal law*, nevertheless they are punishments which can only be imposed because of a person's status as one who has breached that criminal law and been sentenced to imprisonment in the first place. The distinction between allocation and administration of punishment is certainly blurred, even though not flagrantly breached. The British position is preferable. But the issue seems not even to have been perceived in Australia or the US by those whose responsibility it is to let contracts for the private management of prisons.

In this context, it is not altogether surprising that, in Queensland, the issue of sentence planning has also been blurred. The Arthur Gorrie Correctional Centre in Brisbane is a privately managed prison, yet it is the one at which most prisoners are classified and their sentence plans worked out. Their subsequent progress through the system — to lower security ratings, greater privileges, access to programs, half-way or pre-release houses, and so on — is significantly affected by that first contact. In an abstract sense, wherever they are housed and whatever their security or privilege status, they are still prisoners serving punishments allocated by the state; sentence planning does not contravene that principle. However, there is a world of practical difference between the various ends of the custodial continuum and thus the nature of the punishment. Once more, the line between the allocation of punishment and administration is a fuzzy one.

It was probably an error, philosophically and strategically, to entrust private prison managers with the key task which drives the subsequent experiences of prisoners within the prison system. The public prison authorities thereby tend to lose direct control not just of a particular inmate in relation to a particular prison but also of the engine-room of the whole system. It really does seem to be missing the point to state, as does the Deputy Director of the Queensland Corrective Services Commission (Macionis, 1992), that:

This contract breaks significant new ground by contracting the management of the reception function to the private sector. As the Commission's main reception centre, the Arthur Gorrie Correctional Centre performs the initial assessment and classification of offenders and is, thus, *a key part of the Commission's sentence management process*. (Emphasis supplied)

In summary, the experience of contract management to date does suggest that only in Britain has there been sufficient sensitivity to that element of accountability concerned with ensuring that only the administration of punishment, and not its allocation, is devolved to non-government prison operators.

Monitoring
Contract specification
The Australian and British approaches emphasise that the performance of contract managers should be monitored. Effective oversight depends, firstly, on the standards and objectives of the contract being clearly specified. Privatisation compels one to define what one hopes to achieve within the prison system — something which has often been obfuscated or self-contradictory within public systems. In the language of economics, the prison system must become *output-based*, whereas the traditional state model has tended to be overwhelmingly *input-based*.

There has been a degree of disparity between jurisdictions as to how detailed the contracts have been. The NSW Corrective Services Commission is statutorily required, as part of the contract-letting process, to prepare a minimum standards document for incorporation into the contract: *Prisons (Contract Management) Act 1990*, s. 31B (2)(b). However, that document was, in the Commission's only contract, non-prescriptive — along the lines of 'The contractor shall provide educational programs of an appropriate standard', etc. The expectation was that detailed standards could then be worked out on the ground cooperatively with the contractors. This 'suck-it-and-see' approach has led to problems in the early stages.[5] The programs provided were not fully compatible with those provided in the remainder of the prison system, creating unnecessary complexities for transfer in or out of Junee. Similar difficulties were encountered with the provision of industrial programs.

The Queensland Corrective Services Commission (QCSC) has been much more prescriptive. Unfortunately, it has persisted with its attitude that the contract is 'commercial-in-confidence' so that an essential element of accountability—general public scrutiny and evaluation—is missing. Of course, even if the specifications are exemplary, the very fact of secrecy undermines public confidence. However, it is known, for example, that 24 hour a day medical services are required within the institutions, and they are in fact provided—something virtually unheard of in the public part of the system. Similarly, educational and work opportunities have been spelled out with precision. The feel within at least one of the privately managed prisons—Borallon—is certainly that of a sense of purpose, and experienced inmates are still making applications to be put on the wait-list to be transferred there (Harding 1992).

The British contracts are likewise very detailed and specific. An important structural matter is that their terms are set and negotiated not by the public prison authorities (now known as the Prison Service Agency) but by a separate body, the Custodial Contracts Unit (formerly the Remand Contracts Unit). Even before this unit was made structurally distinct from the public prison authorities, it worked to a separate line of accountability within the Home Office.[6] If, inevitably, its cultural expectations as to what would be appropriate and might be achievable were coloured by knowledge of the workings of the public system, nevertheless the notion of having an agency not involved in line responsibility setting contractual terms is a theoretically preferable one.

Harding has argued that British contracts are carefully focused and strong on detail. Performance criteria are spelled out satisfactorily. For all that, Tumim was not entirely happy. Primarily, this was because too much attention had been focused upon the means rather than the ends. He states: 'The agreement does not require the contractors to help the inmates to lead useful lives. The authors of the Agreement may have been unduly influenced by the belief that, as you cannot make the unconvicted work, you cannot be expected to encourage them into activity. The result is lethargy' (Tumim 1993, p. 1). He goes on strongly to criticise the impact which this has had on the prison regime generally.

Tumim's point that penological objectives are in danger of being lost in the minutiae of administrative details contained in management contracts is given point by the Operational Audit carried out by officials of the QCSC as a prerequisite to renewal of CCA's Borallon contract. This document—not generally available but made available to the author by the Commission itself—is, in comparison to Tumim's report on The Wolds, not a cogent one. A team of six went through the prison with their individual check-lists—personnel training, physical security and control, leave of absence, prisoner trust accounts, library, religion, fire safety, and so on — before reporting back to head office, where their individual reports were in effect stapled together. It is thus a welter of unsynthesised detail. At no point does the document address the question: Is Borallon fulfilling the penological objectives of the Commission? One is left with no feeling whatever for whether Borallon is properly focused on outputs and, if so, what those outputs are. The tone is still that of traditional input-based prison management; the wood cannot be seen for the trees.

That is not necessarily to say that the QCSC has actually lost sight of those penological objectives. In fact, other evidence (Harding 1992) suggests that these have been carefully thought through, at least at the level of senior management. However, no outsider and no newcomer to the system could possibly infer this from the scrappy format of the Operational Audit, standing in stark contrast to the approach found in Tumim's report on The Wolds.

In summary, whilst contract-specification skills are certainly improving, there is still not sufficient focus on penological objectives which the contractor should seek to attain.

The monitoring process

In Britain and NSW, the monitoring process is established by statute; in Queensland it is simply an aspect of the contractual arrangements.

Queensland commenced the monitoring process in relation to Borallon with great gusto — a daily presence of the QCSC monitor. The author was informed that the monitor was available to hear prisoner complaints on a regular basis, particularly where any question of disciplinary sanctions was involved. For all that, Moyle (1992, p. 118) has documented what seems to have been a degree of complacency creeping in: 'Originally we were supposed to have an on-site monitor five days per week, but that isn't how it has worked out . . . There have been very few incidents of significance that have occurred here [Borallon].' Moyle estimated that time spent on performance monitoring, as opposed to signing forms and dealing with administrative minutiae, could be as little as one hour per week.

The QCSC's own view is articulated by Macionis (1992):

> [Whilst] it is desirable for the operator to operate on-site during the crucial (set-up) phase . . . as operations mature the need for constant on-site supervision reduces. In the Queensland experience this has been found to be after about 12 months operation, at which time the QCSC has found it is able to move to

a process in which the contractor is formally evaluated for performance against the contract by means of periodic and/or ad hoc formal audits.

In NSW, where the position of the monitor is a statutory office under the Public Sector Management Act (with the presumed intent of imposing a degree of independence from the Commission itself), the title of the appointee was informally changed by the Commission to that of 'liaison officer'. It was evidently considered that this more accurately reflected the role that person should play or at any rate was actually playing during the early establishment period (Harding, 1993; Vinson and Baldry, 1993). Within a year the on-site activities of that office-holder have tailed off, to the point of no more than one week's presence per month (personal communication, Ms Lee Downes, February 1994).

In Britain, Tumim (1993, pp. 2, 31) identified some 'uncertainty about the [respective] roles of Director and Controller' at The Wolds. He felt in particular that there was a potential problem over the status of the controller, who was less experienced and of a lower equivalent grade than the director. Harding observed on a visit to Blakenhurst Prison — the second British one to be placed under contract — that the controller was prepared to let the operators develop their on-site protocols at their own pace, with a view to identifying in the light of these protocols the appropriate control points which should be monitored. Pragmatic and sensible as this is from one perspective, it is arguably from the point of view of accountability not the optimum arrangement.

In summary, the monitor/controller mechanism is already showing signs of having been captured by the contract managers, or, more accurately, *surrendered by the contract-granting authorities*. This is so whether the position is contractually secured or statutorily specified, indicating that this factor is possibly endemic to the nature of the task.

Staffing

A key element of a satisfactory system is suitable staff. Arrangements so far made are on a continuum from nil direct control to ongoing potential power of dismissal by the public authority.

The US position is, broadly speaking, that it is the contractor's responsibility to provide suitable staff and to discharge unsuitable staff, and that the public authority's legitimate interest goes no further than overall contract performance. It is classically output-based, not concerned with any inputs such as screening or training but simply with the end-product.

Queensland goes further, having some stake in inputs as well as outputs. By statute, the Commission possesses the power of veto over the contractor's choice of a 'general manager' to run the prison, and in a parallel way it also may authorise (and thus also refuse to authorise) persons as custodial officers.[7] What is not clear is whether the Commission can withdraw authorisation, once granted, though there is certainly a respectable argument particularly with regard to a general manager that it could do so, at least indirectly (Moyle 1993, p. 237).

In NSW, the model selected is that of prior authorisation by the Commission of both the governor and custodial staff *and* potential withdrawal of that authorisation — but only after 'affording the person concerned a reasonable opportunity to be heard'.[8] Under standard administrative law principles, this provision opens up any such decision to a substantial degree of judicial supervision, thus inhibiting somewhat the power of the Commission itself.

In Britain, there is a power of prior veto over all levels of custodial staff, including the director, as well as a power of revocation at any time if it appears to the Home Secretary that he/she 'is not a fit and proper person' to perform the duties.[9]

The big issue that has arisen in Australia is that of the 'cultural appropriateness' of general managers/governors. As each of the currently active private contractors are derivatives of the two big American players — Corrections Corporation of America and the Wackenhut Corporation — it was predictable that American managers might be brought in to head up the private prisons. This in fact happened in the two prisons with which Wackenhut is associated, Arthur Gorrie and Junee. This should be considered in the context that *prisons are cultural organisms*; thus an American prison or a French prison is each a different cultural organism from an Australian one (Harding 1993).

To illustrate: in America there is the particular issue of how to run effectively and equitably a prison whose population includes many Afro-Americans and Hispanics; in France, north Africans (often Muslims) and blacks; in Australia, above all, Aboriginal people. The deliberations and findings of the Royal Commission into Aboriginal Deaths in Custody (Johnston, 1991) serve to highlight the distinctive cultural issues posed by this part of the prison population. That is not to say, of course, that the excessive representation of Aboriginal people in a typical Australian prison is the only manifestation of a distinct culture; it is simply the most vivid.

In this context, then, one should be wary of importing different cultures; to say this is not to be xenophobic but realistic. This is particularly so where the parent company has been involved on its home front in well-documented problems and failures (MacArthur 1992; Vinson and Baldry 1993). Yet in both Queensland and NSW, ACM Ltd. — the company associated with the Wackenhut Corporation — was permitted to bring in long-term American prison superintendents.

The Commissioner in NSW explained this in terms of 'importing the best in American correctional practice' (personal interview, March 1993) and thus far, it must be said, there are no visible signs of significant cultural conflict. In Queensland, however, there were immediate problems. These included two suicides (one of them allegedly after prisoners had taunted the inmate continually to kill himself whilst custodial officers stood by laughing, the other of a prisoner who was in the process of sueing prison authorities after allegedly being raped twice within the prison) and a riot involving about 30 prisoners. This riot was followed by the laying of charges of 'mutiny' under the Prisons Act — an overkill response which was culturally quite alien to the Australian context. In March 1993, Wackenhut sent the imported general manager back to California to run another of their institutions (Hansen 1993).

The most revealing aspect of this decision was the reaction of the public prison authority or regulator. All new institutions had 'teething problems' and the departure of the manager was 'a matter for his private employers', said the head of the Queensland Corrective Services Commission. Capture, or surrender as I have previously characterised it, had evidently occurred without a struggle or a whimper. A matter of absolutely central concern to the prison system as a whole — managerial performance within a major prison — was no longer perceived as something about which the public authorities should take a proactive role.

The Australian and British systems maintain a considerable degree of input into staff training. The common element is that the custodial officers must have undergone a course approved by the public authorities. In NSW, the private contractor sub-contracted the training to the Corrective Services Commission's own training academy; in both Queensland and Britain the contractor made alternative arrangements drawing upon their own expertise or that of associated groups. There has developed quite a strong policy in all jurisdictions of not recruiting, as base-grade uniformed staff persons with previous experience in the public system.

In summary, the statutory and/or contractual arrangements in Britain and Australia provide ready mechanisms for close regulation of both senior and custodial staff. There is some early evidence that the public authorities may not sufficiently appreciate what a key control-point this is, so that already there has been some slippage.

Financial accountability

The primary control-point is the contract negotiation itself. If the performance standards are properly articulated, if there are efficient costing mechanisms within the public prison system so that comparative costs are ascertainable, then the contract price should be a fair one. As long as the services contracted for are actually supplied (cf. Tumim 1993, pp. 115-6; Queensland Public Sector Management Commission 1993, pp. 124), then it really should be of no consequence whether the contractor is making a profit or a loss.

There is some suggestion that some contractors may have 'lowballed' their bids to get their foot in the door, intending to re-negotiate at an opportune moment (McDonald 1992, pp. 398). There is also clear evidence that the government may find that the job it wants done can be done more cheaply by the public sector, once the employees realise that they must accommodate their work practices to the fact that their monopoly can readily be broken. This was the case in the Northern Territory of Australia (Harding 1992) and subsequently also in Western Australia.

The question whether the private sector is more or less expensive is not as simple to resolve as it might sound (McDonald 1992, pp. 398-404). There are hidden public sector overheads in running the private system, and difficulties as to whether one is comparing like with like. However, comparative cost-effectiveness is not my present concern, merely the question of accountability. Provided the contract has been sensibly negotiated, financial accountability is not so much a separate head as an aspect of monitoring. At this stage, it appears to pose no significant or insuperable problems.

Political accountability

It has been strongly argued that private sector prison managers have a vested interest in high incarceration rates. They will 'be in a position to publish lurid descriptions of violence in prisons, reinforcing a perceived need for increased facilities. This will feed the imagination of the media, creating an environment of fear in the community. Such tactics will ensure that beds are full' (George 1989). Such fears seem far-fetched. In the British and Australian contexts, contract prices are reached on the basis of 100 per cent occupancy; thus, any arguable benefit to the contractor and detriment to the public authority in failure to meet that target is not tied in with incarceration policies in the broad but simply reflects poor management of the contract (Queensland Public Sector Management Commission 1993, pp. 121-25).

A somewhat more cogent argument is that of Lilly and Knepper (1993, p. 47), who see the coalescence of what they call a 'corrections-commercial complex'. This consists of i. private organisations devoted to profiting from imprisonment, ii. government agencies anxious to maintain their continued existence, and iii. professional organisations which sew together an otherwise fragmented group into a powerful alliance. This is not so much capture as everyone voluntarily getting into bed together.

This analysis seems to take insufficient account of other powerful factors. One is that there is a fourth player — government. All around the world there is governmental concern at the vast and burgeoning costs of imprisonment. Whilst privatisation has been to some extent a response to this concern, no governments imagine that it is a permanent solution. Ultimately, there is only one way to bring costs back under control — and that is *to reduce imprisonment levels*. The marginal savings which may flow from privatisation are a drop in the bucket, no more.

Of course, this understanding has not been matched by performance in much of the western world. For the present, prison populations continue to increase. There is already a huge amount of potential 'take-up' for the private sector, not just with existing or expanding populations needing new prisons but also with replacement of decaying stock. McDonald (1992, p. 409) states: 'With the private sector housing so small a proportion of the total number of prisoners behind bars, and with other forces pressing prison populations upwards, it is hard to see a need for private prison providers to lobby for a still more expansive use of imprisonment.'

In summary, it seems unlikely that private operators can through lobbying have a significant effect on incarceration policies. These are driven by other powerful factors, not least a growing recognition that prison populations must be levelled off and preferably reduced if the financial and human costs are to remain tolerable.

THE PUBLIC INTEREST AND ACCOUNTABILITY

The terms of the initial contract

Clearly, the dilemma has been that the public authority is well placed to know what can realistically be written into the initial contract both as to ends (correctional objectives) and as to means (performance standards). It is equally evident that there is a tendency to take the current public system as a benchmark, with expectations of only gradual accretions or improvements. Tumim has documented this with regard to the British system. In NSW, the non-prescriptive terms of the contract were arguably too soft. In Queensland, the very act of secrecy as to precise performance standards has been a weakness.

The optimum system would inject an external element into the contract negotiations, i.e. external to those who continue to operate the public system. The British model, with a specialist Custodial Contracts Unit working to a different line of accountability, comes nearest to this. None of the antipodean systems have quite grasped this point. In Victoria, which has sought tenders for the financing, design, construction and management of three new prisons, the contract process is to be handled by a 'regulator'.[10] This position will be set up administratively within the Ministry of Justice, the umbrella Ministry within which the Corrections Office itself falls. However, the 'regulator' will possess no statutory independence.

In New Zealand, where three new prisons are also expected to be financed, designed, constructed and managed by the private sector, a not dissimilar arrangement will be made.[11] The Deputy Secretary of Justice, who has overall responsibility for the running of the public prison system, will also have responsibility for the arrangements with private sector operators.[12]

Perhaps subconsciously there has been some concern that contract management does not expose too vividly the previous shortcomings of the public system. On the other hand, it must not be forgotten that the public and private institutions must still constitute a *single or unified system*, where for example prisoners can be moved from one institution to another without undue disruption to educational and other programs, changes in disciplinary arrangements, and so on.[13] In this context, using existing standards as a benchmark is more defensible.

On balance, the British system seems preferable. Indeed, it could be strengthened by statutory recognition of the role of the Custodial Contracts Unit.

Monitoring

This should be provided for by statute, rather than contractually or administratively. Britain and NSW have adopted the statutory model, and New Zealand will do so. Queensland has treated monitoring arrangements simply as a contractual provision, though contract managed institutions are subject to the general rules as to periodic audit by the Commission. Victoria will likewise deal with this issue contractually/administratively by use of the 'regulator' device mentioned above.

As already described, there appears to have been a degree of 'capture' of the monitoring arrangements, in some cases amounting to almost a painless surrender. This appears to be endemic to the task. The best available safeguard is for the monitor to be truly independent and at arm's length from the system. The only example discovered so far is that of the British Inspector General of Prisons — a statutory office-holder with his own staff and budget and direct access to Parliament where his reports are tabled.

Value for money

In the US, some of the early privatisation arrangements reflected the need for cash-strapped governments to bypass state bond-raising formalities necessary to raise capital to construct new prisons. This was in turn a response to the spate of court-ordered caps on overcrowded prison populations, orders which ran headlong into the burgeoning numbers of the 1980s (McDonald 1990, p. 102).

Initially that has not been a factor in the antipodes, where no such capital-raising formalities inhibit governments and where courts cannot control overcrowding. The early motivation seemed more related to recurrent costs, as for example in Queensland where ACM's bid to run the Arthur Gorrie prison came in at about 65 per cent of the costs the public system estimated (Harding 1992). However, in New Zealand, Victoria and NSW — where finance, design, construct and manage contracts are starting to be the norm — the need to reduce up-front state outlays has now clearly emerged as a factor in contract management. Related to this is the fact that governments are generally inefficient negotiators with the construction industry, which has become adept at building in cost over-runs; it has been calculated, for example, that the $90 million cost of building a new prison in Western Australia included about $15 million to cover union featherbedding (Harding 1992).

With this new emphasis the concern to reduce aspects of recurrent costs has not, of course, disappeared. The single most important objective, running through all the recent manoeuvres, has been to break down the strong union control over the manning levels and dispositions of uniformed staff. Of course, this relates not just to costs but to regimes; it gets back to the most fundamental consideration and my own starting point, *the historically entrenched negativism of the custodial environment.*

Privatisation has started to put the spotlight on the fact that prison regimes have seemed to be designed at least as much and probably more for the convenience of custodial staff as for prisoner welfare. Staff have often exercised undue control over programs and changes (Vorenberg 1972; Hawkins 1976; Vinson 1982; O'Hare 1990; Woolf 1991). This is in a context where the peer-group subculture is intensely resistant to external challenge (Williams 1983).

In Australia there has even been speculation that a spate of escapes from the Queensland public prison system may have been condoned, if not positively engineered, by officers trying to hold back the pace of reform. Such an assertion is not necessarily fanciful. The inquiry into the 1986 riots in several UK prisons found that at least one outbreak (at Gloucester prison) was actively provoked by officers intent on forestalling reform (HM Inspector of Prisons 1987, pp. 11-21).

There can be no doubt that part of the contract management push has been as much to break down this otherwise impenetrable subculture as to save recurrent expenditure. In the Northern Territory of Australia, the idea of privatising one new prison was floated very much from the point of view of breaking down restrictive work practices so as to enable unit management to be introduced (Harding 1992). When the union complied, privatisation went off the agenda. Much the same has happened in Western Australia, where the union has agreed to implement major changes to work practices as a quid pro quo for the government's not opening up the system to the private sector.[14] In the short term this has been avowedly a money-saving exercise; but the expectation or hope is that it will prove to be a preliminary step to program improvement and enhanced performance.

From this point of view, the public authorities do seem to be showing an awareness that the public is entitled to get value for money, and that this is as much a case of spending a fixed amount more productively as of spending a lesser amount. Privatisation has been a way of bringing this about. It is also evident that there is quite a strong line of thought that the *threat of privatisation* may be sufficient to stimulate organisational change and that, if this is effective, it is preferable to fragmenting the total system between two sectors. In NSW further privatisation is unlikely in the short term because the workforce, even at the prison with the most hard-core uniformed staff, has recognised the need to adopt new work practices (personal conversation with the Commissioner, February 1994).

Either way, there is potential benefit to the community, to prisoners, and to the 'remote public interest'.

Gingering up the public system

This follows naturally from the previous points. There is no point in introducing different systems for their own sakes; the point is to improve the whole. This involves active cross-fertilisation, indeed competition.

Tumim, reviewing The Wolds, identified practices which he 'would like to see replicated in other prisons' (1993, pp. 36-7, 48, 49). However, there was no mechanism which ensured cross-fertilisation across the dual system: 'There is a need to integrate the work of The Wolds and the Prison Service so that the needs of inmates can be better met by a mutual exchange of ideas and staff training opportunities' (1993, p. 27, see also p.116). The NSW Commissioner also considers there has been little or no cross-fertilisation, but rather some internal stimulus to the public system (personal communication, February 1992). The point, then, seems to be that cross-fertilisation is fortuitous at best.

How could it be structured into the total system? The answer is: if there is genuine competition between the sectors *and* accountability to the apex of a common triangle.

Regarding competition, it is essential that *the public system be able to bid against the private sector* for the management of new prisons. The new English arrangements permit this; the corporatised Prisons Service Agency beat off strong private sector competition to win the contract to run the reconstructed Strangeways prison. The contract was awarded by the government on the recommendation of an objective third party, the Custodial Contracts Unit.

No such formal bidding is possible in any of the Australian states — though, as indicated above, the public system is sensitive to what its own costs would be under their existing constraints in running the prison in question. But that is not quite the same thing as reconstructing oneself and then submitting a bid to an independent third party.

In Victoria, it has actively been decided that the general provisions of the *State Owned Enterprises Act 1992*, which provide an apposite vehicle, will *not* be applied to corporatising the public corrections system. In New Zealand, likewise, the public system will not be corporatised; however, it will be able to bid against the private sector for the third new prison due to come on stream. Whether the provider be the public or the private sector, a service agreement will then be entered into with the Deputy Secretary of Justice responsible for corrections. Western Australia seems likely also to adopt the notion of service agreements — but in all probability the system itself will remain solely public.

Even where there can be public sector competition, accountability for performance is crucial. The New Zealand system will leave the deputy secretary, at the apex of the triangle, wearing many hats — adviser to the government on general correctional policy matters, judge between competing private and public providers, monitor through his officers of each of them, and yet in all matters answerable to a political head. This seems to pose an impossible set of dilemmas.[15] The preferable model surely is that of an independent body, judging between competitors and monitoring contract performance. The nearest approximation to that model is that of the British Inspector of Prisons. But because that person lacks any line of responsibility for allocating contracts or setting their terms and because his monitoring is not ongoing but spasmodic, the intense competition and cross-fertilisation that is desirable cannot really flow through his office.

Practice, evaluation and modification

Evaluation is an aspect of cross-fertilisation; it is also a potential safeguard, akin to long-range monitoring. One would expect the public system authorities to have been fully alert to its importance.

In Britain, an independent team from the University of Hull has been evaluating The Wolds from the earliest stages of staff selection and training. In NSW, an officer from the Research and Statistics group within the Department of Corrective Services conceptualised an evaluative study of all aspects of Junee, to commence at the time staff began to be recruited (Bowery 1992). It was as good a proposal as has yet been put up in this area. Yet funding had to be sought *outside* of the department. Evidently, at that stage the Commission did not conceive of such evaluations as being integral to the new approach to management, but rather peripheral. The application for outside moneys was unsuccessful *on the basis that this sort of research par excellence should be carried out as a normal departmental activity.* Subsequently, the Commission has allocated some funds to the research, but of course its commencement was delayed and its scope seems not to be as broad. In Queensland, so far as I am aware there is no formal research project in progress.[16] There has been a considerable amount of negotiation and, ultimately, antagonism between one particular researcher and the Commission along with one of the contract managers. This has led to a situation where access to information has had to be sought formally — and unsuccessfully — under the Freedom of Information Act (Moyle 1994a, 1994b). Most recently, the Commission has declined to instruct the contract managers to permit the researcher access to their institution, apparently on the basis that they lack the contractual right or power to do so.

Whatever the rights and wrongs of this saga, and acknowledging the readiness with which the contract managers have generally permitted short-term access to the institution to a wide range of persons including journalists and other researchers, this does nevertheless sound like an ethos where the notion that benefits may flow from proper evaluation is not strongly appreciated.

In summary, in these early days the systems are still, at best, groping towards the notion that research and evaluation is integral to developing practice.

A MODEL OF ACCOUNTABILITY

A model is required which is both *contractor focused* and *sensitive to the remote and abstract public interest*. None of the models we have seen quite measure up. This is because they have evolved in a context where the public system both allocated contractors as principals to private sector agents and then purported to regulate the new sector. Even in Britain, where new structural arrangements have cut out the principal/agent confusion, accountability has uneasily been superimposed through the use of a pre-existing independent body (HM Inspector of Prisons) which was first established to oversee the public system only.

The optimum arrangement for maximising the benefits of privatisation and minimising the potential hazards would be as follows. An independent statutory office holder — let us call it the Prisons Commissioner — with suitable staff, would be charged with specifying contractual performance standards in relation to new prisons. Tenders would then be sought from the private sector *and* from a fully corporatised public sector. The contract would be awarded by the Prisons Commissioner not just on the basis of cost but taking into account reliability, range of services offered, and so on. Monitoring in the prisons (public or private) would be carried out by staff working to the Commissioner. Major inspections or audits would be carried out from time to time by other staff from that office. Management contracts would run for a reasonable period and would be renewable, but new tenders would have to be submitted in open competition after, say, eight years. Without being unitary, the systems would be sufficiently congruent for easy transfer of prisoners, without prejudice to programs. Management conferences involving persons from both parts of the system would be convened by the Commissioner from time to time. The overall strategy would be the attainment of different but equal standards across the system. An explicit part of the overall planning — in which the Commissioner would be consulted by the ministerial agency or department responsible for penal policy — would be to ensure that neither part of the system was squeezed out artificially by the other (e.g. by 'lowballing' bids). All this would progressively be extended to existing prisons.[17] Figure 2 illustrates this model.

Under such arrangements, there would be natural ebb and flow between the parts of the system as contracts expired and new tenders were sought. The public sector should have the inside running most of the time, particularly as it gets used to the discipline of outputs — something which is in any case beginning to happen across all aspects of the public sector. Its efficiency should be enhanced also when it realises it is above all a player, not also a regulator. But the private sector would undoubtedly continue to pick up some contracts, and there would be some potential synergies from this which have not yet been properly explored — for example, the sector's participation in related post-release programs or implementation of community-based orders.

Prisons policy has been arid for a long time. Possibly, reform can occur from within. However, to allow that belief to form the cornerstone of one's strategy for a less bad prison system is to allow hope to triumph over experience. In the late 20th century, some different structural arrangements must be tried. Contract management by the private sector poses real hazards. That is why it is so important to construct a model of accountability which provides a framework within which the performance of not only the new private sector but also the old public sector may be fundamentally improved.

Notes

1. The term 'contract management' is preferred to that of privatisation because it encompasses the widest variety of arrangements for the involvement of the non-government sector in the delivery of correctional services. These may be for-profit organisations, charities such as the Salvation Army, or other NGOs;

Figure 2

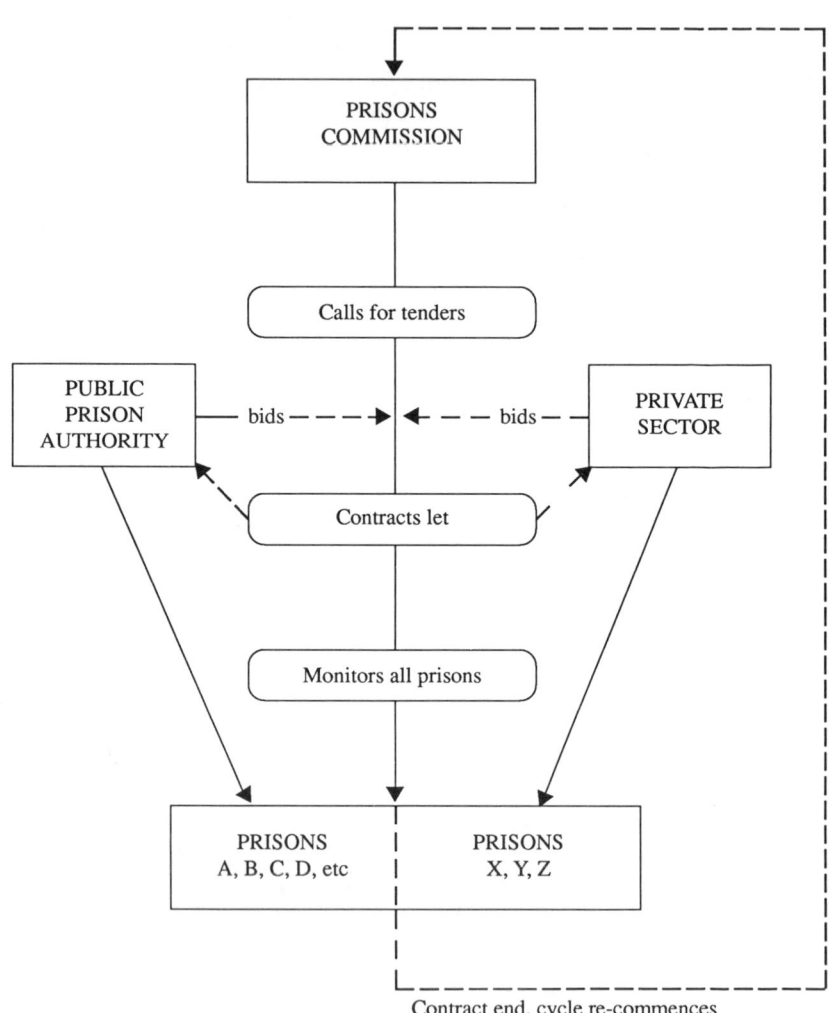

Contract end, cycle re-commences

the contracted services may be partial (one aspect of a correctional service, such as health programs) or total; they may be institutional or community based; they may relate to juveniles or adults; they may involve government or non-government ownership of the physical plant used for the service delivery; or they may relate to non-criminal justice functions (e.g. detention of illegal immigrants) or justice-related ones. However, in the context of this paper, in practice it is only private sector organisations which have shown interest in bidding against the public system to operate prisons.

2. Australia: three prisons housing approximately 1220 inmates, which is about 8 per cent of the total prison population; Britain: three prisons housing approximately 2000 inmates, which is about 4 per cent of the total prison population; US: as at the end of 1990, 44 prisons housing approximately 15,000 inmates, which was at that time about 1.5 per cent of the total prison and local jail population (McDonald 1992, pp. 386-90). In each of these jurisdictions, other contractual possibilities are being actively pursued.

3. Managed under contract by the Corrections Company of Australia—a consortium comprised of Corrections Corporation of America, the Australian-owned John Holland construction group and the Australian public company Wormald's Security Ltd.

4. At the time the 1991 Act was passed this was HM Prison Service, a sub-department of the Home Office. Subsequently, this has been corporatised under the name of the Prison Service Agency. There are slight tensions of accountability in this arrangement because the authority within the Home Office responsible for the letting of contracts to manage prisons, the Custodial Contracts Unit, is not part of the same line of responsibility as are the controllers, who are generally mid-level Governor grades from the PSA.

5. Junee was only opened in March 1993, becoming fully operational by about August.

6. On 1 April, 1994 the unit was renamed the Contracts and Competition Group, to reflect the philosophy that much of its future work will involve market-testing (i.e. checking the ability of the Prison Service Agency to run any given prison at least as cost-effectively as the private sector has). That re-designation of both name and duties seems to have drawn the group more closely within the mainstream hierarchy, though the reporting line is still directly to the Director General.

7. *Corrective Services Act 1988*, (Qld) s. 18; *Corrective Services (Administration) Act 1988*, (Qld) s. 19(2).

8. *Prisons (Contract Management) Amendment Act 1990*, (NSW) s. 31C .

9. *Criminal Justice Act 1991*, (Qld) s. 85, Schedule 10.

10. One with a capacity of 600 to replace the maximum security Pentridge prison; one with capacity of 600 as a remand prison; and one with a capacity of 125 for female sentenced and unsentenced prisoners. Expressions of interest were to be lodged by February 1994; the prisons are to become operational 30 months after the letting of contracts.

11. The first two are as follows: a 250 bed remand prison in central Auckland and

a 350 bed medium security institution in South Auckland. A third regional prison, with a capacity of 350-500, is expected to come on line quite soon thereafter.

12. This flows from the general terms of the Penal Institutions Act. The contract management structures are provided for in the Penal Institutions Amendment Bill, which was introduced into Parliament in 1993, was referred to a Select Committee, then sent back to the House with some suggested modifications before Parliament was prorogued prior to the 1993 general election. The Bill in its Select Committee form will now be re-presented to Parliament some time in March 1994 and is expected to pass without further amendment.

13. This has been a problem with the English arrangements, mainly because of union attitudes which prevent prisoners once admitted to a privately operated prison from being transferred to one whose officers are members of the Prison Officers Association.

14. The Northern Territory went to the extent of seeking tenders and drawing up a short list. In Western Australia it was enough that the idea was floated in a report reviewing governmental activities; expressions of interest were not formally sought: see Young, A. 1994, The *West Australian*, 21 January, p. 12.

15. Since this was written, organisational changes within the New Zealand Department of Justice (May 1994) have created a model closely akin to that set out below. Decisions as to contract management and the terms of any such contract will be made by the General Manager Criminal Justice Department; whilst responsibility for the operation of corrections generally, including publicly managed and contract managed prisons, will rest with the General Manager Corrections Operations. Each of these positions reports to the Secretary of Justice. Contract monitors are to be appointed by the Secretary. In this way the system will attempt to maintain effective checks and balances.

16. It should be noted however that Moyle conducted extensive field research at Borallon Correctional Centre 1991. The main findings of this field research are due to be published in 1995.

17. The difficulties of this are recognised; in effect, an existing prison may have to be temporarily shut down (as happened during the re-building of Strangeways in Britain) to free it up for private sector contract management. It is the intention of the New Zealand authorities ultimately to go down this line.

References

Bowery, M. 1992, 'Private versus Public Prisons: A Case Study of Junee Correctional Centre', Research Proposal, N.S.W. Department of Corrective Services, unpublished.

Broadhurst, R., and Maller, R. 1990, 'The Recidivism of Prisoners Released for the First Time: Reconsidering the Effectiveness Question', 23 *Australian and New Zealand Journal of Criminology*, vol. 23, pp. 88-104.

Cross, R. 1971, *Punishment, Prison and the Public: An Assessment of Penal Reform in Twentieth Century England by an Armchair Penologist*, Stevens and Sons, London.

Dinitz, S. 1981, 'Are Safe and Humane Prisons Possible?' *Australian and New Zealand Journal of Criminology*, vol. 14, pp. 3-19.

George, A. 1989, 'The State Tries an Escape', *Legal Service Bulletin*, vol. 14, pp. 53-57.

Grabosky, P., and Braithwaite, J. 1986, *Of Manners Gentle: Enforcement Strategies of Australian Business Regulatory Agencies*, Oxford University Press, Melbourne.

Hallenstein, H. 1989, *Finding of Inquisition held at a Coroner's Court, Melbourne, into the Deaths of James Richard Loughnan and Others*, Office of the Victoria State Coroner, Melbourne.

Hansen, P. 1993, 'Prison Boss Quits', *Brisbane Sunday Mail*, 28 March 1993

Harding, R. 1992, 'Private Prisons in Australia', *Trends and Issues in Crime and Criminal Justice*, no. 36, Australian Institute of Criminology, Canberra.

—— 1993, 'Inside Trading', *The Bulletin*, 6 April 1993.

Hawkins, G. 1976, *The Prison: Policy and Practice*, University of Chicago Press, Chicago.

Her Majesty's Inspector of Prisons 1987, *Report of an Inquiry into the Disturbances in Prison Service Establishments in England between 29 April/2 May 1986*, HMSO, London.

Johnston, e. 1991, *Final Report of the Royal Commission into Aboriginal Deaths in Custody*, Australian Government Publishing Service, Canberra.

Lilly, J., and Knepper, P. 1993, 'The Corrections-Commercial Complex', *Prison Service Journal*, vol. 87, pp. 43-52.

MacArthur, S. 1992, 'Private prison operator admits mismanagement', *The Australian*, 11 March 1992.

Macionis, S. 1992, 'Contract Management in Corrections: The Queensland Experience', in *Conference Proceedings: Private Sector and Community Involvement in the Criminal Justice System*, Australian Institute of Criminology, (forthcoming).

McDonald, D. 1992, 'Private Penal Institutions', *Crime and Justice: A Review of Research*, vol. 16, pp. 361-419.

McGivern, J. 1988, *Report of the Enquiry into the Causes of the Riot, Fire and Hostage-taking at Fremantle Prison on 4th/5th January 1988*, Department of Corrective Services, Perth.

Morris, N. 1974, *The Future of Imprisonment*, University of Chicago Press, Chicago.

Moyle, P. 1992, 'Privatising Prisons: The Underlying Issues', *Alternative Law Journal*, vol. 17, pp. 114-119.

—— 1993, 'Privatisation of Prisons in New South Wales and Queensland: A Review of Some Key Developments in Australia', *The Howard Journal of Criminal Justice*, vol. 32, pp. 231-250.

—— 1994a, 'Private Prison Research in Queensland, Australia: A case study of Borallon Correctional Centre, 1991', *British Journal of Criminology*, Autumn, (in press). See also chapter 5.

—— 1994b, 'Contracting for Private Prisons in Queensland—Lessons for Penal

Policy', Paper presented to Occasional Seminar, no. 2, 24 February, 1994, Australian Institute of Criminology, *Socio-Legal Bulletin*, April, (in press).

Nagle, J. 1978, *Report of an Inquiry into the New South Wales Department of Corrective Services*, N.S.W. Government Printer, Sydney.

O'Hare, 1990, The Privatisation of Imprisonment: A Managerial Perspective', in *Private Prisons and the Public Interest*, (ed) D. McDonald, Rutgers University Press, New Brunswick, N.J.

Queensland Public Sector Management Commission 1993, *Review of the Queensland Corrective Services Commission*, State Government Printer, Brisbane, December.

Radzinowicz, L. 1988, Letter to *The Times*, 22 September 1988, referred to in Shaw (1992).

Shaw, S. 1989, 'Penal Sanctions: Private Affluence or Public Squalor?', in *Punishment for Profit?*, M. Farrell, Institute for the Study and Treatment of Delinquency, London.

— 1992, 'The Short History of Prison Privatisation', *Prison Service Journal*, vol. 87, pp. 30-32.

Tumim, S. 1993, *Wolds Remand Prison: Report by H. M. Chief Inspector of Prisons*, Home Office, London.

Vinson, T. 1982, *Wilful Obstruction: The Frustration of Prison Reform*, Methuen, Sydney.

Vinson, T., and Baldry, e. 1993, 'It's jackpot for some in bottom-line jails', *The Sydney Morning Herald*, 30 December 1993.

Vorenberg, J. 1972, 'The War on Crime: The First Five Years', *The Atlantic Monthly*, May.

Weiss, R. 1991, 'The Bitter Lessons Forgotten?" in 'Attica: 1971-91—A Commemorative Issue', *Social Justice*, vol. 18, pp. 1-12.

Williams, T. 1983, 'Custody and Conflict: An Organisational Study of Prison Officers' Roles and Attitudes', *Australian and New Zealand Journal of Criminology*, vol. 16, pp. 44-55.

Woolf, H. 1991, *Prison Disturbances, April 1990: Report of An Inquiry*, Cm 1456, HMSO, London.

* This is a revised version of a paper presented to a conference entitled Prisons 2000, University of Leicester, April 8-10, 1994.

4

The industrial issues of private prisons: a union's perspective

David Belton

Abstract: This chapter provides a description of the Prison Officers Association of Australia's (POAA) objectives and policy on the privatisation of corrections. A brief summary of the experience of Australasian prison officers in various states is given with particular emphasis on the development of private sector involvement in corrections.

Finally a case study of Western Australia is outlined focusing upon the development of an appropriate union response that opposes privatisation yet embraces support of all prison officers irrespective of whether they are public or private sector employees. This consultative approach is provided as a practical example of how genuine industrial reform can occur without necessarily involving the private sector.

The recent and continuing intrusion by the private sector into Australian corrections is an issue of major concern to unions representing prison/correctional officers. The purpose of this paper is to outline the POAA's policy and activity in this area, particularly in regard to the privatisation of correctional functions.

The POAA is not a union in its own right. It is an informal association of unions that represent prison officers in the Australian states and territories. More recently, the POAA has invited the participation of the New Zealand Public Service Association and the Correctional Employees Association of Papua New Guinea, and sought the involvement of prison officers employed by the private sector within Queensland and New South Wales.

The current objectives of the association are as follows:

- to foster and maintain harmonious relations between persons employed in various states in prison or corrective services as designated by those states;
- to improve and maintain, by all lawful means at their disposal, the working conditions, salaries and increments and protect the general interests of participant members/groups;
- to promote, develop and encourage the humane treatment, care, custody control and supervision of incarcerated offenders;
- to provide opportunities for individual members and participant groups to acquire and disseminate knowledge and understanding of all relevant aspects of the prison/correctional system;
- to consider and determine, by means of Annual Conference, all such matters proposed by state groups or individuals which, in the opinion of the Executive Council, affect the interests of the profession;
- to provide, as far as practicable, legal, monetary or other assistance to member groups or states. Such assistance is to be determined by Executive Council;
- to collect from participants a reasonable fee, and to judiciously use this to enable the association to effectively function in the pursuit of its stated objectives. Such a fee is to be determined each year at the Annual Conference;
- to standardise the rank(s) of prison officers between states;
- to be a policy making body which makes recommendations to states; where policies are accepted, the onus shall lie on the state to implement them.

The POAA's current policy position in respect to private sector involvement in corrections is brief and to the point. The POAA:

- opposes the privatisation of prisons and other corrections functions;
- will seek to ensure that appropriate unions provide competent industrial representation on behalf of corrections/prison officers irrespective of whether they are public or private sector workers;
- invites the participation and affiliation of corrections/prison

officers irrespective of whether they are public or private sector workers;

- intends that the POAA Executive draft a detailed policy position on privatisation including a course of action to be pursued to achieve the above objectives;
- calls on the Queensland government to honour its pre-election promise to terminate the Borallon contract and prevent the making of profits from essential government services;
- calls on the Queensland government to make available all information relating to the contractual arrangements and obligations entered into by the previous National Queensland government on behalf of the taxpayers of Queensland.

The policy position of the POAA reflects both union opposition to the privatisation of public services and a reaction to the intrusion of the private sector into the jurisdictions of unions affiliated with, or associated with, the POAA. It is useful to summarise the experience of prison officers and their Unions in each of those jurisdictions.

Queensland
Subsequent to the commissioning and receipt of the Kennedy Report (1988) the conservative Bjelke-Petersen National Party government decided to privatise Borallon Prison. That prison opened under the contract administration of Corrections Corporation of Australia in January, 1990. Upon election to office, the Goss Labor government failed to honour a pre-election pledge to discontinue the project.

Following failed negotiations between government and the Queensland State Service Union (QSSU) the Goss administration in March, 1992 awarded the management contract for the Wacol Remand and Reception Prison to Australasian Correctional Management Ltd (ACM). The early operational history of the Arthur Gorrie Centre includes disturbances, fires, violence and deaths in custody.

Early in 1994 Corrections Minister Paul Brady advised the Queensland branch of the State Public Service Federation that the Queensland government was moving towards re-opening Woodford Correctional facility and that late in 1994 expressions of interest from the public and private sector would be called for.

New South Wales
In May 1993, the conservative Liberal NSW government opened the 600 bed Junee facility which is managed by ACM Ltd. Little direct knowledge of the operational experience of Junee is known. It is

believed that there had been difficulties which may explain the fact that the former senior superintendent of the maximum security Goulburn Prison is currently the acting assistant superintendent of the Junee Prison, while still remaining a Government employee. There has been speculation about proposals to have Junee downgraded to minimum security or to use it as a facility for short-term visits. It is thought the latter proposal may have arisen due to difficulties associated with prisoner visits because of the remote location of Junee.

The NSW conservative Liberal government intends to construct a new 400 bed prison facility at Silverwater. The construction and management of the new prison will be put to tender. The NSW Corrective Services Department intends to submit a bid. ACM is actively recruiting senior personnel from the NSW Corrections Department.

The NSW branch of the State Public Service Federation reports that the threat of privatisation is regularly used as an industrial lever in negotiations.

Northern Territory
In July 1991 the conservative National Party Northern Territory government called for expressions of interest in the design, construction and management of the new prison to be built in Alice Springs. Subsequent to discussions and negotiations with the Prison Officers Association, a sub-section of the Liquor Hospitality and Miscellaneous Workers Union, the government decided to maintain the ownership and manage the prison.

Victoria, Tasmania, South Australia and Western Australia
In these states, prison officers and their unions can cite many examples where the prospect of private prisons in part or whole has been used by government to influence the response of prison officers and their unions to a range of work issues.

Victoria
In December, 1993 the conservative Liberal Victorian government announced it would close Fairlea Women's Prison, close Pentridge Prison and build three new prisons which are to be privately managed. The government has also de-regulated the labour market. Twenty per cent cuts to the corrections budget have been forecast. A representative of the Victorian branch of the State Public Service Federation asserts that the Liberal government in Victoria appears 'hellbent on discrediting public sector prisons and is treating its own employees with contempt'.

South Australia

The recently elected conservative Liberal South Australian govern-ment has announced its privatisation plans. The new 60 bed Mt Gambier facility is to be offered to private contractors and the intention is to privatise the yet to be constructed 400 bed multi-purpose prison which will include the women's prison. Cadell and Port Lincoln prisons are under threat of closure and the South Australian government demanded that costs be on a par with Victoria's with 33 per cent budget cuts speculated.

Tasmania

The Tasmanian Minister for Corrections has made a public commit-ment not to privatise Tasmanian prisons.

Papua New Guinea

The Correctional Employees Association of Papua New Guinea cited the two major issues of concern to them as being privatisation and deregulation of the labour market.

New Zealand

Late in 1992, the New Zealand government proposed to privatise two yet to be constructed prisons. Prison farms would operate privately, employing inmates on contracts. Court custody and prison transport were also to be privatised. Prison health services were to be contracted out as well as most correctional functions other than core custodial functions. Since the November 1993 election privatisation of correc-tions appears not to have been pursued.

WHY THE UNIONS OPPOSE PRIVATISATION

Prior to discussing union opposition to privatisation, it is worth outlining POAA policy with respect to officers employed in prisons or correctional establishments owned and/or operated by the private sector. In establishing the fundamentals of its policy, and that is all that exists to date, the POAA recognises that its responsibility in represent-ing prison officers goes beyond the public sector. Whilst the POAA is committed to the retention of correctional functions within the public sector and is highly critical of the intrusion of the private sector into corrections, the POAA is determined to ensure industrial justice is delivered to officers within private correctional facilities. The POAA in criticising and opposing the private sector intrusion into corrections is very keen to ensure that the integrity and competence of prison officers employed in the private sector is not tarnished or questioned merely by association.

Whilst for the purposes of this paper it is impossible to canvass in detail the constitutions and policies of each of the unions affiliated or associated with the POAA, it is fair to say that those unions are supportive of a society that is democratic and delivers legal, social, economic and industrial justice in the context of a mixed economy where the public and private sector co-exist in an appropriately regulated environment. The POAA is not blindly anti-private sector. It is opposed to private sector ownership and/or management of correctional functions.

The POAA opposes the privatisation of corrections activities and prisons in particular for reasons that are wide ranging and go beyond ideology. Prison officers and their unions are justifiably concerned that the intrusion of the private sector into corrections represents a threat to existing wages and working conditions. It is interesting to note that despite the recent development of private sector involvement in corrections, this involvement is not a new thing.

Vallance, in her prize winning essay, 'Private Prison Management: Panacea or Pretence' cites John Howard's 'The State of Prisons' (1777) and Jeremy Bentham's 'Panopticon' (1791) to demonstrate the appalling record of early private sector involvement in custodial matters. That record is one of non-payment of officers, brutal abuse of prisoners and appalling conditions for both (Vallance 1991, pp. 397-398).

In the United States privately managed prisons operated from the mid-19th century up to the 1930s when the government resumed total control of prison management. Vallance cites one commentator who said of this period:

> The history of private sector involvement in corrections is unbelievably bleak, a well documented tale of inmate abuse and political corruption. In many instances, private contractors worked inmates to death, beat or killed them for minor rule infractions, or failed to provide inmates with the quantity and quality of life's necessities (food, clothing, shelter etc) specified in their often meticulously drafted contracts. (Dilulio 1988, p. 2)

The 1980s saw a renewed trend towards privatisation of corrections emerge in the US. The POAA notes that interest came from the south-eastern states in particular. The union movement needs no reminding that those states have a poor labour relations record, their race relations are appalling and their commitment to social equity objectives almost non-existent.

The POAA also notes that the most strident advocates of private sector involvement in corrections, other than the enterprises themselves, are conservative political forces also advocating and implementing deregulation of the labour market. It is clear to prison officers and their unions that the motive of those who advocate deregulation and privatisation is to maximise profits through a low wage structure. A low wage structure for prison officers will not advance the efficiency of corrections, it may in fact prejudice it. The actions of the private sector in other areas of industry will demonstrate this.

The Australian mining industry is a case in point. The industry has traditionally shown scant regard for the environment. Reacting to public concern, Australian governments have introduced a range of regulating measures designed to ensure that mining companies involved themselves in rehabilitation of those areas mined. Mining companies have vigorously opposed such moves. It is not uncommon to witness sophisticated advertising campaigns by the Australian mining industry and individual companies promoting themselves as responsible corporate citizens on the basis of post-mining rehabilitation, whilst at the same time running a constant campaign to be allowed to explore and mine in national parks and heritage areas.

The oil industry is another case in point. The 1973 oil crisis hit New Zealand very hard. Oil companies were seen as being too powerful and having little regard for the environment. To improve its public image Mobil Oil NZ Ltd mounted a sophisticated public relations exercise involving a fuel economy advertising campaign, energy audits for commercial or industrial customers, and the promotion of activities to demonstrate to the community that it was a good corporate citizen. At the same time, that company was importing and marketing transformer oils containing polychlorinated biphenyls into New Zealand knowing that they were banned in the US.

Harding (1992) finds no evidence to suggest that private sector involvement in corrections in Queensland has created an environment in which private sector interests influence government policy. 'This strongly suggests that what ever is driving correctional policy in Queensland, it is certainly not a lobby in support of high imprisonment rates to underwrite private prisons', he says. The POAA, on the other hand, has grave fears that this unassailability of government policy will be compromised as private sector involvement in Australasian corrections expands.

US academics Lilly and Knepper (1992) describe the workings of the phenomenon they have entitled the 'corrections commercial complex':

- all participants in the corrections sub-government share a close working relationship supported by the flow of information, influence and money;
- there is a distinct overlap between the for-profit companies and professional organisations, and the interests of the federal agencies' maintained by the flow of influence and personnel;
- the corrections commercial complex operates without public scrutiny and exercises enormous influence over corrections policy;
- the corrections commercial complex shows signs of becoming a fixture within the national policy area.

Lilly and Knepper claim that in the US there is a growing body of evidence to suggest that corrections budgets are soaring, with disturbing amounts of waste and inefficiency and massive defects in new corrections construction and prison services. They report that Ohio, California and Connecticut have cut millions from their education budgets while increasing their corrections budgets at unprecedented rates.

The POAA believes that the intrusion of the private sector into Australasian corrections combined with the social divisiveness of a deregulated low wage labour market, a laissez-faire commercial environment and conservative-sponsored 'truth in sentencing' policies, will lead to a substantial increase in corrections budgets. This will be at the expense of other important areas of government responsibility such as health, education and welfare services.

The POAA supports the comment by eminent criminologist, Sir Leon Rudzinowicz (1988):

> In a democracy grounded on the rule of law and public accountability, the enforcement of penal legislation which includes prisoners deprived of their liberty while awaiting trial, should be the undiluted responsibility of the State. It is one thing for private companies to provide services for the prison system, it is an altogether different matter for bodies whose motivation is primarily commercial to have coercive powers over prisoners.

The POAA is of the view that private sector involvement in corrections, with its attendant profit motivation, has the potential to prejudice humanitarian aspects of corrections. Earlier in this paper, reference was made to the denial of basic human needs in private US correctional facilities despite the authorities' best endeavours to ensure those needs were provided for through regulating the contractual arrangements.

The POAA is concerned that any lowering of standards of care and provision of services has the potential to prejudice the safety and welfare of officers employed in those institutions. This concern goes beyond questions of immediate safety to the treatment of officers by the employer in the event of external criticism of a private institution's actions. It is feared that employers may well 'serve up' an officer or officers without recourse to due process and/or representation. Given that the privatisation of corrections has emerged from the south-eastern states of the US, embraced by conservative laissez-faire anti-union administrations in the United Kingdom, New Zealand, Queensland and NSW, union fears about the welfare of officers are legitimate.

A number of commentators have claimed that undue union influence is itself a factor inclining policy makers toward private sector involvement in corrections. Harding (1992) points to a number of observations that: 'Custodial Staff have in the past tended to exercise undue control over programs and change'. The POAA is disturbed by such assertions. Not that such assertions do not have an element of truth, but because privatisation is no remedy for 'subcultural' or 'institutional myopia'. Surely the focus for change should be within the public sector. The POAA is of the view that whatever flaws exist within the ranks of the public sector, the potential for the same flaws exists within the private sector. And indeed, such failings are already apparent within the private sector in other industries.

Western Australia

To identify the potential for cultural and industrial change it is useful to examine the West Australian experience. Delegates from all Australian states, Papua New Guinea and New Zealand attended the POAA 1992 Conference held in Perth, Western Australia where the WA Prison Officers Union received positive written and verbal comment from visiting prison officers about the operations and facilities of the WA prison system. The POAA is of the view that the current WA corrections experience may provide a legitimate alternative in terms of the change process required in corrections so that they deliver to the community and government a just, humane and cost efficient service.

Like other corrections systems, the WA system felt the effects of the recession. The WA government was strapped for cash and told government departments they must meet their budgets.

The 1980s was a period of significant change for WA corrections. It was a period of rapid modernisation and expansion of physical facilities culminating in the opening of the new Casuarina Prison and the closure of the 'Dickensian' Fremantle Gaol. The Prisons Department amalgamated with the Parole Board and became the Department of Corrective Services which was divisionalised into areas of Community Based Corrections, Prison Operations, Building Services and Corporate. In July 1993, the Department of Corrective Services was amalgamated with Crown Law, Court Services and the Juvenile Justices division of the Department of Social Welfare to form the new Ministry of Justice. The '80s was a period where the role of officers was expanded and enhanced with the implementation of Unit Management occurring progressively through the early '90s.

Early into the 92/93 budget year, it rapidly became apparent that the Department of Corrective Services would have trouble meeting its budget and its overtime budget in particular. Whilst there were initial differences of opinion between the WA Prison Officers Union and the department as to the cause for the budget difficulty and what should be done about it, an agreed cooperative approach to the management of the problem was negotiated. An overall operational review would be conducted by a joint group which would oversee institutional reviews at every prison. It was a process which involved everyone, uniformed officers, their union and administration, cooperating to achieve common goals.

These goals included:

- cooperating with budget management;
- ensuring the budget was met and that there was no possibility of reductions in officers wages, conditions and entitlements;
- ensuring the continued positive involvement of officers and their union in the decision making processes which affect their working lives;
- creating the opportunity to improve the working environment;
- ensuring that sick leave is not the result of poor job design, poor management, poor rostering, poor safety/security or misuse.

The process was not about:

- reductions in conditions;
- reductions in staff levels.

- the total elimination of overtime;
- a reduction of, or restriction of, access to sick leave.

Additional features of the program are worth noting:

- the process involved the tabling and discussion of the department's overall and individual institutional budgets;
- the agenda was not confined only to traditional industrial issues, but included all operational and administrative issues;
- the program is not short term and it is hoped that it develops into a permanent consultative feature.

Early results have included:

- departmental directors and senior union officials addressing joint meetings of prison administrative and uniformed staff to explain the process and seek positive participation;
- a prison superintendent and that prison's union representative successfully delivering a sophisticated proposal for that prison's future operations to the Department of Corrective Services corporate executive.

The operational review process was endorsed by the newly elected Liberal Attorney General the Hon. C. Edwards. This process was acknowledged in the Report of the Independent Commission to Review Public Sector Finances. The Commission observed, 'Relations have improved and enterprise bargaining with the union is progressing' (WA Government 1993).

Whilst the independent commission acknowledged the operational review, it went on to recommend that:

- costly and inefficient labour practices are evident and should be removed under enterprise bargaining agreement;
- a country prison be privatised to allow for bench marking;
- two prisons be closed; and
- manning levels should be reduced to achieve $5.9 million in savings.

The government established a sub-committee of Cabinet which includes the Premier and senior Ministers to oversee departmental responses to the recommendations of the independent commission.

The WA Prison Officers Union in opposing privatisation, advised government it was committed to savings and efficiencies in return for a commitment from government that it would not proceed with a program of privatisation of prisons. In December, 1993 government responded with a demand that by January 17, 1994 it required an agreement that would save 10 per cent or $8 million from the Prison Operations Division of the newly formed Ministry of Justice budget. Agreement was reached, in principle, on a package of labour reforms negotiated between the union and the Ministry of Justice. The reform package was submitted to the Cabinet sub-committee with advice that the package was to be subject to government commitments not to privatise and would also be subject to a ballot of all members of the union. The Cabinet sub-committee's response, interpreted as a 'soft green light' was to seek more detailed particulars in the form of a draft agreement.

The fundamental elements of the package include the conversion of the system of payment for prison officers from a weekly wage plus penalties and allowances to a single annual salary, paid fortnightly. The annual salary will be comprised of the current base rate, shift penalties, and an extra amount in return for working a 40-hour week (instead of a 38-hour week). A further amount in consideration for the trade off of the 'day in lieu' option will also be taken into account. Where an officer is rostered off duty on a public holiday an amount will be paid in advance as part of the salary in lieu of overtime in return for an agreement that officers may be required to work up to an additional 80 hours or 10 shifts per annum.

Should these reforms be accepted by Government and the Unions members, the effect will be:

- officers who work shifts would work between 17 and 27 additional shifts per annum and receive monetary increases via the annual salary of between $4000 and $5000;
- officers who work week days only would work an additional 12 days and receive an increase of $1500;
- the employer, the Ministry of Justice, would then have available to it an excess of 20,000 working days which equates to over 100 officers' positions which when combined with other agreed areas of staff rationalisation, would produce savings of $5 million;
- the salary concept which includes an amount in lieu of overtime effectively does away with overtime as it is currently practised and produces $8 million in savings;
- a total savings of $13 million of which government recoups $8 million, with $5 million being diverted to salary increase for officers;

- a greatly enhanced budget forecast and accounting system for the Ministry of Justice with consistent earnings for officers.

Other elements subject to discussion between the parties include voluntary redundancy, clearance of long service leave, sick leave, management practices, 12-hour shift systems, improved rank structure and career path, permanent part-time/job share and prisoner management issues. At the time of writing it remains to be determined whether the package of reforms progresses from agreement in principle to full agreement and implementation.

From time to time the WA government appears shaky on the issue given the conflict which exists between the Liberal government's pro-privatisation, anti-union ideology and the promise of genuine economic reform inherent in this package.

The union's members are alarmed on the one hand at the increasing intrusion of the private sector into the Australasian corrections environment, bringing with it lower wages and conditions including casualisation, and on the other hand the radical nature of the proposed reforms which will, in some people's view, erode valued conditions of employment. Some in the union believe this will decrease potential additional income-earning capacity through the removal of the overtime component that has for many years been a part of the working environment for prison officers.

The union's members are subject to pressures associated with job security whilst they try to cope with increased prison musters in an environment of diminishing resources. The Minister for Corrections has also expressed a pro-privatisation, pro-labour market deregulation approach noting that prison officers are 'paid beyond community standards'.

The POAA is of the view that genuine consultative labour relations is the true alternative to labour market de-regulation, privatisation and unfettered management prerogative. Institutional or subcultural myopia can be overcome through information sharing, education, and genuine participation. There is an enormous pool of unrecognised information and talent amongst the ranks of prison officers. Correctional administrators and policy makers are urged to turn their attention to the world's enduring successful economies, particularly those which don't enjoy vast natural mineral or primary resource wealth. Those Northern European (and more recently Japanese) economies have, as an ongoing feature, genuine participation and consultation with the workforce and their unions. They have not privatised their corrective functions.

The POAA opposition to privatisation does not extend to specific criticism of any of the companies currently engaged in, or proposing to become involved in, Australian corrections. This is not to say that this will not be the case in the future as the track record develops or information comes to light about the propriety or otherwise of their actions or modus operandi. The POAA will actively involve itself in support of officers employed in private sector correctional enterprises. It is inappropriate that profitability comes about through the exploitation of workers through inferior wage structures and employment conditions.

The POAA is conscious that corrective services are not of themselves, generators of revenue. Corrective services have very limited opportunities in this regard. Corrective services are paid for by the taxpayer. The private sector has a legitimate right to exist. Our view is that the private sector's proper role in a society with a mixed economy is to involve itself in the pursuit of profit through true wealth generating activities. The involvement of the private sector in corrections is not economic activity of a wealth generating nature.

The POAA is of the view that the current infatuation of conservative administrators with private sector corrective activities is resulting in misconceived social experiments already discredited in other times and places. Despite a slick public relations and marketing campaign, neither the private sector nor governments involved with them can point to any demonstrable long-term benefits to society from the privatisation of corrective services or functions.

References

Commission of Review into Corrective Services in Queensland 1988, *Final Report*, (J. J. Kennedy, Commissioner), Queensland Government Printer, Brisbane.

DiIulio, J. 1988, *Private Prisons*, US National Institute of Justice, Crime File Study Guide, no. 3, p. 3.

Harding, R. 1992, 'Private Prisons in Australia', *Trends and Issues in Crime and Criminal Justice*, Australian Institute of Criminology, May.

Kennedy Report. *See* Commission of Review into Corrective Services in Queensland.

Lilly, J. R. and Knepper, P. 1992, 'Corrections Commercial Complex', *Prisons Service Journal*, Issue 87.

Rudzinowicz, Sir L. 1988, *London Times*, 22 September 1988.

Vallance, S. 1991, 'Private Prison Management: Panacea or Pretence', *Australian Journal of Public Administration*, vol. 50, no. 3, September, pp. 397-398.

Western Australian Government, *Report of the Independent Commission to Review Public Sector Finances — Agenda for Reform*, vol. 2, August, pp. 323-329.

5

Privatisation and industrial relations: ACM's experience

Debra Diplock and Wayne Calabrese

*Abstract: This chapter gives an outline of Australasian Correctional Services'
structure focusing on Australasian Correctional Management Pty Ltd's (ACM)
impact on industrial relations strategies within its corrections centres. Both Junee
and Arthur Gorrie Correctional Centres, which were awarded to ACM, are
discussed from their implementation to operational stages with particular reference
to ACM's philosophy.*

This chapter examines the history of Australasian Correctional
Management Pty Ltd (ACM) and the impact of industrial relations
strategies on the reform process within the company's private correctional centres. In order to gain an appreciation of ACM's role in the
management of private correctional centres it is helpful to examine the
context in which ACM was established and operates.

This can be best illustrated with Figure 1: ACS company structure
showing parent & operating companies. As can be seen in the diagram
ACM's parent company WCC is an equal partner in Australasian
Correctional Services with Theiss Contractors Pty Ltd (Theiss).

Australasian Correctional Services (ACS) is an Australian company specifically established for the provision of private sector financing, design, construction, management and operational correctional services. ACS is owned in equal shares by Wackenhut Corrections Corporation (WCC), and Theiss Contractors Pty Ltd (Theiss), one of Australia's oldest and most experienced design and construction companies. ACS and ACM operate jointly in responding to government tenders with an integrated systems approach to the privatisation of correctional centres. ACS offers expertise in design and construction whilst ACM provides expertise in the management of correctional centres.

ACM was, until recently, a joint venture company formed by two worldwide security firms, ADT and Wackenhut. ACM became a wholly owned subsidiary of WCC on 28 January 1994. Wackenhut Corrections Corporation (WCC), the world's premier provider of private correctional design, finance, construction and management services, is a wholly owned subsidiary of The Wackenhut Corporation which was founded in 1954 by Mr George Wackenhut, a former FBI employee. The Wackenhut Corporation provides security services around the world and has over 40,000 employees and 125 offices in the United States and some 40 other countries.

WCC currently manages nine correctional centres in the US and has recently been awarded a contract with its joint venture partner, Serco, to manage an 800 bed remand and reception centre in Doncaster, England.

ACM has become the largest Australian private corrections management company with the contract to manage the Junee Correctional Centre, a 600 bed centre, awarded in August 1991 by the New South Wales government and a second contract awarded in April 1992 by the Queensland government to manage the Arthur Gorrie Correctional Centre in Brisbane, a 380 bed remand and reception centre. On 7 August 1991 the NSW government awarded the contract for the design, construction and management of the Junee Correctional Centre to ACS. On the same day ACS entered into two sub-contracts, the first with Theiss for the design and construction of the centre and the second with ACM for its management and operation. ACM was awarded the contract by the Queensland government to manage the Arthur Gorrie Correctional Centre in early 1992. ACS did not play an active role in this process as the Queensland government had designed and constructed the centre before the decision to privatise its management and operation was made. Therefore, a single contract was awarded to ACM to manage the centre.

These two management contracts were won by ACM largely because

Figure 1: Australasian Correctional Services (ACS):
Company structure showing parent and operating companies.

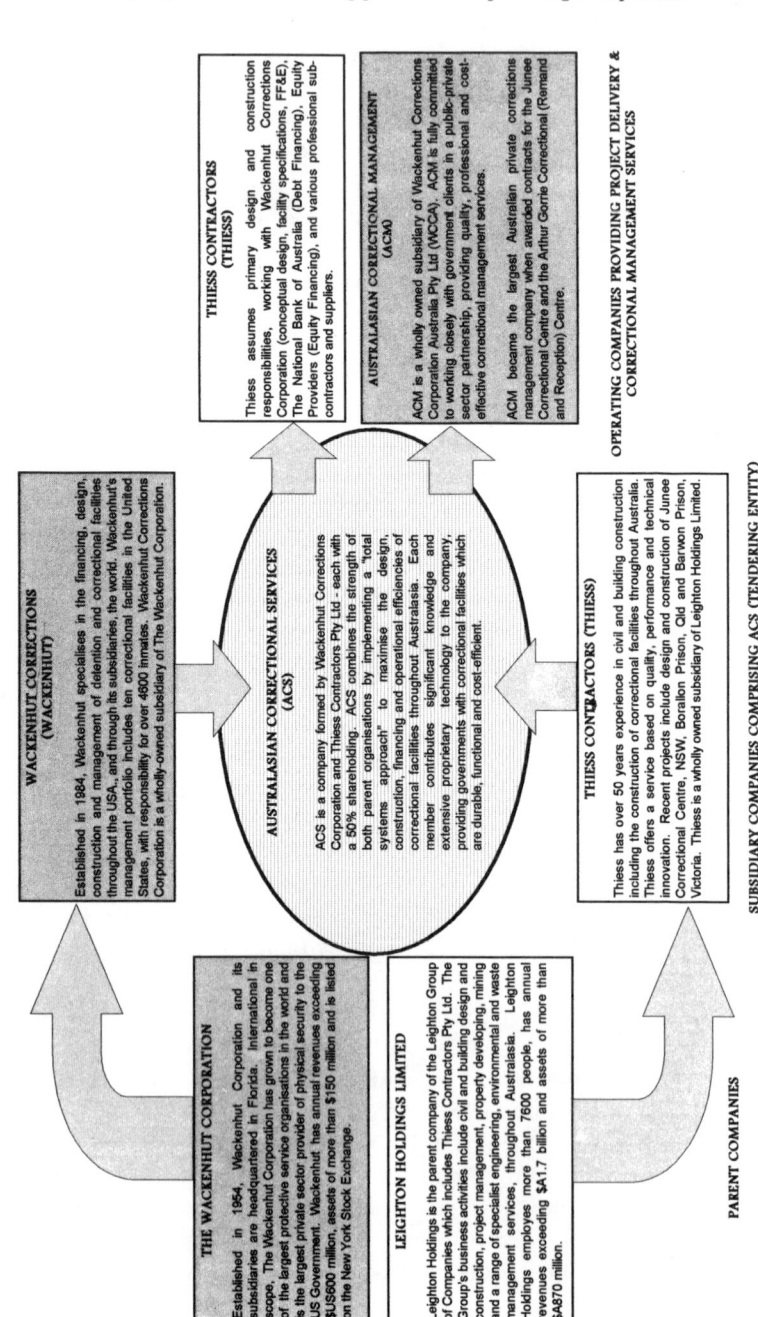

THIESS CONTRACTORS (THIESS)

Thiess assumes primary design and construction responsibilities, working with Wackenhut Corrections Corporation (conceptual design, facility specifications, FF&E), The National Bank of Australia (Debt Financing), Equity Providers (Equity Financing), and various professional sub-contractors and suppliers.

AUSTRALASIAN CORRECTIONAL MANAGEMENT (ACM)

ACM is a wholly owned subsidiary of Wackenhut Corrections Corporation Australia Pty Ltd (WCCA). ACM is fully committed to working closely with government clients in a public-private sector partnership, providing quality, professional and cost-effective correctional management services.

ACM became the largest Australian private corrections management company when awarded contracts for the Junee Correctional Centre and the Arthur Gorrie Correctional (Remand and Reception) Centre.

OPERATING COMPANIES PROVIDING PROJECT DELIVERY & CORRECTIONAL MANAGEMENT SERVICES

WACKENHUT CORRECTIONS (WACKENHUT)

Established in 1984, Wackenhut specialises in the financing, design, construction and management of detention and correctional facilities throughout the USA, and through its subsidiaries, the world. Wackenhut's management portfolio includes ten correctional facilities in the United States, with responsibility for over 4600 inmates. Wackenhut Corrections Corporation is a wholly-owned subsidiary of The Wackenhut Corporation.

AUSTRALASIAN CORRECTIONAL SERVICES (ACS)

ACS is a company formed by Wackenhut Corrections Corporation and Thiess Contractors Pty Ltd - each with a 50% shareholding. ACS combines the strength of both parent organisations by implementing a "total systems approach" to maximise the design, construction, financing and operational efficiencies of correctional facilities throughout Australasia. Each member contributes significant knowledge and extensive proprietary technology to the company, providing governments with correctional facilities which are durable, functional and cost-efficient.

THE WACKENHUT CORPORATION

Established in 1954, Wackenhut Corporation and its subsidiaries are headquartered in Florida. International in scope, The Wackenhut Corporation has grown to become one of the largest protective service organisations in the world and is the largest private sector provider of physical security to the US Government. Wackenhut has annual revenues exceeding $US600 million, assets of more than $150 million and is listed on the New York Stock Exchange.

LEIGHTON HOLDINGS LIMITED

Leighton Holdings is the parent company of the Leighton Group of Companies which includes Thiess Contractors Pty Ltd. The Group's business activities include civil and building design and construction, project management, property developing, mining and a range of specialist engineering, environmental and waste management services, throughout Australasia. Leighton Holdings employs more than 7600 people, has annual revenues exceeding $A1.7 billion and assets of more than $A870 million.

THIESS CONTRACTORS (THIESS)

Thiess has over 50 years experience in civil and building construction including the construction of correctional facilities throughout Australia. Thiess offers a service based on quality, performance and technical innovation. Recent projects include design and construction of Junee Correctional Centre, NSW, Borallon Prison, Qld and Barwon Prison, Victoria. Thiess is a wholly owned subsidiary of Leighton Holdings Limited.

SUBSIDIARY COMPANIES COMPRISING ACS (TENDERING ENTITY)

PARENT COMPANIES

of the progressive and innovative practices the company has to offer in corrections management. ACM was able to demonstrate that the experience and knowledge of its parent company Wackenhut Corrections Corporation (WCC) would provide 'best practice' correctional management and inmate rehabilitation initiatives aimed at reducing recidivism, in a cost effective manner.

During the late 1980s, the beginning of the recession in Australia, the state and federal governments were faced with the obligation to provide more services to taxpayers with less funding. Government departments and statutory authorities were being asked to reduce costs without reducing the number and quality of services they provided. In fact many government agencies were being pressured to improve the quality of their services. It was in this environment that private sector options were being considered as viable alternatives. The various state corrections departments were not excluded from these pressures and began to review the idea of privatisation within corrections. These reviews led to the conclusion that there was a distinct economic advantage in the privatisation of correctional centre management and construction. In addition to the economic advantages other benefits gained from a public/private partnership were innovation in management and operational procedures, cost accounting, specialised automated systems and the introduction of attitudinal and cultural change. Additionally, the government obtains an opportunity to measure its own performance against lessons learnt from contracting with and monitoring the performance of private operators.

In general, the major reasons for the privatisation of prisons can be summarised in three words: Cost, Culture and Innovation. ACM's contribution to each one of these is reflected in the company's policies and procedures.

ACM's correctional management and operating mission is to provide a safe, secure and humane correctional environment wherein offenders are afforded meaningful opportunities for self-understanding and improvement through individual and group counselling, health, education, work skills and life-skills programs. The primary principles of the ACM correctional philosophy are:

- the dignity and rights of each offender are to be recognised and respected;
- the loss of the offender's liberty is his/her sole punishment; the conditions of that lost liberty should contribute to the offender's overall rehabilitation, consistent with the good order and discipline of the centre;

- offender programs, in order to be effective, must address the offender's individual needs and circumstances of criminal behaviour, with particular emphasis on the special needs of offender minority populations;
- the correction of offender behaviour is a continuum of care that begins and ends in the community; to be effective, offender programs must encourage maximum understanding from and interaction with the community;
- the officers and staff of the entire organisation must be supported with safe and equitable work conditions, meaningful career opportunities, highest quality equipment and technology, and ongoing professional training;
- correctional programs are to be offered to offenders without respect to colour, gender, marital status, physical disability, religion, political affiliation, or national origin, except as may be consistent with meeting the needs of a disadvantaged individual or group.

In attempting to illustrate the benefits of privatisation of the management of correctional centres, particularly with respect to the role of industrial relations in assisting with achieving cost advantages, cultural change and innovation, it is useful to begin with an examination of the main features of each centre and conclude with an analysis of the industrial relations mechanisms at the Junee Correctional Centre.

THE JUNEE CORRECTIONAL CENTRE

As the NSW government was considering the privatisation issue for NSW, representatives from the Department of Corrective Services visited the US to observe the benefits of private corrections management. They visited public and private correctional facilities and met with government and private correctional management and government leaders. For two years the NSW Department of Corrective Services researched and monitored the effects of private correctional centres in the US. The government, once satisfied that privatisation was a viable alternative, announced expressions of interest were being called to design, construct and manage a new prison in NSW.

Legislation providing for the contract management of correctional centres was passed by the NSW government in 1990 and the *Prisons (Contract Management) Act* was proclaimed on 25 February 1991. As a result of the legislation:

- minimum standards were developed with which the management company had to comply. This exercise meant that minimum standards were actually documented for the first time;
- the legislation provided for the appointment of a monitor or liaison officer who reports to the Commissioner of Corrective Services on a regular basis regarding the adherence of the contractual obligations of the management company. The monitor or liaison officer is based on site at Junee and has unrestricted access to the staff and the centre;
- the legislation also provided that a community advisory council be established (members are to be appointed by and report to the Minister).

The process of expressions of interest, tenders and contracts took approximately a year to complete. The NSW Public Works Department was responsible for the design and construction phase and the Department of Corrective Services was responsible for the contracting relationship with the management company.

The NSW Department of Corrective Services 1990/91 Annual Report states: 'The Junee prison will provide an opportunity for the private sector to prove it can be more cost effective and innovative in the design, construction and management of prisons. The privately managed prison will also provide a yardstick by which publicly managed prisons can be assessed and act as a catalyst for change in the existing prison system.'

In an effort to review the advantages of privatisation the Department of Corrective Services have commissioned external consultants to undertake a series of research studies at various stages of the development of the project. The research unit within the Department of Corrective Services also has plans to evaluate the effectiveness of initiatives at Junee, with emphasis on those that are considered to be cost effective and innovative. Regular statistics will also be collected and collated for comparison with government prisons.

The prison was built on 106 hectares, two kilometres outside Junee, a small country town (about 360 kilometres SW of Sydney). The residents were experiencing the pain of unemployment as the railway, the town's main industry for the last 150 years was downsizing and employees were being made redundant. The town's leaders knew that the construction of the new prison would bring immediate life back to their town; however, it took several months for the residents to overcome their apprehension of having a goal so close to their community. A well-integrated process of community liaison by both

Figure 2: Junee prison.

the government and ACM ensured the concerns of the local residents were addressed and resolved. Junee residents are now amongst the strongest supporters of the correctional centre.

The Premier of NSW, The Hon. John Fahey MP said at the opening of the correctional centre in March 1993, 'This project, which I know the people of Junee have supported enthusiastically shows how the government and private sector can work in harmony to the ultimate benefit of the taxpayer'.

The Junee Correctional Centre is the first correctional facility in Australia to be designed, constructed and managed by the private sector. It was completed within budget ahead of schedule and is the most cost-efficient correctional centre in the country.

Project Information:

Cost to build:	$53 million.
Construction Period:	August 1991 – March 1993
Number of Beds:	600 total; 500 medium security, 100 minimum security.
Opening:	5 April 1993.
Project Delivery:	Australasian Correctional Services.
Design and Construction:	Theiss Contractors Pty Ltd.
Operation:	Australasian Correctional Management.

Five hundred of the centre's offenders are housed in the four medium security housing units of four pods each. The remaining 100 offenders are accommodated in the centre's minimum security compound.

The Junee Correctional Centre is managed and operated in accordance with unit management principles. Each housing unit is managed by a unit manager with a unit management team comprised of a case manager, counsellor and correctional officers. Each offender is accorded individual case review, including a review of classification, achievement of needs and objectives and programs participation. In so far as is possible, decisions regarding the management of offenders within each unit are made by the unit management team, through appropriate delegations.

Junee Correctional Centre has a 2250 square metre industry building which provides work opportunities for approximately 200 inmates. The primary industries are electronic assembly and manufacture of electrical cable and plugs. Private companies lease the space from ACM and pay ACM for the produced products. ACM in turn provides the inmate labour and pays employees in accordance with the NSW Department of Corrective Services industry wage guidelines.

THE ARTHUR GORRIE CORRECTIONAL CENTRE

ACM was selected by the Queensland Corrective Services Commission (QCSC) in March 1992 through a competitive tender process to operate its new remand and reception centre, located at Wacol. This centre, the Arthur Gorrie Correctional Centre, was built to replace the Boggo Road prison, parts of which were constructed at the turn of the century. The selection of a private sector corrections management company to operate this facility is a continuation of a policy adopted earlier by the Queensland government when it selected a private company to manage its Borallon Correctional Centre.

ACM is responsible for all aspects of the centre's operation, including:

- the intake and processing of all remandees from police custody and to and from the courts;
- calculation and processing of offender fines, penalties, and bail payments;
- intake and processing of all sentenced offenders from the courts;
- preparation of sentence management plans in accordance with QCSC regulations and requirements;
- provision of custodial care to immigrant detainees under a sub-contract arrangement between the state and federal governments;
- management of a young offenders' unit;
- management of a sentenced custody population.

As a remand and reception centre, Arthur Gorrie accommodates all classifications of offenders and has often served as a placement centre of 'last resort' for problem inmates which the QCSC has sought to place in a secure environment. It is the largest correctional centre in Queensland and is the only privately operated remand and reception centre in Australia.

Prior to and during the tendering process for these two contracts, ACM began a full review of all local customs and practices. Efforts were made to ensure local people were recruited and links were established with government leaders and local businesses. While attempting to assimilate into the local environment ACM also had to retain the characteristics that place it on the cutting edge of corrections management. ACM was in the enviable position of creating a company that had no previous history or culture. Both sites, Junee and Arthur Gorrie, were greenfield sites.

Each correctional centre is a largely autonomous enterprise

operating under guidelines established by ACM's corporate office, located in Sydney. The company is managed by a chief executive officer and four general managers: Operations, Administration and Finance, Human Resources and Health Services. All general managers serve as both a resource and monitor of centre operations. ACM manages its corporate affairs in accordance with a complete set of corporate policies and procedures, which are supported in turn by site specific policies and procedures manuals for each centre. These policies and procedures incorporate all aspects of ACM's contractual obligations and 'best practice' methodologies.

The centres are separate enterprises with specific missions and objectives and are structured in such a way that there are four or five functional departments each with a department manager who reports directly to the general manager or the Governor of the Centre. The functional departments work together in small 'task' oriented teams. For example, a small team at the Junee correctional centre was recently tasked with recommending options for establishing a system of allowing inmates to make reverse charge telephone calls from Junee. This group met regularly each week for an hour and within six weeks presented centre management with a viable option which will reduce the current difficulties in reverse charge telephone calls for inmates.

INDUSTRIAL RELATIONS

When looking at the impact of industrial relations on the changes that are occurring within organisations it is important to realise that industrial relations cannot be insulated from the changing influences within society. Industrial relations is not about drafting an industrial agreement or award and walking away until the next appearance at the Industrial Relations Commission. It is no longer about 'them' and 'us'; it is about management and the way people in the organisation are expected to perform their jobs in accordance with company and enterprise objectives.

ACM's progressive human resource policies and procedures have been instrumental in creating an organisational culture that encourages team work, an emphasis on customer service and a commitment to the company's philosophy. The underlying principles are consistency, fairness, equity and accountability. ACM human resource policies are regarded by ACM managers and employees as both innovative and practical. These policies are a combination of 'best practices' from both cultures, the US and Australia, and are incorporated in first line supervisors' and managers' job descriptions. The

Figure 3: Arthur Gorrie Correctional Centre.

message from the Chief Executive Officer in the employees handbook highlights ACM's philosophy.

Dear Employee

Welcome to the Australasian Correctional Management organisation.

ACM is dedicated to providing professional correctional management services to its government clients through out Australasia. As an ACM employee, you are expected to know and represent the Company's goals and principles. In return, you can expect to be provided with comprehensive training and guidance designed to enhance your career goals and job satisfaction. ACM's commitment to professionalism and integrity depends upon the co-operation and personal commitment of every employee within the organisation. Effective communication within established channels ensures that no positive ideas for improvement of our practices and procedures will go unheard. Your constructive opinions and ideas are valued highly.

This Handbook is one of the means by which you will learn about ACM and its expectations of you as an employee, as well as ACM's responsibilities to you and its clients. Become familiar with its contents and if you have questions or concerns, raise them with your supervisor. The most important assets of any service organisation are its employees. Together we can and will maintain ACM's position of strength and potential for growth as the premier provider of contract correctional management services throughout Australia.

As ACM did not have the constraints of the entrenched unions with which the government prison system was tied, there was an opportunity to review all available industrial options and compare the effectiveness of each one in contributing to the objectives of the company and enterprise. This exercise was undertaken prior to the recruitment of personnel at both Arthur Gorrie and Junee. There were no established awards or agreements for staff employed in private correctional facilities. The only precedent was Borallon Correctional Centre in Queensland, who had negotiated an agreement for correctional officers with the Queensland branch of the Liquor and Hospitality Miscellaneous Workers Union (LHMWU) in the late 1980s.

In view of this precedent, ACM began negotiations with the LHMWU Queensland branch (then known as the Federated Miscellaneous Workers Union), to establish an agreement for correctional officers employed at Arthur Gorrie. This agreement was very similar to that developed for Borallon. However, ACM placed greater emphasis on multi-skilling of correctional officers.

The role of industrial relations strategies in contributing to prison reform in the private sector can best be demonstrated by examining the industrial initiatives at Junee. An initial review of the options for Junee highlighted the need to pursue enterprise specific agreements in order to meet the stated company objectives and goals. Whilst ACM understood that enterprise agreements in themselves do not provide magic answers to productivity and high morale, it was understood that as a tool in the hands of skilled managers and supervisors, enterprise agreements ensure greater efficiency and enhance communication with staff.

INDUSTRIAL RELATIONS AT JUNEE

Taking advantage of the innovative NSW state industrial legislation, two enterprise agreements were negotiated at the correctional centre. Approximately 80 per cent of the workforce at Junee are employed under an enterprise agreement registered pursuant to section 126 of the NSW *Industrial Relations Act 1991*. Two enterprise agreements currently operate at the centre, one for custodial officers and one for non-custodial employees. Both agreements are based on the concept of an aggregate annual salary without penalty rates or allowances and are designed to satisfy the following enterprise requirements:

- flexible and equitable rostering, particularly for correctional officers; the practice of working in a dedicated post is discouraged. All correctional officers should be able to work in any post in the centre;
- enhancement of 'total quality management' principles and a commitment to continuous improvement;
- the encouragement of multi-skilling of all staff;
- merit based selection and promotions. (Years of service and seniority are not significant factors in these processes);
- simplified payroll and rostering procedures;
- plain English agreements that are easily understood.

The Junee Custodial Officers Enterprise Agreement covers all correctional officers and senior correctional officers. This agreement was negotiated with the LHMWU (NSW branch), on behalf of the correctional officers. As ACM had already formed a professional and practical working relationship with the LHMWU in Queensland, it was logical to continue the relationship. This agreement was registered on 30 March 1993 and remains in force for 12 months.

This agreement between ACM and the LHMWU creates a single union coverage for correctional officers at Junee and is intended to provide for the elimination of demarcations and rationalisation of coverage by industrial organisations of employees within the enterprise. As this was the first enterprise agreement under NSW legislation for both ACM and the LHMWU it was agreed the minimum standard for an agreement of one year would be appropriate so that both parties would have an opportunity to understand the requirements of the enterprise as it developed.

The Junee Non-Custodial Employees Enterprise Agreement was registered on 29 July 1993 and remains in force for 18 months. This agreement replaces the following NSW state awards:

- Clerks (state);
- Nurses etc, other than in hospitals etc (state);
- Storemen and Packers-General (state);
- Canteen etc, Workers (state);
- Teacher (non government business colleges) (state);
- Miscellaneous workers'– general services (state);
- Landscape gardeners etc (state).

The following categories of staff are covered by the terms and conditions of this agreement: registered nurses, clerks, cooks, counsellors, teachers, recreation specialists, maintenance technicians, storekeepers, groundskeepers, cleaners. The salaries for the classifications are the only aspects of the agreement that differ; all other terms and conditions apply equally to all classifications covered by the agreement.

Annual performance appraisals are mandatory for all staff and salaries are reviewed annually by ACM. Clause 3.1 of the agreement states: 'It is ACM practice to review employees' wage rates annually. Adjustments, if any will be made based upon the employee's performance, achievement of established objectives, company financial condition and cost of living indicators.'

There is no union representation for any of these groups; the employees negotiated the agreement directly with ACM after commencing employment. Prior to the registration of the agreement a secret ballot was conducted by the State Electoral Office for all staff covered by the agreement. The result was 100 per cent in favour of the agreement as proposed.

The flexibility of both these agreements allows for greater and immediate responsiveness of our service delivery to inmates, particularly in allowing for efficient and effective unit management. The benefit of the flexibility of these agreements is reflected in the procedure of inmate disciplinary interviews, previously conducted by the governor of the centre. These interviews are now conducted by an inter-disciplinary panel of employees within each unit and result when an inmate fails to respond to an instruction or commits an offence within the centre. The panel consists of the unit manager, the case manager, the counsellor and a correctional officer. Each member provides input towards the final recommendation for presentation to the governor. This team approach towards making informed group decisions at the 'coal face' ensures better recommendations are made and appropriate disciplinary actions are taken.

Inmate programs can be provided during evenings as well as during the day as staff can arrange their working hours to accommodate their own needs in accordance with those of the enterprise. These programs can also be tailored to the skills needed to work in the specific industries at the centre.

Another example of the flexibility within the working environment can be demonstrated by the attitudes of the registered nurses on site. The nurses work an equitable roster providing 24-hour medical coverage and organise their working arrangements amongst themselves. During the enterprise agreement negotiations, the nurses requested that they all receive the same annual salary rather than receiving payment based on the traditional 'years of service' model. They felt this pay structure would enhance their *esprit de corps* and assist them to work as a more cohesive team. This attitude to team work has manifested itself in many ways and has had a very positive influence throughout the centre. There is no doubt that there is a direct correlation between the level of team work amongst the health professionals and the reduced need to transport injured inmates to outside hospitals.

Custodial staff at each facility receive regular training (at least 40 hours of scheduled training each year), and are encouraged to attend seminars whenever possible. The more highly trained the staff, the more skills they have for contributing to the operation of the centre. A US suicide prevention expert, Joseph Rowan, attended both facilities in January this year to provide training on suicide prevention for employees and inmates. The training was mandatory for every staff member (including the office staff) at each centre. Joseph Rowan states that all employees have a responsibility to assist in the prevention of deaths in custody. This is in fact reflected in ACM's suicide prevention policy and procedures and highlights the philosophy that all employees contribute to the management of the centre, and do not simply perform within the confines of their prescribed job descriptions.

The workforce at Junee form part of the local community and work closely together. Any industrial action arising from demarcation disputes would be detrimental to productivity and good industrial relations. ACM employees feel proud to be part of an organisation that is playing a key role in providing innovative and responsive inmate programs. The staff understand their performance directly affects ACM's future growth and business success. This awareness provides a high level of motivation for the employees who enjoy the challenge of becoming successful and respected leaders in their fields of expertise. Annual salary reviews based on performance and opportunities for rapid career advancement and secondments both interstate and overseas, encourage attitudes of excellence amongst the staff.

When ACM began the recruitment process for staff at Junee the selection criteria, to the surprise of many, did not include as a mandatory requirement previous prison experience. The major criterion in the recruitment of staff was to select employees from the local area, who could demonstrate an ability to communicate effectively. Good interpersonal skills were considered to be more important than previous correctional experience. This approach to recruitment means that employees begin work without any preconceived ideas as to how a prison should function. The comprehensive pre-service training provided by ACM for all new staff equips them with the skills and knowledge they need to effectively perform their tasks.

ACM employees are not public sector employees and as such are not employed under the same terms and conditions as government employees. However, agreements in both Queensland and NSW with the correctional officers and the LHMWU were challenged in the Industrial Relations Commission by the respective state registered unions. In Queensland the State Services Union of Employees (QSSU) lodged an application in the Commission (No. B280 of 1992) seeking exclusive coverage of employees engaged in, or in connection with, the provision of custodial correctional services at the Wacol Remand and Reception Centre. After a lengthy hearing, the Commission refused the QSSU's application.

In NSW applications were made by the Federated Miscellaneous Workers Union (FMWU) and by the Public Service Association of NSW (PSA). Both sought to have private correctional officers included under their respective awards. The proceedings had been underway for several months when the two unions involved agreed to withdraw their applications. The status quo currently remains with the LHMWU representing the correctional officers at Junee and Arthur Gorrie.

It will be interesting to observe the outcomes of future coverage issues. The issue of union coverage of correctional officers in private correctional centres has not been fully settled, and will no doubt raise its head again in the future. ACM's experience strongly suggests that site specific agreements are the only way to achieve true efficiencies. They not only reflect the requirements of the enterprise but are more likely to truly represent the needs of the employees.

The culture of ACM has been firmly established and is reflected in the organisation structure, company objectives, decision making processes and employee job descriptions. Greenfield sites and new employees provide opportunities for setting ground rules and providing directions that encourage innovation without the barriers and obstacles of past practice. Enterprise agreements play a major role in facilitating the implementation of company policies and procedures. Industry based agreements would make this task extremely difficult.

ACM acknowledges the importance of good industrial relations and the role it plays in contributing to the overall success of the mission. Without well integrated industrial processes ACM would not be leading the field in the business of private correctional management.

Part II

Private contract management of prisons in Queensland and New South Wales, Australia: recent developments

6

USA prison privateers: neo-colonialists in a southern land

Eileen Baldry

Abstract: Colonisation may not only be imposed but invited. Recently New South Wales, Queensland, Victoria and New Zealand prison systems have been casting around for solutions to the problems of increasing costs and unsuccessful methods which create confrontation and violence and leave ex-inmates unable to integrate into their society. At the same time, private prisons entrepreneurs from the United States have been promoting their corporations as solutions. The unseemly rush by NZ and Australian correctional departments to privatise leaves major questions unanswered. What are the models we are buying? What are the credentials of the American corporations (Corrections Corporation of America and Wakenhut) we have invited in? Why are we not only allowing, but asking for US colonisation of our corrections systems? What are the implications of such a move?

The current contracting of Australian prisons to private corporations with their bases in the United States is only the most recent in the saga of US entrepreneurial expansion. It can be paralleled with the export for profit of nuclear power, health care systems and toxic chemicals by large US transnational corporations and the attempted 'colonisation' of those industries in countries outside the US. Each of these exercises has concealed vital information from the receiving country, and has been accompanied by extravagant claims concerning the benefits of the commodity being 'sold'. Each has necessitated the introduction of culturally foreign attitudes and personnel, and each has talked about economic imperatives to the exclusion of argument about social cohesion, well-being and citizens' rights. All have attempted expansion into foreign markets at the self-same time that expansion in the US was declining or under threat. The introduction of the US private prison model to Australia and its ready acceptance has been an exercise in entrepreneurial colonisation hastily invited and given without proper investigation. This chapter examines the process by which private for-profit prison corporations have been granted contracts in Australia.

SELLERS AND BUYERS

With the advent of the Coalition government in NSW early in 1988, came the new Minister for Corrective Services, Michael Yabsley. Within months discussions were taking place with private prison corporations. In November 1988 the John Holland Group sponsored a promotional meeting in Sydney for Corrections Corporation of America (CCA) with Mr Yabsley chairing the session. The promotion (letter to author 18 November 1988) claimed that CCA had specialist skills in corrections management, finance, business, planning and construction and that it had experience in all aspects of corrections. The reality was that CCA had only been running since 1983, had only become a public company in 1986 and at the time of the promotion was only running nine facilities, all of them juvenile, work house or minimum security centres (Larson 1988). What CCA was doing is well described by its chairman and founder, Beasley: 'You just sell it like you were selling cars or real estate or hamburgers' (Larson 1988). In the US, it is alleged that Beasley also used his political contacts — he is a former head of the Republican Party in Tennessee — and that three of the commissioners who voted in 1984 to give CCA the contract to run Silverdale prison farm were later granted contracts with the prison (Savitz 1989). These allegations do not appear to have been legally challenged. At the time of the Australian promotional tour, CCA was making a loss (Larson 1988).

As it turned out, CCA (together with Wormald and Holland Holdings) — in its Australian incarnation, Corrections Corporation of Australia — was first off the rank in Queensland, winning the Borallon contract. A much newer player in the US corrections field, Wackenhut Corporation in the form of Australasian Correctional Services (with

Thiess Contractors and ADT Security) won the first NSW contract to both build and under the name Australasian Correctional Management (Wackenhut and ADT), manage Junee Correctional Centre. It should have been thoroughly disconcerting for the people of NSW, on the eve of the opening of Junee, to read in the *Sydney Morning Herald* (20 March 1993) 'little is known about the American based companies' and to be told in three lines all the journalist could glean from government and the company itself about Wackenhut.

Much could have been known, had the government of the day properly scrutinised it. The Public Accounts Committee, NSW Parliament (1992), in its report on the procedure used to award the Junee contract, indicates that the security clearances that gave attention to 'the integrity of the shortlisted companies . . . and the principles of those companies' were undertaken by the Special Investigation Unit of the Department of Corrective Services — surely ill-equipped for such a task. As with Queensland, NSW appears to have naively 'bought' the lines served up by the American companies: that private prisons have proved much more efficient, safe and rehabilitative than state prisons, that they provide a benchmark against which to measure the performance of publicly run prisons (Department of Corrective Services NSW 1992, p. 4) and that they solve numerous problems faced by the state including overcrowding, escalating costs and recalcitrant unions (Kennedy 1988, p. 97; Kleinwort Benson 1989, p. 5.1, 5.4, 5.6).

What background did Wackenhut have to be granted the management of Junee? According to *Business Week* (17 December 1990) Wackenhut Corporation, founded in 1955 by George Wackenhut (still the head) a former FBI agent, mainly provided security and surveillance services until the early 1980s when it began seeking diversification. It tried to capitalise on President Reagan's 1984 invitation to privatise anything that could be privatised by moving into emergency medical services and airport crash and rescue services. These proved unfruitful for the company so in 1987 it turned to private prisons, a government responsibility Reagan's privatisation committee had recommended as being in need of private sector take-over (Donahue 1989, pp. 5-8). It is predicted by *Business Week* (17 December 1990) to be destined for more success in prisons than its other privatisation attempts.

Donahue (1989, p. 151) listed Wackenhut as the newest player in private corrections, and at that stage noted that it, along with Bechtel (famed as the contractor which built GE's worst performing and most contaminated nuclear power station — the Tarapur Atomic Power Station) had contracts to build and run two prisons in Texas. In November 1990, Wackenhut opened its first medium security prison

(*Business Week*, 17 December 1990). Wackenhut therefore had barely entered the private prison arena in 1989 when Michael Yabsley stated to NSW Parliament that on June 13, he had 'met with representatives of the Wackenhut Corporation, a well established and respected group experienced in the operations of privatised prisons' (Hansard July 26, 1989, p. 8506).

Wackenhut's major experience had been as one of the world's largest total security service companies, providing services such as protecting facilities like nuclear power plants, petroleum reserves and US overseas corporate offices and embassies and providing security training for government and private clients (*Business Week* 17 December 1990; Committee on Interior and Insular Affairs 1992, p. 1). To run Australasian Correctional Management (ACM), Wackenhut sent two senior managers, Calabrese and Barncastle from the USA and Grigas and a retired prison governor from the Massachusetts Department of Corrections, to run the Junee prison (*Sun Herald*, 20 December 1992). This is, of course, in no way a comment on particular individuals. The senior staff of ACM have assisted the author, been hospitable and appear to be implementing a non-abusive and efficient system at Junee. But it indicates that US corporations are colonising, not only with models and ideologies, but with personnel in the same way as 19th century imperialist countries did.

USA PRISON CRISIS

The decision by Queensland and NSW governments to contract these private-for-profit corporations with their parent companies in the US to run prisons needs to be understood in the context of the development and ethos of the private prison industry in the US, because local circumstances cannot account for it. It is universally agreed that these, and similar corporations, rose like rockets in the mid to late 1980s in the US due to very particular circumstances (Donahue 1989, Taylor and Pease 1989, Vallance 1991, Chan 1992). These circumstances were:

- unprecedented growth in detention centre, jail and prison populations and expenditures. Expenditures at all levels of corrections (federal, state and local) had virtually doubled from 1980 to 1985 (from $6901 million to $13,034 million); the rate of incarceration per 100,000 for state and federal institutions alone (not including local jails) had risen from 139 in 1980 to 200 in 1985 (Bureau of the Census 1988);
- litigation by inmates and injunctions against numerous prison

authorities requiring overcrowding and below standard accommodation to be rectified. For example, in 1982 Texas was under threat by a federal judge with an $800,000 a day fine unless it alleviated overcrowding in its prisons (*Business Week*, 20 April 1982);

- the inability of many states faced with massive growth in prisoner numbers to raise the capital to build new cells (for example the economic disaster experienced by southern states that had the highest prison populations, like Texas). There was also an unwillingness to change the 'lock-em-up' policies which largely had led to the overcrowding problem (Donahue 1989, p. 151);

- the political ethos of the day which was characterised by an official in the following way: 'by the second Reagan term, officials took to joking that virtually any proposal could become administrative policy if it carried the label "privatisation"' (Donahue 1989, p. 5).

The cultural, economic and political setting which fostered the move to privatise prisons in the US was just not present in Australia (Vallance 1991; Chan 1992). The enormous growth in NSW prisoner numbers only began with Michael Yabsley's term as minister. In 1988 the NSW rate was 101 per 100,000. By 1991 it was 129 (Walker 1992, Table D6) — a disaster by Australian standards, but nothing like the US. In 1988 NSW was not facing a crisis of massive overcrowding, litigation or lack of public funds to build prisons. The Minister's policies, by his own admission, were contributing to the increase in prisoner numbers in NSW whilst the rest of the Australian states were maintaining, not increasing their rates of imprisonment. The Minister was granted budget funds for capital works to finish and build Lithgow, Windsor and Junee prisons. The capital was not put up by a private company to build Junee, as was being done in the US to avoid the state standing the capital cost. There were some very obvious directions the government could have taken to overcome growing numbers and the need for more programs in prisons. One solution was to put fewer people in prison. This chapter is not the place to canvass the well trod ground of arguing the case that larger numbers in prison do not reduce crime nor improve the possibility of rehabilitation of offenders. Suffice it to note that after almost a decade of private prisons in the US, Mr Conyers, Chair of the House Committee on Government Operations and Senior Members of the Congressional Black Caucus stated: 'The only beneficiary of our distorted "lock-em-up" criminal justice policies is prison construction, not crime control or prevention' (*New York Times*, 11 February 1993).

COMPARISON WITH US NUCLEAR POWER AND OTHER INDUSTRIES

To understand something of why Australia has so precipitously embraced private prison corporations and their product, it may be useful to note the client state nature of Australia's relationship to the US (Pusey 1991, p. xii) and to look at similar US entrepreneurial activity in other areas. This will take us away from prisons for the moment, but it is a necessary and most pertinent excursion.

In 1953 President Eisenhower launched the 'Atoms for Peace' program at the UN. A major motive behind this program was to ensure American enterprise industry captured the bulk of the global market for nuclear power plants (Lowry 1989). The Atomic Energy Act of 1946 was amended in 1954 to entice entrepreneurial activity despite the well-known dangers of nuclear power production and despite the fact that not one plant had been completed in the US. The risks and lack of evaluation on reactors were not mentioned in the rush to sell to international markets. In fact 'almost anything was acceptable if it did not interrupt the expansion of the atomic empire world wide' (Lowry 1989, p. 13). From the early 1960s nuclear reactors in the US were experiencing severe problems — fatalities, leakages, contaminations, major accidents, non-productivity, out of court settlements and massive secret expenditure on 'clean-ups' (Pringle and Spigelman 1983). None of this was made available to prospective customers. This entrepreneurial colonisation gained momentum in the early and mid 1970s for it was at that time that American state governments and local communities began waking up to the lemons they had been sold and started cancelling existing orders and not placing new ones. Since 1974, no new order for a nuclear reactor has been made in the US and all existing orders have been either cancelled or indefinitely deferred (May 1989, p. 338). The product though is still promoted, particularly to third world countries, as the answer to their power problems.

The self-same story emerges when the US sale of toxic chemicals internationally is examined. US companies, having developed a product and having the profit motive above all others, promote their products before full trials on the safety of the chemicals have been done, or even more immorally, after the product has been deemed unsafe for US consumption by government regulatory bodies. Exports of such products from US ports rose by 12 per cent in 1991 compared to 1990 figures, according to government shipping records (FASE 1993). These included DDT, banned for more than 20 years in the US, dieldrin also banned, and chlordane, heptachlor and carbofuron all severely restricted. US companies that cannot sell their product to their own citizens can make a profit selling it to the expendable citizens of other countries.

New South Wales has recently granted the right to Australian Medical Enterprises (AME) formerly Markalinga, a subsidiary of National Medical Enterprises (NME), to buy the four private hospitals in the St George area and the AME is negotiating to build and run a private hospital adjacent to the St George Public Hospital (*Sydney Morning Herald*, 17 October 1992; *Sydney Morning Herald*, 6 March 1993). The aggressive moves by US private medical and hospital companies into Australia are of the same ilk as the two earlier examples. The US health system is acknowledged, even by President Clinton (*Sun Herald*, 19 September 1993), to be the worst in the 'developed' world with 14 per cent of GDP (compared with Australia's 8 per cent) being spent on health but with some 60 million people being inadequately covered and 37 million not covered at all. Private hospitals, nursing homes, psychiatric hospitals and clinics dominate the system and devour the budget.

The Report of the Senate Select Committee on Private Hospitals and Nursing Homes tabled in the Australian Parliament in 1987 voiced concern over the emergence of foreign-owned, mainly US-based, corporate chains in the private health sector in Australia (chapter 6). The Committee was presented with rationales for foreign corporations running private hospitals:

- high standards of services and efficiency are introduced;
- these private hospitals become yardsticks for state run hospitals;
- foreign personnel bring more advanced practices. (pp. 253-254)

It is no coincidence that these are almost identical with the private prison rationales discussed earlier and are just as spurious. It was noted by the committee that no evidence was given in support of them and that in fact, the 'advantage of overseas input was unmeasured' (p. 254). It was also noted that in the US these corporations have been associated with rising health care costs, contrary to their claims (p. 267 & Chapter 7), and with monopolistic tendencies (p. 267) and that the intention of US corporations was to dominate the private hospital system in Australia (p. 260). The committee could see no evidence of benefit but rather of harm to Australian citizens in the expansion of US private health corporations. The committee concluded that the uncontrolled entry of foreign-owned hospital chains into Australia was contrary to the national interest (p. 266).

NME, the parent corporation of AME, mentioned earlier as attempting to operate in the St George district, has a string of allegations against it for defrauding the US federal government of $750 million and is facing lawsuits from 13 insurance companies and various civil litigants over allegations of false imprisonment, insurance fraud, violation of constitutional rights, battery, assault, negligence, conspiracy, medical malpractice and personal injury (Four Corners 19 October 1992; *Sydney Morning Herald*, 6 March 1993). The FBI recently raided the head offices of the corporation on allegations of criminal misconduct (*The Australian*, 28 August 1993; *Telegraph Mirror*, 28 August 1993). This very company is trying to colonise the Australian health care system at the same time as its profitability in the US is under threat. Not only is it under individual threat, but the whole US health care system is facing massive change precisely because of the style of health care system created by the private sector: that is it is not accountable enough to government, is inefficient, is overpriced and is inequitable. Ironically, the US is favourably evaluating the Australian Medicare system in an attempt to work out a universal health care system (*Sun Herald*, 19 September 1993).

PRIVATE PRISONS

To return to private prisons. The foregoing examples of US international entrepreneurial activities which have been in the interests of the profit making companies, but not necessarily in the interests of the receiving citizens, are being repeated in the case of prisons.

To this day, there is no evidence that private prisons are more cost effective than public ones. The corporations say they are, but the figures do not sustain that claim. Juvenile detention has been the field in which private companies have had the longest time to prove their success. There has been a fairly steady rate over the last decade in the US of about one third of all juveniles in detention being held in private centres.

Between 1983 and 1987, the comparative cost of keeping a juvenile in public as opposed to private custody was virtually equal but if anything the public cost had a lower growth rate than the private: in 1983 the per resident operating cost for private was $21,300, for public $22,000; the comparative 1987 cost was $27,800 against $27,000 (Bureau of the Census 1988, Table 332 p. 192). As usual, the public detention centres had to contend with the more difficult detainees, that is older, more violent juveniles and more black offenders (Bureau of the Census 1988, p. 192; Donahue 1989, p. 159). This cost comparison does not, of course, measure quality, but even on the privateers' own terms the cost outcome is not a success. With adult centres, the recent introduction of private prisons and the fact that virtually all of them, until two years ago, were minimum classification with rights to refuse certain difficult prisoners (for example, HIV positive and violent prisoners) makes it very difficult to compare costs (Donahue 1989, pp. 155-158).

Nevertheless, when Australian governments were deciding in favour of private prisons, partly on the basis of lower costs, the evidence was highly equivocal. Both Curran (1988) and Donahue (1989) in their separate cost comparisons found very little evidence of cost efficiencies. Recent newspaper reports are even more condemnatory of the costs of private prisons with headlines such as 'Prisons run out of cells, money and choices' (New York Times, 28 May 1993) and 'It's a bust. Promoters keep pushing privately run prisons to job-hungry towns.' (*Wall Street Journal*, 18 June 1991). As has been shown to be the case with nuclear power, toxic chemicals and private medical services, the costs both financially and to community well-being may well prove in the long run to be not only nothing like the savings and benefits promised, but to be very high and socially negative.

Just as in the 1950s with nuclear reactors, none of these companies have had any long-term experience in running adult correctional centres despite their claims. At the time Queensland and NSW governments were signing up private prison companies, not even 1 per cent of US prisoners were in private 'facilities' (Matthews 1989, p. 35; Donahue 1989, p. 158; Vallance 1991, p. 398). Australia has obligingly turned over approximately 9 per cent of its prison population for US companies to run their experiment here whilst only one state in the US, Texas, is increasing its stake in private prisons (*New York Times*, 28 May 1993). It would appear that American officials are reluctant to expand involvement in their own jurisdiction.

As private prison corporations see a decline in business in the US, they move to establish their profit-making businesses elsewhere in the world. The number of states contracting adult prison management to private corporations has not met their expectations. As long ago as 1991, some states were abandoning their private contracts as they ran out and officials were pulling prisoners out of private prisons for financial or bad management reasons (*Wall Street Journal*, 18 June 1991). The same paper stated: 'Once hailed as a quick fix for the nation's overcrowded prisons, privatisation is turning into quicksand for the companies and communities involved'. One DC prison official, Mr Graves, said that his state received a 'tremendous number of un-solicited proposals from prison entrepreneurs. We have no business for them.' (*Wall Street Journal*, 18 June 1991). Apparently Australia is kindly opening its market whilst the US is closing its. Politicians and citizens in the US are realising that education and health are taking second place to cell construction but with no effect on the crime rate and they are putting pressure on justice officials to turn to therapeutic options and put an end to the cell building boom that 'has made corrections a one million inmate, $25 bil. a year industry—the world's largest and costliest prison system' (*New York Times*, 28 May 1993).

The most worrying aspect is the acceptability of the US private corporations' style and behaviour. As with nuclear power, chemical and health corporations, some highly questionable activities undertaken by private corrections corporations in the US have been and are the subject of various investigations. It was promised by the NSW Minister of Corrective Services in 1989 that proper scrutiny would be made and maintained of any private organisation running NSW prisons. In fact Mr Yabsley assured the NSW public that 'the government will be looking for a far higher standard of probity and ethics than one would ever get from any of the Whelan family companies.' (Hansard September 13, 1989, p. 9878). By the time the Kleinwort Benson Report (September 1989) was presented, the Minister had already met with, and been very impressed by, Wackenhut executives. That report gave the NSW government the unequivocal recommendation that private prison operators could more easily, efficiently and effectively build and operate a prison in NSW than the public sector (ibid). It also stated that it had reviewed a wide variety of material relating to private sector involvement. The evidence quoted for such a claim is unacceptably thin. There is no evidence cited in the report that the consultants investigated any of the private prison corporations nor is there any evidence other than the Public Accounts Committee Report 73 discussed earlier, that any detailed investigation was made subsequent to that report of the two relevant US parent companies, CCA and Wackenhut. In 1990/91 no fewer than nine Corrective Services staff visited private prisons in the US (Department of Corrective Services NSW 1991, p. 144) but there does not appear to be any public evidence of those visitors exploring the probity of the parent corporations.

Junee Prison is subject to the same scrutiny as state institutions concerning discipline and prisoner management. Inmates can complain to the Ombudsman, there is an official visitor and the Independent Commission Against Corruption has the right to investigate alleged corrupt practices. Corrective Services has also appointed its own liaison officer with the prison. The Minister also promised another level of monitoring, a Community Advisory

Council. Although the council was formed it has had a somewhat chequered career, not meeting over the three month period during which Junee was opening and setting up its management operations, surely a critical time, and having some lack of clarity concerning its role. NSW citizens have found the same problem as their Queensland compatriots in gaining copies of what should be a public document, the contract between the state government and the private prison contractor. The contract is exempt from the Freedom of Information Act provisions due to commercial secrecy and therefore the exact terms on which the government has delegated responsibility to ACM for the care and control of inmates are inaccessible to citizens of NSW.

What of the probity and ethics of the Wackenhut Corporation? In July 1992 the Committee on Interior and Insular Affairs of the US House of Representatives One Hundred Second Congress published a report on 'Alyeska Pipeline Service Company Covert Operation' (CIIA 1992). The Committee had heard allegations of misconduct on the part of Alyeska and its contracted security agent Wackenhut during 1990-1991. Alyeska operates the trans-Alaska pipeline on behalf of seven oil companies (including Exxon of the 'Exxon Valdez' fame). In July 1991 a Charles Hamel, strong critic of Alyeska, informed the committee that he had been the victim of a 'sting' operation conducted by Wackenhut's Special Investigation Division on behalf of Alyeska allegedly with the purpose of preventing him from providing the committee with relevant documents on environmental health and safety breaches. At the time the committee was holding an ongoing investigation of the 'Exxon Valdez' oil spill. The committee found that,

> Wackenhut agents watched Hamel's home, picked through his trash, obtained his personal credit, banking and long-distance telephone records, as well as information about his divorce, his family, his ownership of property, his business disputes with Exxon, and virtually all his activities in the environmental arena. Wackenhut also gathered information on and extended its covert operations in varying ways to individuals and organisation also known to be Alyeska critics. (CIIA 1992, p. 3).

The committee, in a majority report, concluded that Alyeska intended to interfere with the committee's on-going investigations and blunt the effect of damaging disclosures about its misdeeds. It found also that Alyeska and Wackenhut obstructed the committee's investigation 'by withholding and possibly destroying and altering key documents and records of the covert activities.' (CIIA, p. 3). It believes these actions constituted violations of a section of the Constitution of the US. It also believes that federal and state criminal laws may have been violated by Wackenhut: obtaining AT&T telephone records without permission; obtaining private credit and financial reports under false pretences; secretly recording private conversations; possessing and transporting interstate devices designed for surreptitious interception of communications; obtaining under false pretences the free use of valuable computer software, and permanently removing documents from Hamel's home which did not belong to Wackenhut or Alyeska. The committee has sent its findings to the Department of Justice and various states for consideration of criminal and/or civil action against Alyeska and Wackenhut. Alyeska has, in the meantime, publicly apologised to the people of Alaska for the nature of the investigation. A minority report, tabled by Republican members of the committee, disagreed with the majority's interpretation of events, but did not dispute that Wackenhut had investigated Mr Hamel using the methods described.

CONCLUSION

Apart from the fact that, by introducing private prisons, Australian states are merely adding to the imprisonment mentality already rife rather than encouraging shifts away from it, wider cultural and social matters have been raised in this chapter. Australia has entered an era in which it looms as an attractive market for US multinationals wishing to transplant commercial service and cultural models. Private prisons are but a part of that market potential and have to be understood against the general background sketched in the previous pages. Australian state governments seem not to have considered either the propriety of contracting such corporations to run their prisons or the cultural ethos such a colonisation brings with it. Nor did NSW and Queensland governments appear to properly scrutinise multinational contractors. There has been much discussion of Australia's need to stand independently and forge its unique identity apart from Britain. It may well be though, as Michael Pusey has postulated, that as Australia has lost the cladding of its colonial heritage it has been left exposed to a 'recolonisation in the alien framework of a totalitarian American "business democracy"' (Pusey 1991, p. xii). As UK commentators Taylor and Pease (1989, p. 192) point out, 'We [may well] . . . have opened our gates to a particularly unpleasant Trojan Horse'.

References

Abraham, M. 1985, *The Lessons of Bhopal*, IOCU, Penang.

Bureau of the Census 1988, 1991 and 1992, *Statistical Abstract of the United States*, US Government Printing Office, Washington.

Chan, J. B. L. 1992, 'The Privatisation of Punishment: A Review of the Key Issues', *Australian Journal of Social Issues*, vol. 27, no. 4, November.

Commission of Review into Corrective Services in Queensland 1988, *Final Report*, (J. J. Kennedy, Commissioner), Queensland Government Printer, Brisbane.

Committee on Interior and Insular Affairs 1992, *Alyeska Pipeline Service Company Covert Operation Report*, US Government Printing Office, Washington.

Curran, D. 1988, 'Destructuring, Privatisation and the Promise of Juvenile Diversion', *Crime and Delinquency*, vol. 34, no. 4, pp. 363-78.

Department of Corrective Services NSW 1992, *Annual Report 1991/1992*, NSW Government Printing Service, Regents Park.

Donahue, J. D. 1989, *The Privatisation Decision*, Basic Books, N.Y.

FASE 1993, *Exporting Banned and Hazardous Pesticide, 1991 Statistics*, FASe, Los Angeles.

George, A. 1989, 'The State Tries an Escape', *Legal Services Bulletin*, vol. 14, no. 2, April, pp. 53-57.

Hansard 1989, July 26, Series 3, vol. 208.

Hansard 1989, September 13, Series 3, vol. 209.

International Organisation of Consumer Unions (IOCU) 1993, *Consumer Interpol Memo*, no. 133, July/August.

Kennedy Report. *See* Commission of Review into Corrective Services in Queensland.

Kenward, M. 1992, 'Can nuclear power ever pay its way?' *New Scientist*, 28 November, pp. 42-44.

Kleinwort Benson Australia Ltd 1989, *Investigation into Private Sector Involvement in the NSW Corrective Services System*, Sydney.

Larsen, E. 1988, 'Captive Company', *Inc*, June, pp. 87-92.

Lowry, D. 1989, 'Introduction' in *The Greenpeace Book of the Nuclear Age*, (ed) J. May, Victor Gallancz, London.

Matthews, R. (ed) 1989, *Privatising Criminal Justice*, Sage, London.

May, J. 1989, *The Greenpeace Book of the Nuclear Age*, Victor Gollancz, London.

Pringle, P. and Spigelman, J. 1983, *The Nuclear Barons*, Sphere Books, London.

Public Accounts Committee Report No. 73, *Infrastructure Management and Financing in NSW*, NSW Government Printer, Sydney.

Pusey, M. 1991, *Economic Rationalism in Canberra*, Cambridge University Press, Oakleigh.

Savitz, E. J. 1989, 'Pros and Cons: The Jury is still out on Private Prisons', *Barrons*, November 6, pp. 13, 22-26.

Senate Select Committee on Private Hospitals and Nursing Homes 1987, *Private Hospitals in Australia: their conduct, administration and ownership*, Australian Government Publishing Service, Canberra.

Taylor, M. and Pease, K. 1989, 'Private Prisons and Penal Purpose' in *Privatising Criminal Justice*, (ed) R. Matthews, Sage, London.

Vallance, S. 1991, 'Private Prison Management: Panacea or Pretence' *Australian Journal of Public Administration*, vol. 50, no. 3, September, pp. 397-413.

Walker, J. 1992, *Australian Prisoners 1991*, Australian Institute of Criminology, Canberra.

World Watch Institute, Greenpeace & WISOE 1992, *The World Nuclear Industry Status Report*.

7

Private prison research in Queensland, Australia: a case study of Borallon Correctional Centre, 1991

Paul Moyle[1]

Abstract: This chapter identifies the legislative and policy basis for the Queensland government's introduction of Borallon Correctional Centre including the contractual and regulatory arrangements between the Queensland Corrective Services Commission (QCSC) and Corrections Corporation of Australia (CCA). In July 1991, field research was conducted at Borallon Correctional Centre and other agencies, using a semi-structured interview research methodology to collect data from 56 people. The findings of this chapter suggested that in the area of industrial and work issues, employees of CCA and Wormald were in a weak bargaining position with little input into decision making. It was also found that the profit motive dominated policy formation in the area of training and programs. Staff-inmate relations were positive with few reported violent incidents and communications were open. The issue for private contract management is whether it will provide the impetus and/or mechanism for progressive correctional reform. The chapter, unfortunately, leaves the issue open. Poor monitoring by the QCSC means that there is a dearth of detailed information — tender evaluations, tender documents, contractual arrangements, and financial and policy information held by QCSC and

CCA. Only when this data is available will it be possible to undertake a comprehensive evaluation of the privatisation initiative.

Private contract management of prisons within Australia has attracted considerable academic and public interest over the past three years. Borallon Correctional Centre is the first privately contract managed correctional centre in Australia. It opened in January 1990 at a cost of $22 million to build with a contract fee of $9.7 million for the 1991 financial year. The centre is located 60 km west of Brisbane and holds 244 male medium security inmates. It is operated by Correction Corporation of Australia (CCA).

The role of private contract management of corrections in Queensland's penal reform process is being extensively debated. The private sector has been seen by senior members of the Queensland Corrective Services Commission (QCSC) as a conduit to initiate change by reforming and improving efficiency in corrections. A significant strategy of the Commission has been the linking of efficiency, including the re-structuring of custodial and community corrections functions of officers into a single correctional officer stream. This has involved a 'revised classification system and emphasis on a collaborative and participative approach between correctional officers and offenders in the day to day management of correctional centres' (QCSC 1992a, p. 37). Private contract management has been used by the QCSC as a method to introduce more flexible work practices across the corrections system.

Any single motive for the QCSC's rapid adoption of private contract management is difficult to identify. It is possible that the escalating cost of custodial corrections was a significant factor in its decision to privately contract manage Borallon Correctional Centre. The QCSC Quarterly Position Assessment for the period July 1 to March 31, 1992 focuses on an overview of recurrent expenditure and concluded that the total corrections budget for this period was $82.637 million with overtime expenditure being over budget, exceeding the annual budget by $1 million early in February 1992. The assessment also revealed revenue generated from industries was under budget by $1.088 million and noted that a lack of change in work practices has led to several centres operating on staffing levels higher than the budget catered for (QCSC, 1992c). The Commission's current over-expenditure has been aggravated by a general increase in the custodial population. This has compelled the Queensland government to explore ways to reduce an increasing drain on its financial resources.

The purpose of this research was to measure the policy justifications for private contract management of correctional centres against the practices at Borallon Correctional Centre. Because of the originality of this research and the newness of private contract management of prisons in Queensland, an open-ended approach was adopted where possible, exploring themes when they emerged. This research was intended to pilot further field research at Borallon, Lotus Glen and Arthur Gorrie Correctional Centres, the QCSC and the Queensland State Service Union (QSSU) in January 1994. Unfortunately, at the time of revision of this paper, the QCSC had not, through its Research and Review Committee, granted approval to conduct further research.

JUSTIFICATIONS FOR PRIVATE CONTRACT MANAGEMENT OF CORRECTIONS IN QUEENSLAND

Policy basis

The implementation of private contract management of corrections was part of a general and substantial reform process of corrective services in Queensland. On February 29, 1988 the Liberal/National Party Cabinet established the Commission of Review into Corrective Services in Queensland (Kennedy Report). The Interim Report outlined a review process that highlighted several points. It was necessary:

- to obtain community involvement;
- to tackle the major issues of 'providing an organisation with dynamic leadership, capable of maintaining the momentum for change [to meet] the need for adequate finances for a modern corrective service' (p. 4);
- to set the agenda for that change by undertaking a 'detailed analysis of the submissions examining policy, the actual running of the system and its administrative problems' (p. 4); and, finally,
- to prepare the infrastructure for change which required the drafting of legislation for the reorganisation of an outdated Prisons Act, lack of procedure manuals, and new organisational structure and awards (p. 5).

The terms of reference for the Commission relating to privatisation stressed that this review was necessary in the public interest and that changes should be contemplated in the organisation, administration and operation of the Queensland prison system. This should include changes in relation to 'the efficiency, management and design of prisons including the cost effectiveness and desirability of introducing private sector involvement in the operation of all or part of the prison system' (Attachments 1988c, p. 2). Remarkably, the Interim Report rejected the option for private sector involvement in corrections. The definition of privatisation used by Jim Kennedy, Chairperson and Commissioner of Review, was unclear in the Interim Report. At one point Kennedy refers to the private sector operating correctional services (a type of total devolution of the correctional services function) (p. 17) yet, in his conclusion, he considers the option of contract management of certain services, ie. specialist security services, escorts, supervision of community detention, counselling and health services. Despite this confusion about which form of privatisation Kennedy was rejecting, he did reject the concept of private contract management of corrections on three principle grounds. He elaborated:

> The market for correctional services is not developed . . . [he also had] reservations about the ethics of the State relinquishing its supervision over sentenced offenders and committing them to the control of companies . . . [and he had] seen little hard evidence to suggest that the private sector would be more efficient than the public sector at providing the management and operation of custodial institutions. (Interim Report 1988b, p. 18)

In the Final Report handed down in August 1988 Kennedy had completely changed his position, now recommending full private sector involvement in corrections. He recommended Borallon Correctional Centre be privatised. Kennedy claimed the reason for this change in position was that he had the 'benefit of detailed discussions with some major companies with an interest in participating in correctional operations' (p. 88).[2] Private companies such as Wormald Security, eventually engaged at Borallon, made proposals to provide perimeter security and control room gate escorts to courts, hospitals and between prisons. Kennedy indicated that his 'chief concern with these submissions was that *they do not go far enough . . . They [Wormald] indicate an unwillingness to become involved directly with prisoners on the night shift or within the prison walls'* (Final Report 1988a, p. 93). [Emphasis supplied]

Kennedy made detailed recommendations with respect to Borallon Correctional Centre. The centre was intended to be a:

> . . . Medium/Low security Centre. Without the disruptive influence and presence of dominating power seeking criminals it can be operated to more efficiently provide genuine corrective services and programs with a lower level of security and staffing,

without internal escorts and with a more relaxed and pleasant work environment for staff, improved and longer visiting arrangements for families and friends, improved sporting facilities and the development of prison teams, better productive work opportunities and training. It will need no cages and no harsh oppressive discipline provided no high risk prisoners are allowed there. It will also provide more security for local residents living nearby as they can be assured that no high risk violent prisoners are housed there. (Final Report 1988a, pp. 96-97)

Kennedy believed that the specific improvements at Borallon Correctional Centre would lead to a generalised improvement across the prison system, leading to the following improvements;

- the problems of finding adequate good staff from within the system would be solved;
- there would be added flexibility;
- the market for corrective institutions in Australia and Queensland would be created;
- there would be an important element of competition for correctional officers which could ultimately lift their status, pay and conditions;
- career prospects for correctional officers and managers would be opened up;
- for the first time there would be competition providing a real measure against which to test the performance and costs of the Queensland Corrective Services.
  The opportunity to do this may not arise again. If Borallon is opened and staffed by the QCSC considerable resistance may arise in any attempt to subsequently privatise it. It is too good an opportunity to miss. (Final Report 1998a, p. 97) [Emphasis supplied]

Legislative basis

The significant legislative change necessary to implement the Kennedy recommendations provided a rare occasion for parliamentary debate on private contract management. It should be noted that the private contract management of Borallon Correctional Centre was only a small part of a larger reform process of Queensland corrections in the late 1980s. The Kennedy Report involved the establishment of a Corrective Services Commission, updating prisoner regimes, the establishment of community correction centres, appointment of official visitors and inspectors, the establishment of home detention, community correction boards and a revision of parole and remissions. Despite this extensive reform, the advantages of private contract management dominated the parliamentary debates about the Corrective Services (Administration) Bill.

On October 27, 1988, in the Legislative Assembly, the Minister for Corrective Services and Administrative Services at the time, Mr Cooper, reflected a general optimistic feeling that private contract management could provide a more efficient and effective corrective service delivery. He noted that privatisation could 'fully open the way for the new Corrective Services Commission to undertake further consultations with unions and other interested parties' (p. 2094). In response to arguments by the opposition (the Labor Party) that privatisation would mean standards would give way in the face of the profit motive, the Hon T. R. Cooper replied:

> The real experience and the real truth of the matter is that privatisation — properly and selectively applied — will generate a more standard conscious, competitive corrective services system. It will allow us to measure performance and standards in a more professional manner, and above all, it will establish a more accountable system than which is now operating. And how do we measure such standards and level of performance? Through a system of permanent audit control. (p. 2095)

There were mixed responses within the Liberal-National Party about whether Borallon should be privatised. Mr Beard, Minister for Mt Isa and Deputy Leader of the Liberal Party, objected to the government delegating the operation of a custodial function to private companies, noting that, 'There are limits to what can be done by private enterprise. The government has certain basic minimal responsibilities . . . I do not believe that the people of Queensland are willing to have private enterprise carry out the function of prison wardens' (pp. 2719-2720).

The Labor Opposition which was to be elected to government in December 1989, and which later affirmed the contract for Borallon with CCA, expressed general agreement with the reform approach of the Bill at the time but wanted the part of the Bill which allowed the privatisation of prisons to be deleted. Mr Milliner, (then member for Everton and subsequently Minister for Justice and Corrective Services), said, 'Privatisation has been advocated in the case of the Borallon institution . . . I do not see how a private organisation can run a prison more effectively than the public sector. It is an area in which privatisation will not work and therefore the opposition does not support that concept' (pp. 2699, 2700).

The Corrective Services (Administration) Bill was passed by a majority of 43 to 29 without amendment and received assent on December 1, 1988. The principle section allowing the operational privatisation of Borallon, and potentially any other new or existing correctional centre, was s19(2)(f). This section enabled the Commission to 'engage a person (other than a commissioner, or an officer or employee of the Commission) or a body of persons to conduct on the Commission's behalf any part of its operations whether under this Act or the *Corrective Services Act 1988*. Where the Commission engaged a body or a person pursuant to s19(2)(f), it may, 'for the purpose of enabling the person or body to conduct those operations, by instrument in writing authorize any person to discharge such of the functions and exercise such of the powers of a general manager, custodial corrections officer or community correctional officer appointed under this Act as are specified in the instrument.'

Apart from the legislative mandate to contract the management of Borallon, the QCSC's own directorate gave itself a policy mandate to implement private contract management in Queensland. In February 1989, the Deputy Director General and the Director of Corporate Services visited the US and the UK to examine the contract management of prisons in those countries. They visited eight privately managed correctional facilities ranging from remand and reception facilities to community based centres run for juvenile offenders. Several senior correctional officials were consulted. The purpose of the trip was to allow the Commission to gain expertise in setting up and administering a privately managed centre. The authors of the report concluded that they saw 'no reason for concern with the Queensland Corrective Services Commission continuing to develop the proposal for the private sector operation of Borallon Correctional Centre' (QCSC 1989b, p. iv).[3]

THE ARRANGEMENTS AT BORALLON CORRECTIONAL CENTRE

Tendering Process and Company Profile

In December 1988, the QCSC called for expressions of interest to contract manage Borallon Correctional Centre. According to its 1989 annual report, five organisations submitted comprehensive proposals, two of which were asked to submit formal tenders. The criteria used by the Commission to evaluate the proposals were, 'Respectability and

financial viability of the company; Quality of the proposal; and Cost'
(1989a, p. 27). CCA was the successful tenderer and the contract was
signed on October 10, 1989.

CCA is a company incorporated in Queensland and is a joint
arrangement of equal shares between Wormald Security (a subsidiary
of Racal Chubb Holding Pty Ltd), Corrections Corporation of
America, one of the largest operators of private prisons in America,
and John Holland Holdings Ltd. The CCA Prospectus indicates it
provides a 'private sector alternative in the area of corrective services to
Governments in Australia and South East Asia . . . [with] comprehensive integrated . . . [services including] the planning, design, construction, financing and management of correctional facilities'. John
Holland Holdings Ltd provides construction and design advice.
Wormald Security provides recruitment advice and places security and
custodial staff at Borallon. Corrections Corporation of America
provides the leadership for policy in its Australian operations by its
influence on decision making through representation on the Australian
Board of Directors. Of the seven directors for CCA, the President,
Chief Executive Officer and Director of Corrections Corporation
America are all on the Australian Board.

None of the criteria or evaluation processes have been placed on the
public record for scrutiny and little is understood about the inter-
relationship between CCA and Corrections Corporation of America.
This is an area which deserves closer scrutiny and public debate (see
postscript).

Inmate Composition

In July 1991, Borallon had design capacity for 244 medium and
maximum security male inmates. Borallon had never been used to
house maximum/high security inmates. At the time of the research,
Borallon had 237 inmates, 194 in medium security, 35 in low security
and 8 in open security. What was remarkable about the contract to
manage Borallon Correctional Centre is that CCA had the highest
number of exclusions of any correctional centre in Queensland. In
1991/92 it was a medium security classified centre for mainstream
prisoners with exclusions that included:

- prisoners subject to extradition or deportation;
- reception prisoners (sentenced and/or remand) direct from courts/
  police;
- prisoners requiring extended hospital or infirmary care;
- prisoners who have escaped or attempted to escape during the

preceding twelve months from a high, medium or low security institution or while on escort;

• prisoners who have had serious breaches of regulations, e.g. violent assaultive behaviour on either other prisoners or staff during existing and/or previous periods' of imprisonment within the preceding twelve months;

• prisoners with a documented recent history of psychiatric or emotional behavioural disturbance;

• prisoners who have been involved in the taking of a hostage while in legal custody;

• genuine protection/high risk prisoners;

• prisoners identified as suffering from communicable diseases (Hepatitis B and AIDS). (QCSC 1992b, p. 2)

TABLE 1
Inmate profile at Borallon Correctional Centre

Offences
(Source for all Tables, Assessment Manager, Borallon Correctional Centre, Manual Count of Records, July 1991, unpublished)

Murder	13.6%
Armed·robbery	14.76%
Sex offences	11.82%
Drug related	11.82%
Break, enter and larceny	11.82%
Other violent	17.29%
Other non-violent	9.28%
Driving offences	8.86%
Arson	0.84%

TABLE 2
Inmate profile at Borallon Correctional Centre

Length of sentence

Under 1 year	10.6%
1 year-5 years	43.03%
6 years-10 years	24.47%
11 years-15 years	4.63%
16 years-20 years	2.53%
21 years-25 years	0.84%
Life	13.90%

TABLE 3
Inmate profile at Borallon Correctional Centre

Ages		Education Benchmark	
18 years-20 years	15.18%	No schooling	3
21 years-25 years	23.62%	Year 10	210
26 years-35 years	32.91%	Senior Certificate	8
Over 35 years	28.28%	TAFE qualifications	11
		Tertiary qualifications	5
Employed at time of offence	98		
Unemployed	72		

With respect to Table 1, it is interesting to note the high percentage of persons convicted of murder and other violent offences. These persons must have been downgraded to at least at a medium classification and would not have shown violent behaviour within the preceding twelve months. The unusually high number of exclusions given to Borallon allows it to refuse any inmate who has a substantial behavioural problem. It should be noted that the offence for which an inmate is originally convicted is not necessarily an indicator of whether he will be violent whilst incarcerated. In other words, the high number of convicted murderers in Borallon (serving life sentences) may improve management of the inmate population by providing stability. This was the case at Borallon (see Findings and discussions — quality of the environment).

Regulatory Arrangements and Operational Standards at Borallon

There are three primary sources for the standard and performance criteria at Borallon Correctional Centre which also apply to public sector correctional centres. The first is the Mandatory Standards for Secure Facilities for Audit Purposes. This document contains minimum standards of performance for:

- centre management and operations, including management and organisation, personnel and training, financial management, community interaction and fire, safety and occupational health;
- centre security and control, including physical security and control and special treatment, separate confinement and disciplinary procedures; and
- prisoner management process and ancillary services, including leave of absence and home detention, prisoner records, programs general, farms and industries, health care services, psychological services, recreation, library, religion, food services, prisoner communication, and Aboriginal and Islander prisoners and facilities.

The second source are the legal requirements under the Commission's rules made pursuant to s20(1) of the *Corrective Services (Administration) Act 1988* (Qld). These are periodical specific directives issued by the QCSC to correctional centres touching upon operational matters.

The third source is the general effect of the remaining corrective services legislation. This includes the *Corrective Services Act 1988* (Qld), *Corrective Services (Consequential Amendments) Act 1988* (Qld), *Corrective Services Regulations 1989* (Qld), and the *Corrective Services Act Amendment Act 1990* (Qld). This legislation provides for the appointment of official visitors and the power of inspectors (made pursuant under the Corrective Services Act 1988).

In practise, general manager's rules made pursuant to s17 (1) & (2) of the *Corrective Services Act 1988* provide internal guidance to custodial and program staff. They outline the procedures for the management of inmates and visitors. If these rules are inconsistent with the Commission's rules, then they are ultra vires and the Commission's rules prevail. Borallon Correctional Centre does not issue GM's rules as such, but instead the GM issues routine instructions which are developed from CCA's Policy and Procedures Manual. The Policy and Procedures Manual contains guidelines for general administration, personnel, training, management information and research, records, physical plant, safety and emergency procedures, safety and control, special management residents, food service, sanitation and hygiene, medical and health care services, resident rights, resident rules and discipline, communication, mail and visiting, reception and orientation, classification, resident work programs, resident services and programs, resident release and citizen involvement and volunteers.

What is unique about the identification of standards at Borallon and the regulatory arrangements is the added factor of a contract for the operation and management of Borallon Correctional Centre executed between CCA and the QCSC. The contract to date has been treated as 'commercial-in-confidence'. The author has managed to gain access to parts of the Deed of Agreement for the operation and management of Borallon with the requirement that it be treated with an appropriate degree of confidentiality. Section 9 of the contract requires that details of the contract 'be kept confidential and shall not be made available to any individual or organisation by the Commission or the Contractor without prior written approval of the other party'. Access to the contract has been severely limited to date. In addition, Freedom of Information legislation recently enacted in Queensland is proving to be a slow and cumbersome method to gain information about private contract managed centres in Queensland (see Accountability, monitoring and performance).

To date, access to contractual information, Commission audit documents, and CCA policy and financial information has been dependent on the goodwill and generosity of senior executives within the QCSC and CCA staff. There has been no consistent procedure regarding access to this information with access being dependent upon luck and circumstance rather than the result of a carefully developed policy. From what the author has obtained, the conditions of the original contract provide for various matters. From a regulatory point of view, the most important conditions of the contract are the following sections:

- section 13: Compliance with Acts; which requires CCA to comply with all Commonwealth and state Acts and regulations and rules, by-laws, notices, orders and proclamations made under such Acts;
- section 15: Financial Statements and Annual Reports; which requires CCA to provide the Commission within one month of its annual general meeting, a copy of its audited financial accounts and annual reports;
- section 20: Contract Performance Evaluation; requires that a monitor be appointed to the centre and paid for by the Commission. CCA 'shall provide the Commission with any information required by the Commission to enable it to monitor and assess the quality of the Contractor's performance';
- section 21: Right to Examine Records; provides a right to the Commission for free access at all times to all records including financial, maintenance, employee and prisoner records generated by CCA;
- section 22: Access to the Centre; provides QCSC, including its officers, the Minister and persons nominated by the Minister, access at all times to all areas of the centre; and
- section 29: Not a Partnership; provides that the QCSC is not a partner of CCA, therefore the Commission is not liable for debts or liabilities incurred by CCA.

There is still considerable uncertainty about the effectiveness of the contract and its adequacy as a comprehensive requirement for CCA to manage Borallon Correctional Centre. The difficulty in evaluating the adequacy of the contract is that Annexure F, which provides for minimum specifications for the operation and management of Borallon Correctional Centre, has not been made available to the author. It is unclear whether these minimum specifications include routine requirements with respect to performance of a quantitative and/or qualitative nature. In other words, is CCA required to provide genuine reform and rehabilitation or just improvements in physical containment? (See Accountability, monitoring and performance) If it is to provide reform, how broad are these requirements and how are they to be measured?

An additional requirement at Borallon is that CCA be subjected to operational audits conducted for the Director of Audit and Prisoner Welfare by audit and investigations officers. These reports are un-published and not generally available to the public. In 1992, six operational audits were conducted at Borallon. There is no evidence to suggest that an operational audit was conducted at Borallon in 1991. The operational audits involve an examination of the centre by QCSC audit staff and may include interviewing official visitors. The available reports strongly support the findings of this case study (see Account-ability, monitoring and performance).

METHODOLOGY

A preliminary research methodology and research guide, including a general interview guide, was developed to provide a justification for a qualitative research approach examining three broad areas. These were: the industrial position, the prisoner and custodial officer experience and the regulatory situation, including the implementation and operation of the contract. Given the unexplored situation with regard to the private contract management of correction centres in Australia, a priority of this research was to understand inmates' experiences of the correctional environment, including their im-pressions of the discipline, training opportunities, prison management and officers' attitudes. The research methodology stressed the need to identify the view points of inmates about their environment. The development of the general interview guide recognised that it is important to check the individual's reported experiences against other people's experiences which included checking published and un-published material and analysing a broad range of unpublished policy information held by CCA.

Selected routine instructions were also checked as were employee performance appraisals, internal correspondence and operational audits conducted by the QCSC on Borallon Correctional Centre. It should be noted that all operational audits were undertaken in 1992 and it appears that no operational audits were conducted by the Commission on Borallon in 1990 or 1991.

A total of 56 people were interviewed within four separate organisations, CCA, Wormald, QCSC and the Queensland State Service Union (QSSU). This included incarcerated inmates held at Borallon Correctional Centre.

Within CCA, fifteen people were interviewed — the General Manager (GM), the manager of operations, the administrative manager, the programs manager, the education manager, the branch accountant, a nursing officer, three assistant operation managers, three trade instructors and the sports and activities manager. A life skills teacher was also interviewed who was working on a part time contract basis to provide a stress management course to inmates. All persons were part of the functional organisation of CCA's Borallon facility — four from senior centre management, eight from middle level manager including one female nursing officer, and three from lower middle management. Two members of senior management, (the GM and operations manager), each had more than ten years experience in the public corrections system. Three middle level managers each had between five and ten years experience in the public corrections system. The remaining two from senior centre management, five from middle level management and three from lower level management, had no previous experience in the public corrections system. The life skills tutor had five years experience tutoring in public sector correctional centres. It is interesting to note that in the functional organisation of Borallon, there was a high concentration of public sector correctional experience at a senior level. The middle and lower levels had no personnel with any previous public sector experience.

Within Wormald Security, eight persons were interviewed — an administrative officer, project manager, three male unit security officers, two female unit security officers, and one female senior unit security officer. None of the persons employed by Wormald had previous public corrections security experience. Two male unit security officers had had previous military service of more than ten years each.

It is noteworthy that CCA and Wormald Security operate as two distinct companies within this facility. CCA handles the financial, program and security administration of the centre, developing policies and issuing routine instructions and also providing all levels of management. Wormald Security provides services for staff recruitment and selection and provides staff for all custodial security functions. It would appear in practice that CCA runs the facility.

Five persons from the QCSC, the Director of Audit and Prisoner

Welfare, the Director of Corporate Services (now the Deputy Director General), Manager of Prisoner Welfare, Principal Adviser Policy Research and Analysis, and Contract Monitor were interviewed.

From the QSSU, three persons were interviewed — the General Secretary, an industrial officer (prison officer's industrial section), and the publicity officer. The discussion with the publicity officer was not taped. All interviewees were male.

Twenty-five inmates were interviewed at Borallon. Eleven of them were participants in a four-week course on resolving conflict. The remaining fourteen were interviewed individually. All inmates interviewed were male within the age range of 21 to 50 years. Seven of the 11 inmates in the group situation had spent between one and five years in the public correctional system. The remaining four having spent no time in the public correctional system. Of the 14 inmates interviewed individually, all had been incarcerated in the public system. One inmate had spent less than two years, six inmates had spent between three and five years, and the remaining seven inmates had spent between five and ten years in public correctional centres. The public sector correctional exposure of inmate interviewees was extensive. Seven of the inmates interviewed individually had been incarcerated in more than two other public sector prisons in Queensland for more than one year at each centre. One inmate had been in nine public correctional centres, averaging one year in each prison (a milk run). Two inmates had been imprisoned from more than one year in other jurisdictions. Two inmates had been at Borallon for more than three months, but less than 12 months. Ten inmates had been at Borallon for more than 12 months but less than 18 months.

Apart from one impromptu discussion with eleven inmates in the education area of Borallon Correctional Centre, all other interviews were of approximately one hour duration. They were conducted in private, out of hearing or seeing range of any other person apart from the interviewer. CCA management agreed that the researcher was not obliged to provide a list of persons interviewed or details of questions to be asked, which meant interviewees could be assured of confidentiality and anonymity. It should be noted that no persons in middle and lower level management, inmates or custodial officers are identifiable from the reporting of these results. This is to preserve the confidentiality and anonymity of interviewees which was a condition of the various interviews (see postscript).

Interviews were taped at various locations. Personnel interviewed — CCA or Wormald staff — were taped in their office or work area. Six CCA administrative staff were interviewed in their respective offices located in the administrative block. Eight middle and lower level management staff were interviewed in their offices attached to the industry, recreation and medical sections. Two assistant operation managers were interviewed whilst on night rounds in the accommodation blocks. Eight unit security (Wormald) staff were interviewed in their observation post at their self-contained accommodation module for which they were assigned. Nine inmates were interviewed in the psychologist's room in the accommodation wing. Five inmates were interviewed in the industries area and one in the visits area. Senior executive staff in the QCSC were interviewed in their offices in Brisbane as were executives in the QSSU. The majority of interviews (51) were conducted during 8.30 am and 5.30 pm Monday to Friday. Five interviews were conducted outside these hours, four being in the evening and one on a weekend.

Borallon was chosen for the case study because it was the first operational privately managed correctional centre in Australia, having commenced operations on January 2, 1990. It had, at the time of the research, established sixteen months of operational history. This was sufficient time for CCA to put in place its policy and for the institution to be normalised.

The sampling of interviewees depended on several factors. It was not possible to select a sample in advance from prisoner records held by CCA or the QCSC because the QCSC would not grant access to inmate files without undertaking a complicated procedure of gaining written permission from the inmate for all required information. It was necessary to rely in the first instance on internal validity checks for the interviews, that is, to ask questions that involved a factual answer and later, ask the question in a slightly different way, checking the consistency of the answers. If the responses were consistent, then it is possible to say that the answers were accurate. Limited access was gained to inmate records after one month. All interviews were then checked against antecedent material which was then used as a second validation technique. Interviews that were inconsistent, were rejected.

Of the 56 people interviewed, 55 were tape recorded and transcribed. Validity checks, both internally and against external facts, indicated a high degree of consistency of responses by interviewees. 51 of the 56 were accepted, with the remaining five being rejected. The acceptance rate was 91 per cent. Four of the interviews were rejected because of an inconsistency in responses through external and/or internal validity checks. The other interview was rejected because the interview was conducted within hearing range of a custodial officer who was behind the interviewer but facing the interviewee. The fact the researcher was in a position to ensure anonymity to interviewees, would in part explain the high validity rating for the interviews.

It was not possible to interview female inmates as this was a male prison. Female and male custodial staff were interviewed with a ratio of roughly one to four in favour of male custodial staff. It was necessary to legitimate the research project in the eyes of senior management at Borallon in order to gain access to the centre. This involved providing regular feedback to the GM about the research design and what the researcher's personal attitudes were about private contract management. This meant that the first three days of the research were spent entirely in the administrative block.

A research diary was kept to record additional information which included research notes, daily tasks and additional points or themes raised by interviewees during the course of interviews. CCA placed no requirement upon the researcher to provide details of who was interviewed or the content of the research diary whilst the researcher was in the facility. CCA's position has subsequently changed (and will be analysed in detail in a forthcoming book by Moyle, 1995).

Transcripts, research diary notes, and published and unpublished information was analysed to identify emerging themes in the area of the industrial position, prisoner and custodial officer experience and the regulatory situation, including the implementation and operation of the contract. The point of reference for these emerging themes was the inmates' description of their own experiences in a variety of settings which included work, recreation and rest environments. Several preliminary themes emerged as being significant at Borallon. Some of these were industrial and work issues, the quality of the environment, and the regulatory role of the QCSC with respect to the monitoring, accountability and performance of Borallon Correctional Centre.

FINDINGS AND DISCUSSION

Industrial and Work Issues

Industrial and work issues at Borallon Correctional Centre were far more complex than simply issues of 'pay, hours of work and conditions between public and private sector jails' (Moyle 1993b, p. 243). Recent Australian scholarship has focused on the potential for private contract management to bring about structural change across the system. Harding (1992) has analysed private contract management as a technique to reduce the high recurrent costs associated with employing unionised custodial staff. Harding highlights that, 'within the framework of the highly-unionised stranglehold exercised by uniformed officers, significant cost reduction cannot realistically be sought. Privatisation is a prerequisite of cost reduction, therefore, and as Queensland experience has shown this may well then spread into the public sector' (p. 25).

Likewise, Moyle (1992a) has stressed that privatisation is being used by the QCSC as a strategy to negotiate with the QSSU to implement its reform and efficiency agenda in a broad way. Part of this has involved disciplining individual correctional centres which fail to meet QCSC's budgetary and operational criteria. In some cases the threat of privatisation has been applied irrespective of the quality of the correctional environment. For example, Lotus Glen Correctional Centre, a public centre which won a Human Rights Award, has been threatened with privatisation on several occasions when it failed to comply with budgetary and staffing requirements set by the QCSC. One senior manager at the facility explained:

> We were so sick of being threatened with privatisation that we put a package together asking for tenders to be called for private parties interested in managing Lotus Glen. The management team here would have submitted a tender. If the standard of service of Borallon is anything to go by, we believe we could run a correctional centre much more efficiently and provide better programs than CCA. The QCSC can't be too serious about it though because we haven't heard anything about our proposal in the six months since we submitted it. (Moyle 1992a, p. 115)

Similarly, the Commission has promoted a justification that privatisation will lead to changing 'restrictive work practises . . . [which] could be identified and removed and improved management processes put in place. Private sector involvement, with green field sites and totally new staff complements provided an ideal opportunity to test this hypothesis' (Macionis 1993, p. 6).

These approaches focus on the motivations of the QCSC for implementing private contract management while ignoring CCA's own industrial strategy for this move. Such approaches also fail to understand the agenda of industrial relations of private companies contract managing correctional centres and whether this agenda actually promotes the transfer of skills to the public sector. In other words, there has been an assumption of the inter-connectedness between the private and public sector, that is, private contract management will lead to an improvement in the public sector. Evidence collected at Borallon suggests the QCSC and CCA have adopted an industrial relations strategy that has been relevant to their own interests, often proving antagonistic to genuine negotiations with the QSSU concerning the need to re-structure and re-skill the public sector work force. CCA has adopted an industrial relations strategy which is characterised by a deep mistrust of the public sector. The general manager of Borallon has indicated that his industrial relations strategy involved recruiting officers who do not have previous experience in public corrections systems because:

> Such systems may have inculcated workforce practices, inter-personal deficiencies or other negative or endemic cultures which may have proved fatally inimical to the CCA philosophy and commitment to the then emerging Unit Management concept. Our policy then was to recruit Officer staff who were mostly inexperienced in Corrections but whose history, personal attributes, attitude, selection and aptitude testing gave every indication that they would constitute an Officer force of superior calibre and without the trammels of preconceived ideas in Correctional duties. (Dickson 1993, p. 8)

Research at Borallon suggests that part of the motivation for recruiting custodial staff with little experience in the public sector was to allow the general manager to function both as an employer and industrial negotiator, thus exercising exceptional influence and power over both CCA and Wormald security staff. The Federated Miscellaneous Workers Union (FMWU) had very little input into daily industrial negotiations at Borallon.

CCA had adopted a policy of cutting the costs of custodial corrections by reducing the overall number of custodial staff. This did not lead to a restructuring or an improvement in skills of officers, but instead, involved assigning different ratios, that is, lowering the custodial officer ratio therefore reducing operational costs and maximising profitability. This technique had different effects on different work classifications within Borallon. The GM reported a feeling of control and satisfaction with this situation: 'I was attracted to this job because I can do what I want to do with the staff. I don't have to go to head office and operation committees and those frustrating things. I've had to put up with those things for the past ten years.'

Custodial and senior custodial officers at the unit security levels were concerned about under-staffing in the accommodation blocks. One officer noted:

You've got 32 inmates, 16 in each spine and I have to run back and forwards to monitor phone calls and keep an eye on things. You're supposed to be in two places at once. I can't monitor what's going on in the unit. I would have to grow eyes in the back of my head. On weekends it's worse. Sometimes I have been the only officer for four units. In the early days, we were just paddling around in the water.

A unit supervisor reported that:

the staffing levels are not adequate here. We have a ratio of about two staff to about 80 inmates. When I first started here, we were promised that it would be one officer to 16 inmates. In periods where we have had high unemployment amongst inmates, you have a real problem with shortage of staff. Fortunately, most of us have a good relationship with inmates. But on one occasion, an officer was attacked by an inmate who knocked him down and then managed to knock another officer out and both of them were put in hospital. We raised our concerns that staffing levels were too low, but they are still the same.

The GM did not report that custodial staffing levels were too low, believing instead that staffing levels could be cut further. 'We don't have as many custodial staff as comparable state institutions. Saving on labour costs allow us to increase profits. It is unfortunate that the state institutions have such a large recurrent overtime bill.'

The strategy of having minimal custodial staff and using a high ratio of casual labour worked against multi-skilling of officers. Custodial staff reported they were uneasy about the staffing levels, believing the levels were not adequate to do their work effectively, and many workers felt there was no effective method to deal with their concerns. The use of casual labour raised the possibility that anyone who threatened industrial action over safety matters could be easily dismissed. The GM reported that the role of unions was limited at the centre and casual labour was a strategy necessary to reduce costs:

When something goes wrong, the only thing unions come up with is the need for more staff. Now this is not the case. We have got to look at how effectively those people are doing their jobs. The immediate reaction that we need more staff is a band aid solution which locks you into a recurrent commitment of valuable resources. There are only so many dollars to go around. If it's all going into wages for correctional staff, then your programs will suffer. I've been able to control that. . . . The way we make a dollar here is different to the public sector. I can manage Borallon more cheaply because of our use of casual employees. I only allow essential jobs to be filled and if possible, use casual employees to fill them. It's best for staff to work two to three days per week with no overtime or penalty rates. We target semi-retired persons who have other incomes so they can take a few days off and still pay the bills. We have 87 on the casual list.

Perhaps the most vulnerable workers at Borallon were the inmates. Inmates often have family commitments and are acutely aware of the need to save money if they are to have any chance of re-skilling through job training upon release, and funding basic accommodation to live in the community. Moyle (1993a) identified a conflict between the utilisation of cheap contract labour which was profitable for CCA, and the provision of genuine skilling and trade training which was expensive to provide. Moyle noted in a comparison between Borallon and Lotus Glen Correctional Centres, 'that a business approach had compelled the exploitation of cheap labour' at Borallon (p. 13).

CCA's accountant clarified the source of this conflict between higher cost training and low cost contract work. The accountant reported:

We don't want to be purchasing stock that is too costly. We prefer to have value added growth and with contract packing, the owner comes in and provides the equipment. We provide the cheap labour. There will always be inmates looking for the opportunity to earn $53 per week and that will help our industries section grown. We won't offer apprenticeships because that's too costly to establish and you must understand, we are a company that manages incarcerations, and we have to provide the best remuneration to our share holders. I really can't see any problem with making money from incarceration.

A conflict between a profit motive and the provision of more costly industries based apprenticeships and training programs, was indicated in a conflict between the administration manager and the programs manager at Borallon. When this case study was conducted, the programs manager was responsible for the education and industries sections within the centres. The administration manager responsible for financial profitability clearly resented this dual role, stating, 'You're either a programs manager or an industries manager. You're not both.'

The management of industries was about to be taken away from the programs manager. It was evident that pressure was placed on the programs manager to promote de-skilled contract work which would give higher financial rewards to CCA. As a consequence, the programs manager had abandoned the idea of broad based skills training, i.e. apprenticeships, for inmates. He reported:

> We are not going to seek to train inmates to be apprentices. Their future lies in labouring work that is mainly unskilled. We haven't really made an attempt to take on apprentices or to develop an apprenticeship training scheme as we just don't have the jobs, equipment, experience or financial resources to do so. We have about 50 inmates that are under-employed here. Once we get the new factory set up, we should be able to absorb them into contract work.

Despite the above difficulties inmates appreciated having work, even though it was repetitive and involved acquiring few meaningful skills. One inmate noted the positive effect of having work and also suggested a solution to the problem of CCA focusing on contract packing. He noted:

> It's good having any work at all. I need a job pretty badly. I know if I'm sacked, there are 100 people waiting to jump into the job. A lot of the other blokes know I get $9 a day, but they don't know I'm only paid that when there is a contract. If you're going to privatise, you should do it properly. I would get rid of the whole thing, CCA running the contract labour centre. Bring in companies and rent them the workshop space and let them employ prisoners on award wages. We would pay board and for apprenticeship training costs. Why should CCA be paid to run the centre and also to get the workshop profits?

It was interesting to note that the lack of job security reported by custodial staff employed by Wormald, was also reported by middle level management and nursing staff within CCA organisational structure. CCA staff were all award free. Assistant operation managers were more dependent on promotion from a recommendation given by the GM and therefore more vulnerable if they threatened industrial action. One assistant operations manager reported that he was prepared to accept a flat rate of pay with afternoon and weekend shifts and no union representation because, in the medium term, he had good prospects of getting a promotion in another CCA facility. He elaborated: 'I have never seen any structured conditions of employment. The GM runs this like a family business and he doesn't take kindly to his authority being challenged. CCA has new operations starting up all the time and while I don't have good job security now, sooner or later a vacancy further up will occur.'

CCA's approach to industrial relations drew a negative response from nursing staff who felt they had a right to belong to a union for the purposes of gaining peer advice and consultation. A nursing officer elaborated:

> The GM has made it clear that we don't come under any award because we work at Borallon. We work for CCA. We feel this attitude is terrible, after all, we are professional registered nurses. Why are we any different to other members? A few months ago one of my nurses contacted the union about a safety issue, and when the GM found out, she was told to leave. Because we are private, no-one gives a damn. No-one checks on us. I've invited them . . . [Nursing Federation and nursing managers of public sector correctional centres] to check to see my centre to make sure I'm doing everything I should be. This is especially because I'm new to prisons. I could be doing something that's not quite right for the prison system.

More importantly, there were reports by nursing staff that they felt pressure placed upon them to diagnose because of the minimal time that a doctor was scheduled to provide medical services. The nursing officer elaborated:

> A doctor comes in for two, two-hour sessions per week. He's on 24 hour call, but because of the high cost to call him in, we feel pressure to diagnose the minor stuff. But what if something goes wrong? We are totally responsible and we have no immediate back up. We are required to make on the spot decisions. You're the only medical person all week apart from four hours. I'm going to join the union. I'm not convinced that CCA will back me if I do make a mistake. I'm not convinced they will supply a lawyer if an inmate sues me, or a family sues me for killing somebody. With the pressure we're under somebody could quite easily misdiagnose something.

Further evidence suggests that many workers were unhappy with the industrial relations situation at Borallon mainly because of an unequal bargaining position between staff and the GM of the facility. It is apparent that CCA had carefully devised an organisational structure that promoted and sustained this unequal situation. Many staff reported it was difficult to raise, and receive action concerning, critical issues. Some staff had resigned themselves to the fact that any successful work or condition changes would primarily have to be initiated by the GM.

The Quality of the Environment

One of the rationales outlined by the QCSC for contract management is to achieve an improvement with the correctional environment, specifically to 'bring about cultural and attitudinal change in the management and operation of correctional centres' (Macionis 1993, p. 6). Macionis continues:

> the Commission has articulated its aim to bring about a more rehabilitative environment in its correctional centres where offenders are given opportunities for self-development while in custody. In order to achieve this, custodial staff would need to adopt a much different approach to their work than that of the traditional stony-faced guard on a fixed post. (p. 7)

In 1991 a Criminal Justice Commission Report on Allegations into Employees of the Queensland Prison Service, which later became the QCSC, indicated there was a group of correctional officers opposed to corrections reform. They belonged to what is known as the 'old guard'. This group was,

> openly critical of the philosophies and goals of the Queensland Corrective Services Commission. They universally thought that strict discipline was appropriate in all cases. They belonged to what was described in evidence as the 'lock them up and forget them' school. They were seemingly in opposition to the 'humanizing' policies that were being introduced by the Queensland Corrective Services Commission. (p. 221)

The quality of life for inmates and staff will undoubtedly be improved if this group can be given further training to assist them to embrace modern case management methods. Putting aside the two issues of whether privatisation is a necessary precursor to implementing attitudinal change in the 'old guard',[4] and whether improvements in staff-inmate relations can be transferred to other correctional centres, methods to improve correctional environments should be encouraged.

Better communication within a facility and more humane treatment of staff and inmates is likely to lower levels of violence, boredom, depression and perhaps more significantly, self-mutilation and suicide amongst inmates.

Very recently, there has been intense speculation about the significance of contract management of prisons, and moreover, the impact of this upon public sector programs. Harding (1993) notes, 'that genuine cross-fertilisation is occurring so as to improve the whole system . . . Of course, comprehensive evaluation is needed of [sic] . . . whether such improvements feed through into lower recidivism rates, higher post-release employment rates, less family breakdown, and so on. But prima facie the evidence so far is promising' (pp. 3-4)

Whilst this research does not support the conclusion that cross-fertilisation between Borallon and the public sector has occurred, there is evidence to suggest that at an institutional level, Borallon demonstrates several progressive trends which are certainly unique if one compares Borallon with older more containment oriented correction centres. The GM was well liked by a majority of inmates. This was due in part to an open campus style environment and the establishment of an 'Inmates Needs Committee' where inmates could raise general programs or staff interaction matters. The committee was not designed to raise specific individual matters which were handled through official channels, i.e. recommendations for remissions or disciplinary proceedings. The committee gave inmates a direct route to the GM to discuss general issues. This method of management of inmates yielded impressive results and appeared to empower inmates, allowing them to raise issues on a collective basis concerning the environment at Borallon (cf this approach with the GM's approach to industrial relations). The GM elaborated on the reasoning behind the Inmates Needs Committee:

> I believe in humane containment and the provision of skills such as the work ethic. We can provide them with some opportunities here because I understand that imprisonment is a paradox. They come in here to be taught responsibility, yet we tell them what to wear, when to eat, when to get up, when to go to bed. At Borallon, as far as I can, I try, within the constraints of running a secure institution, to put the responsibility back to the inmate. The inmate needs committee is there to talk about deficiencies in programs and the way the inmates are treated. I believe you can run a medium/low security institution as an open campus without locking doors internally. If you have a good perimeter

security system with people booking inmates from where they live to where they work, inmates recognise this responsibility and respond to the trust. It's a cost effective way to do things.

Inmates responded positively to this conciliatory approach which filtered down to influence inmates' perceptions of officers and officer's perceptions of inmates. In the areas of approaches to security, visits and attitudes to punishment, several progressive trends emerged. One unit security officer elaborates a view which the majority of officers shared: 'We are less security conscious here. It is more open. We don't try to run the place like a military camp and the atmosphere here is less hostile. I don't want to have a stand off with an inmate and we try a dynamic security system here which means you get to know the inmate and try to deal with their problems on a personal level. It's not about having a dozen guys with batons walking around the place.'

The inmates responded positively to this attitude. One inmate commented, 'Officers mix with inmates and they [officers] don't just sit in the fish bowl. The officers don't seem like the screws in Boggo Road. At Boggo, there was a definite line. Cross it and you were bashed. Sometimes the line changed and you'd be bashed anyway. Here I feel I can talk to an officer if you need to and the officer won't mess you around by bringing up stuff you've told him later.'

Borallon had all day Saturday and Sunday inmate visits and custodial officers demonstrated a supportive approach to these. One officer commented, 'You try and make the visit and the place as pleasant as possible. When visitors first came in, they were aggressive, but after a couple of weeks, they changed. They realised you were just doing your job and you can joke with some of them.' What was particularly interesting about visits is that the Inmates Needs Committee was able to have some input into providing facilities for inmate's families, e.g. vending machines and a sand pit for children to play in, thus giving adults time together during the visit. On one occasion, the committee was asked to pay for overtime costs for visits on Christmas Day. This involved a progressive element by allowing inmates to choose if they wanted extra visits, but also contained a regressive element by making inmates pay for a service which normally is provided by the centre. A member of the committee elaborated:

Visits are important to us and I don't feel the officers are too intrusive. On Christmas Day, most of the lads wanted all-day visits and the general manager said okay you can do that but CCA won't pay for the penalty rates and over time. The committee

spoke to other inmates and they all wanted to see their families on
that day. It cost us $1500 for the officers salaries, but what choice
have you got. I'd pay anything I had to see my family on
Christmas Day.

A final point concerning the quality of the environment, was
attitudes to punishment. In this area, it was clear that security staff
adopted a progressive attitude. A custodial officer reported,

Taking them away from their families and taking their freedom is
their punishment. There is no reason to treat them badly once
they are in here. They . . . [officers in public sector prisons] . . .
call us Hotel Borallon because the inmates are supposed to live
in great surroundings but Sir David Longland . . . [a public
sector correctional centre] . . . just down the road is identical to
Borallon. The difference here is that we treat inmates humanely,
and what's the problem with that? I don't mind if they call me
Mary and I call them Fred and I talk to them and try to sort their
problems out. It's better than locking them up and then having to
look over your shoulder when they're let out for exercise.

Inmates responded positively to these attitudes. One inmate noted,
'You can do your time here and not be bashed by screws. I don't feel I'll
be singled out because I'm an inmate. The officers here don't harass
you or single you out and if you're reasonable, they're reasonable back.'

ACCOUNTABILITY, MONITORING AND PERFORMANCE

Accountability, monitoring and the performance of CCA at Borallon
Correctional Centre are all parts of an inter-related process. It is
primarily the responsibility of the QCSC to ensure that the policy and
contractual information, including audits it performs, are placed on
the public record. Evaluations by the QCSC of Borallon's compliance
with its contract obligations including operational audits, financial
information and reports of official visitors, need to be carefully
scrutinised and related to performance indicators including the
standards in the contract. There has been considerable confusion
about the criteria used by the QCSC to evaluate the successful tenderer
for Borallon. Further, the performance criteria developed by the
QCSC, including methods used to monitor Borallon, are uncertain.
This confusion has been caused by the QCSC's refusal to make
available to the public, documents relating to the privatisation

process.[5] This lack of availability of information has led to academic speculation about accountability, monitoring and performance.

Recently the results of a Public Sector Management Commission (PSMC) review of the QCSC (1993) indicated a reason for the QCSC's reluctance to publicly disclose performance criteria. The PSMC noted that: 'Most of the focus . . . [by the QCSC] . . . has been on cost comparisons . . . Little effort has been made to assess the qualitative issues . . . Qualitative comparisons have not been attempted . . . the particular indicators to consider in making qualitative assessments have not been subject to close consideration' (p. 118).

The PSMC urgently recommended that:

> By 30 September 1994, the Queensland Corrective Services Commission, in consultation with the Office of the Cabinet and Treasury, develop a methodology for evaluating contract management of custodial and community corrections centres which includes:
> * the basis on which costs should be compared;
> * the basis on which quality of service can be assessed; and
> * the overall financial and other impacts on the state and the state correctional system of contract-managed centres. (p. 119)

Two approaches to the issues of accountability, monitoring procedures and performance of Borallon have emerged.[6] Harding (1992) has stressed that Borallon is no less accountable than other Queensland prisons. The first reason for this is that Borallon is subject to all corrective services legislation and regulations including the Mandatory Standards for Secure Facilities for Audit Purposes. He elaborates: 'Run-of-the-mill matters within Borallon are no less accountable than in any other Queensland prison; and with the added factor of an official monitor it could even be said that there is greater accountability. Moreover, the endless procession of semi-official visitors which Borallon willingly accepts is in contrast to the secretiveness which some public prison systems still exhibit' (p. 18).

Harding also infers that the very process of drawing up a contract forces the parties to be specific about what they require (compare this conclusion with the PSMC's review findings): 'In the absence of stated objectives, there can hardly be a contract. . . . All these things are capable of being specified—indeed, *must be specified in great detail* if performance criteria are to be laid down for tenderers and if the performance of the successful bidder is to be subsequently audited' (1992, p. 23).

The second approach has involved a reluctance to draw conclusions about whether private contract management promotes efficiency, without proper access and evaluation of contractual and related information. In essence, Moyle (1993a, pp. 7-10; 1992b, pp. 25-27; 1993b, pp. 244-245) argues that the process of accountability is closely linked to mechanisms of monitoring and performance evaluations. In this sense, the level of accountability can only be identified when all of the information has been placed on the public record and has been thoroughly examined. This approach assumes that the state should take special measures above the minimum legislative requirements to oversee private contractors because of the potential conflict of a company's financial interest with the public interest. Moyle has argued that the inaccessibility of contractual arrangements due to CCA's claims to 'commercial confidentiality', inhibits effective evaluation of Borallon's performance. It is of course better to have the information first, before the analysis, and certainly before conclusions are drawn. In its absence, the researcher must draw inferences about the adequacy of accountability, monitoring and performance from whatever sources he/she can find. It is easier to document deficiencies in the account-ability process after information has been evaluated. This approach places the onus on the QCSC to implement institutional arrangements to provide an adequate information flow to the public.

Evaluation of the initial Deed of Agreement made between the QCSC and CCA indicates that the contract refers specifically to existing operational documents and standards with respect to per-formance criteria. In other words, there appear to be no additional performance criteria relating to:

- the quality of the programs provided;
- the provisions of industrial and trade training;
- impact on recidivism rates;
- staff and inmate perceptions of the facility;
- escape rates;
- successful rehabilitation of inmates;
- reducing levels of violence and assault within centres;
- employment rates upon release; and
- the provision and utilisation of amenities. (Moyle 1993a, p. 10.)

This suggests that the QCSC was content to use cost savings as a primary justification for private contract management of Borallon in

1990. It also appears that no significant operational audits were performed by the QCSC on Borallon in 1990 and 1991. Other evidence reveals the QCSC had a poorly defined policy basis for the implementation and application of monitoring Borallon Correctional Centre. In part, this problem has been caused by continued under-staffing and lack of specific expertise within the policy, research and analysis section of the QCSC. The Principal Policy Adviser reported:

> We don't have any formalised research program for Borallon. Private prisons is not an area we have researched at all. We really haven't had the resources to do any research on Borallon because our research department consists of four people and our role is to be involved in the day to day activities of the Commission. Private prisons is certainly an area of interest to us, I mean we are running the first private correctional institution in Australia.

In addition to a lack of broad based policy research into Borallon, it was noticeable that the Director of Audit and Prisoner Welfare believed that no special monitoring measures were necessary in either the evaluation or audit areas for Borallon. The Director of Audit revealed that monitoring was already effectively taking place through inmates who would surely complain to a public sector prison if Borallon was not performing adequately. The Director of Audit reported, 'We haven't done any real evaluation of Borallon at this stage and nor do I think we need to monitor Borallon very closely, either in terms of case management or industrial training. Inmates don't spend their total sentence at Borallon. That means that if people coming from Borallon were not given effective case management, our own [public] centres would be jumping up and down.'

The Director of Audit also indicated,

> We don't have the capacity to monitor the quality of training, either trade or programs, at Borallon. In any case, most of the work at Borallon will be unskilled and your capacity to qualitatively analyse unskilled work is very limited. . . . Ideally the role of the contract monitor should be as an unobtrusive observer. As time goes by, I would see the need for a regular presence at Borallon diminishing and once practices are in place, then the need for continual monitoring of standards will stop.

CCA found the level and type of monitoring performed by the QCSC to be highly satisfactory. The programs manager noted that it was not the role of the QCSC to adopt any responsibility for monitoring program standards. He reported: 'It is not the responsibility of the Queensland Corrective Services Commission Contract Monitor to monitor the quality of our programs. There is not a great deal being done through the Contract Monitor other than I know she is aware that we have programs here and reports that fact back to the QCSC.'

This ambivalent attitude by the Commission towards its monitoring and auditing function assisted in the development of a culture of secrecy within CCA's operations at Borallon Correctional Centre. In response to written and verbal requests for access to basic financial and contractual information, the GM replied, 'It would not be possible for you to get a copy of the contract. We would not consent to it. It is a matter between the company and the Commission and we would not be prepared to release it. We are not about to give you or anyone else in the community a copy of our contract.'[7]

This statement was made in July 1991. On November 12, 1992, to the credit of both CCA and the QCSC, the Deputy Director General gained consent from CCA to provide the researcher with a copy of parts of the initial contract for the management of Borallon and a selected number of audit documents for 1992. The audit documents, whilst they do not cover the period of this research, support the conclusion that monitoring in 1991 was superficial. The reports found the following: that a financial audit had not occurred on prisoners' trust accounts; inadequate care was taken by CCA regarding legal requirements issued to it by the QCSC in relation to offender management; program evaluation at Borallon was a weakness with poorly defined criteria to measure achievement; that it would be preferable to have available a wider range of employment and vocational opportunities; that there was inadequate treatment of a mentally handicapped inmate; and that food packaging and the hygiene of catering was inadequate. Interestingly, the audits noted that staff-inmate relations were excellent.

One of the important dimensions of the finding of this research on the monitoring role is the inadequate policy basis for identifying and monitoring standards of performance at Borallon. This led to a failure by the QCSC to adequately evaluate the performance of CCA. In 1991, the QCSC had given insufficient resources to the audit function and had not adopted a lateral view with respect to the identification and evaluation of qualitative outcomes. Part of the difficulty was the superficial terms and conditions contained in the contract. Nevertheless, specific operational criteria could have been set down by the director of Audit, after the contract was signed, by issuing

Commission's Rules to CCA. Because of the secrecy adopted by the QCSC in 1990/91 concerning documentation on evaluation and on the contract itself, these deficiencies were not identified until 1993 by the PSMC in its review of the QCSC. Judicious use of external expertise and community input may have avoided this failure by the QCSC to fulfil its statutory obligations.

PRIVATISATION AND THE FUTURE: REDEFINING ISSUES

Australian researchers have been optimistic about the possibilities that private contract management raises for the reform of the Australian penal system. Harding (1992) concludes that is it likely that:

> the future of private corrections will turn not so much on cost as *value* . . . Aspects of value include: (i) diversity within the total system; (ii) consequently, competitiveness not only as to cost-effectiveness but more significantly as to service delivery across the public and private sectors of the system; (iii) better utilisation of expensively-trained personnel for specialist tasks, so that for example public correctional staff may increasingly be expected to be program specialists whilst private sector ones will be generalists; (iv) enhanced flexibility and capacity to deliver in different situations or for different groups than the public sector possesses; and (v) an increased sense of community involvement in this most difficult of social responsibilities. (p. 27)

Chan (1992) has been more reluctant to make predictions about the specific effect of private sector involvement on the corrections system. Chan adopts an approach with which the author has some sympathy, being that specific jurisdictional and institutional research is necessary before preliminary conclusions can be drawn. She elaborates:

> Privatisation of prisons is still at a very early stage of development and there has been little systematic evaluation of these initiatives. . . . I have chosen to leave open the possibility that progressive changes may result from the privatisation of punishment, while insisting on a scrupulous examination of each privatisation initiative. . . . Specific instances of privatisation must be judged on their own merits and, if necessary, contested within their own institutional and legal contexts. (p. 244)

The findings of this preliminary case study indicate that private contract management has not as yet offered better service delivery across the public and private spheres, nor has it led to better utilisation of personnel or enhanced flexibility and capacity to deliver services to groups or increased community involvement. Moyle (1993c, pp. 13-14) has indicated how such objectives may be achieved. Modifying McLaren's (1992, pp. 78-80) principles of effective intervention, specific strategies for better utilisation of personnel or enhanced flexibility to deliver services could include:

- the requirement that private companies use programs that stress social learning models treating criminal attitudes and behaviours as learned habits which could be changed by teaching and re-enforcing new non-criminal attitudes and behaviours;
- an obligation to identify cross-organisational measures and provide detailed statements that ensure clear rules and sanctions that are applied in a vivid, understandable and certain way. Discretion where possible should be reduced to avoid the possibility of a conflict of interest between private commercial interest and inmate's rights. In no case should private companies be given the power to hear and determine breaches of discipline, perform a remand and reception function or have a determining influence on parole and remissions;
- the need for private companies to specify how they will build incentive systems into their daily regimes that reward pro-social alternatives to criminal styles of thinking, feeling and behaviour. Companies should detail education programs in practical, personal and social problem solving areas and where possible use ex-addicts in the intervention and planning of programs to serve as credible models. This should allow for neutralising or mobilising the offender's peer group so that less opportunity to re-inforce anti-social criminal attitudes occurs;
- the obligation for private companies to provide promotional opportunities for staff who display a capacity to develop empathetic relationships with offenders based on open communication and trust and offenders being treated in a flexible and enthusiastic way;
- private companies should also provide for a range of interventions some of which should include community resources and input which establish positive links between the institutions and the community;
- costing and payments under the contract should allow for interventions to be run by staff who are given proper training and adequate supervision so that the effectiveness of the intervention and the number of hours of the intervention is not diluted

because of financial stringency or other management considerations;

- finally, in the tendering and implementation phase private companies should be encouraged to submit tenders that provide a combination of tools to be used to change criminal behaviour rather than relying on a single method of intervention. This should include, where possible, proper post-release training and supervision so that the inmate can be successfully integrated into the community. Private companies should be encouraged to use a multiple modality approach with combinations of intervention types, such as vocational or academic training and group counselling, being used at the same time, or successively.

These important principles may still be potentially obtainable but it is evident the QCSC has failed to develop the necessary policy basis to achieve these reforms. Part of the reason for this failure has been a lack of expertise within the QCSC, and also a failure to utilise the community expertise. Issues such as commercial confidentiality and the QCSC's reluctance to provide access to documentation have seriously undermined its objectives of achieving progressive penal reform.

Before a genuine improvement in the quality of corrective services can occur, the QCSC needs to rethink and justify its objectives for private contract management. This should include the identification of *qualitative tests to ensure that Borallon achieves specific outcomes that are superior to existing public correction centres*. The development of policy by the QCSC should set standards and identify the requirements for CCA, based on the QCSC's own agenda for penal reform, rather than responding to difficulties as they emerge in a reactive way. This would require the Commission to identify specific issues that private contract management raises, such as the effect of the profit motive on administration, industrial training, custodial and programs functions of CCA, and how proper monitoring safeguards can be put in place. It is clear that each area presents ethical, legal and political issues that must be set against policy development. At Borallon for example, a conflict between the attitudes of the administrative and financial managers toward inmate labour (through the use of a value added approach) needs immediate attention.

One important result of this case study is that it commences the theory-building process by identifying qualitative issues concerning the operation of Borallon Correctional Centre. The research indicates some of the immensely complex issues that such an initiative raises and highlights the need for a more detailed and systematic assessment of the private sector's role in corrections. The task for researchers is to ignore general and vague claims about the advantages and disadvantages of private contract management and to build instead a thorough and detailed picture of the rationale, identifying the policy and practices of privatised correctional centres at an institutional level. Ultimately, the successful study of private contract management is dependent upon the goodwill of the responsible agencies which must provide access to facilities and documentation for the completion of detailed studies. The successful evaluation of the private contract initiative is only possible if regulatory agencies are prepared in practice to be open and accountable. As interest in corrections reform is high in Queensland, it is hoped that these standards will apply and the problems identified in this research will be overcome.

This case study indicates much more work is needed in order to develop a clearer understanding of private contract management's relationship to penal reform. Further study is needed to provide a comprehensive evaluation of the Australian jurisdictions undertaking this policy with greater emphasis on comparisons across jurisdictional boundaries. Private contract management clearly presents an opportunity for change but whether this change will be just a replacement of public sector prisons with equivalent private sector ones, or whether it will lead to a fundamental re-evaluation of the purpose and restructuring of the operations of corrections, will depend upon the availability and encouragement of informed debate and detailed academic criticism. Above all, we rely upon the willingness of regulatory agencies to engage in this process. Without the latter, it will be a difficult task to identify the necessary elements for a more effective and efficient corrections system.

The next step is to design studies which integrate and identify what improvements, if any, private contract management can achieve. Several questions require exploration. First, how can measurements be put into place to enhance the transfer of improvements from the private sector to the public sector within a less confrontationist framework? What objectives should form the basis of a system of corrections and how can they be linked to the reform process of privatisation? How will jurisdictional and cultural differences in Australian states effect the implementation of change? What framework should be developed to set the boundaries if any, on the mix of private and public sector involvement in corrections?[8]

POSTSCRIPT

Five months after submitting this paper to Corrections Corporation of Australia Pty Ltd for their comments I received a response from both the GM of Borallon Correctional Centre and CCA's Company Secretary. Without fully commenting upon and evaluating the validity and relevance of their comments, (see Moyle, 1995 forthcoming), I have decided to publish their remarks so that readers may be aware of their views. The GM believes this case study shows, 'An almost complete lack of understanding about both the history and complexities of managing prisoners in the 1990s. It contains a number of mistakes in reference to industrial arrangements . . . falsely interprets a number of Corrections Corporation of Australia's policy and procedures . . . [and] . . . you [the author] have chosen in your paper to mainly present negative comments.'

After a request for specific clarification of these issues since no examples were provided, the company secretary wrote:

> At no stage did Corrections Corporation of America attempt to dominate proceedings or direct the manner in which the company was to operate in Australia . . . You [the author] make comment as to the considerable uncertainty about the effectiveness of the contract. This is again unfair as you appear to be drawing conclusions from insignificant information . . . You *refer to the audit of a prison* . . . For your information the best audit a prison can have is by its prisoners . . . Perhaps you could explain to us why you have used leading questions to people interviewed rather than obtain objective information as to the real operation of the centre . . . *It is simple to draw conclusions from leading questions made to people who are not familiar with the total operation of a centre and who are only entitled to comment upon their particular jobs.* [Emphasis supplied]

AUTHOR'S NOTE

The audits referred to were conducted by the QCSC, a statutory authority entrusted by the Queensland government to monitor prisons (see section Accountability, monitoring and performance in this chapter).

It is interesting to note that open ended questions were used which allowed the interviewee to relate his/her experiences with very little intervention from the interviewer. The general interview guide did not contain, nor does transcript material indicate that any leading questions were used. It should also be noted that interviews were conducted anonymously and confidentially in accordance; with university's experimentation ethics review committee guidelines for research involving human participants. The quotes used were transposed and retained for safe keeping by the researcher. No member of CCA's Senior Executive has been given the original or copies of transcript material. Neither the GM nor the Company Secretary would know who, apart from themselves, was interviewed, nor would they be aware of the specific questions asked.

About the author's evaluation of the historical complexities, industrial arrangements and private prisons policy in Queensland, I will allow the readers to from their own conclusions.

Notes

1. A version of this chapter was presented at the British Criminology Conference, Cardiff, Wales, July 28-31, 1993. It will appear in the *British Journal of Criminology*, Autumn, 1994. This chapter was completed as preliminary work for a PhD at the Faculty of Law, University of New South Wales. The assistance of George Zdenkowski is acknowledged both in the supervision of the research and the preparation of this chapter. Special thanks to Peter Burns who proof read the chapter.

2. Commissioner Kennedy's background was predominantly in the private sector and he had no previous legal training or experience in the corrections area. He was a Fellow of the Institute of Chartered Accountants and a certified public accountant. His past positions included chairman of Pan Australian Mining Ltd, director of Daily Sun and Sunday Sun Newspapers, chairman of the Queensland Government's Small Business Development Corporation, and director of Brisbane TV Ltd – BTQ Channel 7. At the time of writing the report he was Director of Pacific Dunlop Ltd, Chairman of Kennedy's Pty Ltd and Associated Companies and Trusts and Director of Santos Ltd.

3. Subsequently, Stan Macionis (1993), Deputy Director General of the QCSC, for the first time publicly indicated that the rationale of the Commission to introduce contract management was based on the benefits of introducing competition, removing restrictive work practices, bringing about cultural and attitudinal change and introducing a more rehabilitative environment in its correction centres. These matters were first discussed in the Kennedy Report in 1988.

4. Moyle (1993a) has argued that officers from the 'old guard' show considerable capacity to adapt to new systems of case management provided they are given sufficient training and time to adjust to new sentence management principles.

In studies conducted at Lotus Glen Correctional Centre in 1991, several officers from the 'old guard' had changed their work practices to a more modern and progressive approach (see especially pp. 10-12).

5. Between 1989 and 1992, the author had made six written requests and several verbal requests for this information. These requests had been made to several officers of the QCSC including the Director General, the Director of Decision Support, the Principal Policy Adviser, and the Director of Audit and Prisoner Welfare and included approaches to the operations manager and GM of Borallon. In 1992, Freedom of Information legislation was introduced in Queensland and the author has made two written applications under this legislation for the above documents. At the time of writing, the Commission had refused access to audit reports, tender documents and contracts for the operation and management of Borallon and Arthur Gorrie Correctional Centres, invoking all possible exemptions available to deny access under the *Freedom of Information Act*. It is now possible for the author to appeal directly to the Information Commissioner. For a review of this refusal see Moyle 1994.

6. It is important to stress that both approaches are legitimate and useful. Harding's approach has to a limited extent forced the Commission to justify the positive inferences he draws about accountability, monitoring and performance. Moyle's approach tends to yield specific information more slowly, as part of the objective is to compel the Commission to provide further information for the public record. This has been a slow and frustrating process.

7. It would appear that the requirement for consent to release the contract derives from Section 9 of the Deed of Agreement for the operation and management of Borallon. Section 9 reads, 'Details of the Contract between the Commission and the Contractor shall be kept confidential and shall not be made available to any individual or organisation by the Commission or the Contractor without prior written approval of the other party'.

8. Since this case study, the Commission has privatised a remand and reception centre (Arthur Gorrie Correctional Centre), which performs the classification procedure for inmates, thus influencing the way inmates move through the corrections system. This further blurring of the boundaries between the allocation and administration of punishment, raises special concerns about how far privatisation should be allowed to proceed. There have been recent allegations that Australasian Corrections Management (ACM), the private company the manages Arthur Gorrie, provided inadequate care and treatment for inmates which caused a major riot, leading to the burning of a unit and about $100,000 worth of damage. (Moyle 1993c)

References

Chan, Janet 1992, 'The Privatisation of Punishment: A Review of the Key Issues', *Australian Journal of Social Issues*, vol. 27, no. 4, November.

Commission of Review into Corrective Services in Queensland 1988a, *Final Report*, (J. J. Kennedy, Commissioner), Queensland Government Printer, Brisbane.

— 1988b, *Interim Report*, (J. J. Kennedy, Commissioner), Queensland Government Printer, Brisbane.

— 1988c, *Volume II, Attachments*, (J. J. Kennedy, Commissioner), Queensland Government Printer, Brisbane.

Criminal Justice Commission 1991, *Report on a Public Inquiry Into Certain Allegations Against Employees of the Queensland Prison Service and its Successor, The Queensland Corrective Services Commission*, (Sir Max Bingham, Chairman), Queensland Government Printer, Brisbane.

Dickson, Brian 1992, 'The Challenge of Change', in D. Biles and J. Vernon (eds), *Australian Institute of Criminology Conference Proceedings on Private Sector and Community Involvement in the Criminal Justice System*, no. 23. AIC, Canberra.

Final Report. See Commission of Review into Corrective Services in Queensland.

Harding, Richard 1992, 'Prison Privatisation in Australia: A Glimpse of the Future', *Current Issues in Criminal Justice*, vol. 4, no. 1, pp. 9-27.

— 1993, 'Privatising Prisons: Principle and Practice', unpublished.

Interim Report. *See* Commission of Review into Corrective Services in Queensland.

Kennedy Report. *See* Commission of Review into Corrective Services in Queensland.

Macionis, Stan 1992, 'The Queensland Experience', in D. Biles and J. Vernon (eds), *Australian Institute of Criminology Conference Proceedings on Private Sector and Community Involvement in the Criminal Justice System*, no. 23, AIC, Canberra.

McLaren, Kay 1992, *Reducing Reoffending: What Works Now*, Department of Justice Penal Division, New Zealand.

Moyle, Paul 1991, Borallon Correctional Centre Field Research Notes, unpublished.

— 1992a, 'Privatising Prisons The Underlying Issues', *Alternative Law Journal*, vol. 17, no. 3, June, pp. 114-119.

— 1992b, 'Practical and Legislative Restrictions to Access of Information for Private Prison Research in Queensland', *Socio-Legal Bulletin*, no. 7, Spring, pp. 24-30.

— 1993a, 'Private Adult Custodial Corrections in Queensland and the First Wave: A Critical Reflection on the First Three Years — Reform or Regression?', in D. Biles and J. Vernon (eds), *Australian Institute of Criminology Conference Proceedings on Private Sector and Community Involvement in the Criminal Justice System*, no. 23, AIC, Canberra.

— 1993b, 'Privatisation of Prisons in New South Wales and Queensland: A Review of Some Key Developments', *The Howard Journal of Criminal Justice*, vol. 32, no. 3, August, pp. 231-250.

—— 1993c, 'Privatisation of Prisons in Australia—Lessons from Queensland', *Culture and Policy*, vol. 5, pp. 205-222.

—— 1994, 'Contracting for Private Prisons in Queensland—Lessons for Penal Policy', Paper presented to the Prisons 2000 Conference, University of Leicester, April in *Socio-Legal Bulletin*, no. 12, Autumn, pp. 16-22.

Public Sector Management Commission 1993, *Review of the Queensland Corrective Services Commission*, Queensland Government Printer, Brisbane.

Queensland Corrective Services Commission 1989a, *Annual Report*, Government Printer, Brisbane.

—— 1989b, Report of Visit to Examine Non-Government Sector Operation of Correctional Facilities, unpublished.

—— 1992a, *Annual Report 1991/92*, Government Printer, Brisbane.

—— 1992b, Correctional Centre Prisoner Classification and Categories, unpublished.

—— 1992c, Public Finance Standards Quarterly Position Assessment, unpublished.

Queensland, Legislative Assembly 1988, *Debates*, vol. 310.

Volume II, Attachments. *See* Commission of Review into Corrective Services in Queensland.

8

Contract management in corrections: the Queensland experience

Stan Macionis

Abstract: The Queensland Corrective Services Commission (QCSC) was the first correctional jurisdiction in the southern hemisphere to contract the full operation and management of a correctional centre to the private sector when a contract for the management and operation of Borallon Correctional Centre was awarded to Corrections Corporation of Australia (CCA) in November 1989.

This chapter will examine the experience of the QCSC with the contract management of Commission facilities by first outlining the history of private sector involvement in corrections in Queensland from 1989 to 1993. This will include the Commission's community corrections centres whose management has been contracted to community organisations as well as the two correctional centres contracted to the private sector.

The Commission's rationale for utilisation of the private sector will then be explored, starting with the Kennedy Commission of Review recommendation for contracting the operation of Borallon Correctional Centre to the private sector. The rationale for subsequent decisions to contract out the management of Commission facilities will then be outlined, including the unprecedented utilisation of the private sector in managing the reception function as has occurred with the Arthur Gorrie Correctional Centre.

The chapter will then focus on contractual arrangements including tender specification, tender evaluation processes and the contractual mechanisms for imposing accountability for performance on the contractor. Day to day operational arrangements and in particular contract monitoring will also be explained.

Finally, the chapter will provide the Commission's view as to the effectiveness of the private sector in the management of correctional centres, including cost comparisons between the CCA managed Borallon Correctional Centre and the Commission operated Lotus Glen Correctional Centre.

HISTORY OF CONTRACT MANAGEMENT IN QUEENSLAND CORRECTIONS

Kennedy Review

The Queensland Corrective Services Commission (QCSC) came into being in 1988 following an extensive review into the provision of correctional services in Queensland by Mr J. J. Kennedy. The recommendations of Kennedy's landmark report provided a blue print for correctional reform and were adopted by the Queensland Parliament with the support of the major political parties.

In his report, Kennedy recommended that one prison under the jurisdiction of the QCSC should be operated and managed by the private sector under contract to the Commission. His rationale for this recommendation was to create a market for corrective institutions in Australia and in particular, Queensland. This would for the first time introduce competition, providing a real measure against which to test the performance and costs of the state operated system.

Borallon Correctional Centre

In accordance with Kennedy's recommendation, the QCSC called tenders for the management of the Borallon Correctional Centre, near Brisbane, which was due for completion in 1989. As a result a contract for the management of the centre, for three years with an option for a further two years, was awarded to Corrections Corporation of Australia (CCA) in November 1989. CCA was a newly formed Queensland based company made up of a consortium of Corrections Corporation of America, Wormald Security and John Holland Constructions.

Following a change in government in December 1989, the newly elected Labor government decided to honour the recently concluded contract despite Labor Party policy which opposed private sector managed prisons.

The centre commenced operation on 2 January, 1990 as a 240 bed facility for medium, low and open security prisoners. The centre initially accommodated a significant proportion of low and open security prisoners but, after about the first 12 months of operation, settled into a prisoner mix of predominantly medium security prisoners with around 10 per cent of the population as low and open security prisoners.

Community Corrections Centres

The enabling legislation for the QCSC included provision for the establishment of community corrections centres — best described as half-way houses where prisoners nearing the end of their custodial sentences could be supervised in a community setting while undergoing programs or release to work as the final stage of re-integration into the community.

Initially, the Commission established one female and two male community corrections centres operated by staff employed in its community corrections arm. Each of these could accommodate around 20 offenders. During 1990, discussions took place with several community groups regarding the operation of community corrections centres by those groups under contract to the Commission in much the same way that CCA operated Borallon Correctional Centre under contract.

The attraction of such arrangements was threefold. First, unlike the Borallon situation, most of the community groups already had substantially completed accommodation facilities which would preclude the need for infrastructure development by the Commission. Second, different groups offered expertise in different types of programs or in dealing with particular offender groups. Third, as for prisons, it was considered beneficial to introduce an element of competition with similar Commission operated facilities which could lead to improved cost-effectiveness in their operation.

As a result, the following contracts for operation of community corrections centres were entered into with various community groups during 1990 and 1991:

- Gwandalan Community Corrections Centre — Brisbane Tribal Council — programs and a release to work facility for Aboriginal and Torres Strait Islander offenders; 25 bed capacity;
- Maconochie Lodge Community Corrections Centre — Shaftesbury Citizenship Centre — work skills and educational programs for younger offenders; 24 bed capacity;
- St Vincent's Community Corrections Centre — Society of St

Vincent De Paul—programs and an inner-city release to work facility for offenders; 27 bed capacity;
- Goodspell Park Community Corrections Centre—Link-up (De La Salle Brothers)—programs for young offenders in a rural location; six bed facility; and
- Tarragindi Lodge Community Corrections Centre—Link-Up (De La Salle Brothers)—programs for female young offenders; six bed facility.

In addition, the Commission entered into contracts with the Association for the Care and Resettlement of Offenders (ACRO) for the operation of two so-called half-way houses. These are similar facilities to community corrections centres, but are not designated as such and do not provide 24 hour a day, seven day a week supervision. As such, these are used to accommodate minimum risk offenders on release to work or administratively transferred to these facilities in order to participate in approved work or development programs.

Remand and Reception (Arthur Gorrie) Centre

As part of its infrastructure redevelopment program, the Commission undertook the construction of a new, modern, campus-style remand and reception centre to replace the infamous Boggo Road prison, parts of which were constructed at the turn of the century.

In mid 1991, the Commission commenced negotiations with the staff union with a view to obtaining agreement to new work practices and procedures to apply at the remand and reception facility when it opened in 1992. These negotiations were unable to bring about any agreement to changes in work practices. As a result, the Board of the Commission informed the government in October 1991 that it intended to proceed to call tenders for the private sector management of this facility rather than transport the old Boggo Road culture and work practices to the new facility.

Following the registration of expressions of interest, seven companies were invited to tender for the contract. In March 1992, Cabinet approved Australasian Correctional Management (ACM) as the successful tenderer. The contract is for five years with an option for a further two years. ACM is comprised of a consortium of Wackenhut and ADT, an Australian based security company.

This contract breaks significant new ground by contracting the management of the reception function to the private sector. As the Commission's main reception centre, the Arthur Gorrie Centre performs the initial assessment and classification of offenders and is, thus, a key part of the Commission's sentence management process.

The new remand and reception centre commenced operation under the management of ACM in June 1992 and the old Boggo Road prison was decommissioned in July 1992.

In summary, in a span of less than three years the QCSC moved from a situation where all correctional facilities were managed and operated by Commission staff to one where two of its eleven correctional centres and five of its seven community corrections centres were managed under contract by the private sector/community groups.

THE RATIONALE FOR CONTRACT MANAGEMENT

It has been stated that Queensland was the first jurisdiction in Australasia to experiment with 'privatisation' of correctional facilities. Two points of clarification need to be made in relation to this statement.

First, 'privatisation' is not the most appropriate term to use with respect to the involvement of the private sector in corrections in Queensland. This is because the State remains the owner of the physical infrastructure (at least in the case of correctional centres), the prisoners remain 'state' prisoners and can and do transfer between private sector and state operated institutions during their sentence, and the state continues to fund the operation of the facilities. In fact, the difference between the state and privately operated facilities is that the latter are managed on behalf of the QCSC by a private sector organisation, under contract, which employs its own staff. Clearly, contract management is a more appropriate term to use in this context.

Second, contract management by the private sector is not a new concept in the administration of corrections in Queensland or in other jurisdictions. Many services have traditionally been contracted to the private sector by the various state operated correctional jurisdictions. These include medical services, cleaning services, maintenance agreements for electronic equipment, vehicle supplies and their servicing, management consultants, etc.

Thus, the private contract management of a correctional centre by the private sector, while a significant departure from the mere provision of auxiliary services, is hardly a revolutionary development.

What, then, is the rationale for taking this significant step? Four main considerations have underpinned the QCSC's decisions in relation to the use of contract management.

As already stated, Kennedy in his review, foresaw the benefits of introducing competition with state operated facilities. Competition would allow the performance of privately and publicly managed facilities to be compared. It would thus provide a stimulus for improved performance by state prison operators and facilitate cross-fertilisation of ideas between the private and public sectors.

The second consideration influencing the OCSC's decisions has been that of cost. There was a perception in Queensland that correctional centres, as with many other jurisdictions, could be managed more efficiently if restrictive work practices could be eliminated and improved management processes put into place. Private sector involvement with greenfield sites and totally new staff provided an ideal opportunity to test this hypothesis. Experience in Queensland with contract management by the private sector has confirmed that the scope for substantial improvements in cost efficiency exists with state operated facilities, particularly correctional centres. The most dramatic illustration of this has been with the new remand and reception centre where the QCSC estimated that to manage and operate the facility itself would cost between $16 million and $18 million per annum depending on whether certain work practices could be altered. The contract eventually entered into with Australasian Correctional Management resulted in a total cost to the QCSC of the order of $12 million per annum to manage and operate the facility.

The third consideration has been the need to bring about cultural and attitudinal change in the management and operation of correctional centres. The QCSC, as well as looking for efficiency improvements, has also sought to improve the effectiveness of the system of corrections in Queensland.

Specifically, the Commission's aim has been to bring about a more rehabilitative environment in its correctional centres where offenders can be given opportunities for self-development while in custody. In order to achieve this, the entrenched attitudes of 'old guard' custodial staff would need to change. In a contemporary correctional environment, based on unit management principles, custodial staff are expected to have substantial interaction with offenders and to have the skills to contribute to the rehabilitation of the offenders under their care. The changed approach required on the part of custodial staff could be glibly put as a shift from controlling to facilitating. The extent of behavioural and attitudinal change required on the part of many currently serving custodial staff in order to operationalise these changes cannot be overstated. It has, in fact, been difficult to bring about the type of cultural change required. Private sector involvement has provided an opportunity to establish centres where staff could be recruited with skills and attitudes commensurate with today's philosophy and direction.

Finally, experience with the private sector is providing the QCSC with comparative information which will assist in assessing future options for the development of correctional services in Queensland.

COMMISSION/CONTRACTOR RELATIONSHIPS

Having determined to proceed with private sector involvement in the administration of corrections, the question arises as to the interworking of the privately managed centre(s) with the remainder of the correctional system and with QCSC management.

Operational Autonomy

The approach taken in Queensland has been to grant the management of the contracted centres as much autonomy in their day to day operations as practicable. The reasons for this are twofold.

First, the organisational structures currently in place in the QCSC are based on the concept of correctional centres as discrete, self-contained organisational units headed by a general manager responsible for the full range of organisational objectives including security, finance, rehabilitation and industries. The idea is that correctional centres are the fundamental building blocks or units of the correctional system and that the role of central office is one of policy formulation, planning and co-ordination rather than that of direct management. In this organisational structure the limits to the autonomy of each GM are only set by primary and subordinate legislation, the need for consistency when applicable, the need to co-ordinate issues, and the abilities and initiative of the individual GM. Maximum extension of autonomy to operate private sector managed centres is thus consistent with this internal organisational environment.

Second, contract management in Queensland has been undertaken on the basis of contracts which, in general, specify outcomes rather than processes. This gives the operator the maximum degree of freedom to manage the centre using different approaches to those traditionally adopted in the state-run system as long as specified outcomes are achieved. That is, autonomy goes hand in hand with accountability for results.

Corporate Level Relationships

In the same way that QCSC operated centres have a QCSC central office, the contract managed centres have a corporate central office to which they are accountable for agreed outcomes. Technically the contract is, in each case, between the QCSC and the corporate entity rather than the centre management. Thus, while day to day operational issues will, in general, be sorted out at officer level with the GM of the contracted centre, policy matters, major contract compliance issues and contract disputes and/or renegotiations take place between the QCSC central office and the corporate office of the contractor.

Contract Evaluation
The contracts between the QCSC and private sector operators contain a 'minimum performance specifications' section which specifies the required outcomes under headings such as: food services; physical security and control; centre prisoner management; health services; and psychological services.

These specifications form the basis for on-going evaluation of each contractor's performance by the Commission's audit section and, in particular, the contract auditor assigned to the particular centre. Feedback is also obtained from those QCSC staff who provide day to day operational support to the contracted centres, particularly with respect to security and prisoner management issues.

Formal evaluations of contractor performance also occur through ad hoc audits and a particularly thorough audit and evaluation is undertaken prior to the decision being taken on exercising the option to extend the contract.

There is currently strong interest in academia regarding performance evaluation and comparison of publicly and privately managed facilities. The Commission is looking to these academics to contribute to increasing the effectiveness of comparative performance evaluation techniques.

OPERATIONAL CONSIDERATIONS

Entering into contract with a private sector operator for the management of a correctional centre raises some unique issues regarding the day-to-day operations of corrective services. Of particular importance are the areas of: day-to-day operational interface; consistency in dealing with offenders; meeting mandatory legislative requirements; role of Contract Monitors/Auditor or Liaison Officers; and the provision of centrally controlled operational support agencies.

Day-to-Day Interface

As with all correctional centres, contract managed centres need to ensure effective operational interfaces not only between the centre and central office but also between the contracted centre and other centres. Care must be taken to ensure commercial and contract considerations are not violated. Any tendency by officials to intervene in the day-to-day operations of the centre must be vigorously resisted. Correctional officials must focus on the desired outcomes and standards, and should not become involved in how the contractor achieves these outcomes.

Success depends on a clearly defined reporting structure so that matters are dealt with on a day-to-day basis. Such a relationship must aim to facilitate communication. It is essential that the contractor receives the same information pertinent to good correctional management as the rest of the organisation. Likewise incidents in the private centre that have the potential to impact, particularly negatively, on the wider correctional community must be communicated to the correctional administration in a timely manner.

The reporting relationships established at the operational level must also be such that they facilitate the transfer of responsibility for inmates/offenders transitioning through the system. Procedures for property transfer, details of visits etc. must be maintained.

Sentence Management

An inmate should be able to expect a consistent minimum standard of treatment, privileges and conditions — regardless of where he/she is accommodated. It is therefore vital that agreements with private sector suppliers of correctional services specify the minimum procedures to apply for the routine management of inmates. Such specifications should apply, at the very least, to the following: a common data base and information management system; standards and scales for clothing issue; visits; use of telephones; medical treatment; and privileges.

In these areas it is appropriate for the contract specifications to be prescriptive. In addition the contractor should ensure the correctional jurisdiction is kept aware of any improvements in those service areas to again ensure a degree of uniformity throughout the system.

Legislation

The minimum requirements under legislation must also be clearly specified and routine procedures for implementing the law must be agreed in place. Ready access to persons having legal obligation or authority must be available, with contractors using common instruments of delegation and recording procedures.

State legislation can lack the flexibility needed to permit the smooth transition to private sector management. Although the Queensland legislation made some allowance for private sector involvement, with the letting of a tender for the second facility it became apparent that amendments were needed to the legislation if maximum benefit and efficiency was to be gained from contract management.

A major lesson from the Queensland experience was that careful legislative review and amendment should be carried out prior to entering into a contract management situation. Particular areas to note include: delegation of statutory power; provision for contractors to exercise routine legal obligations; authority for contractors to exercise powers under related Acts; and power to discipline prisoners.

Operational Support

The cost of the contract may well become prohibitive if the contractor is required to duplicate the full range of operational support services such as transport, escort and specialist dog squad. This is especially so in locations where such external services are already provided to state operated facilities. In such cases economy of scale can be achieved by incorporating the conditions for use of those services in the contract. However there is a danger that contractors may overly rely on such centrally provided services as a means of reducing their costs. Therefore if the state retains the responsibility for providing such services, careful agreement must be reached on such things as: circumstances in which they can be used; conditions of use; frequency of response; legal liability; circumstances where use will be a direct cost to the contractor, e.g. escapes; and command and control.

Any such agreement should stipulate the method for requesting such support and the approving authority and its responsibilities. Care must be taken to ensure that the contractor's access to these services is consistent with that of any other centre.

Monitoring the Contract

Contract management, particularly in the early stages, will raise a number of issues that would not normally arise in a state operated facility. These are normally caused by differing interpretations of contract provisions and unfamiliarity with procedures or legislation. The long-term success of the relationship between the correctional jurisdiction and private contractors will be ensured if such issues are dealt with promptly and to each party's satisfaction. The resolution of such issues from a remote central office is often impractical, slow and inappropriate to the problem as it is perceived on the ground. The use of an officer employed by the state jurisdiction but located on site can be beneficial in these circumstances.

In Queensland this on-site role has been variously undertaken by liaison officers, contract monitors and contract auditors. While each role has some common duties, they have been used to provide a different emphasis at different times during the life of the contract.

The liaison officer. This role has proven beneficial during the pre-commissioning and set up period, from the time the contract is awarded until the centre is fully operational. The role of the liaison officer is to ensure the smooth implementation of the contract. Considerable work is involved in ensuring that all aspects prescribed by the contract are in place prior to the centre opening.

The monitor. Once the centre is fully operational there is a need for the correctional jurisdiction to carefully monitor the contractor's performance against the contract and specifications. Instances will occur where adjustments will need to be made to the formal arrangements. These will occur as the centre settles into a routine. In this role the monitor provides a day to day capacity to evaluate performance. It has been found desirable for the monitor to operate on site during this critical phase.

The auditor. As operations mature, the need for constant on-site supervision reduces. In the Queensland experience this has been after about 12 months operation, at which time the QCSC has found it is able to move to a process in which the contractor is formally evaluated for performance against the contract by means of periodic and/or ad hoc formal audits.

CONTRACT DEVELOPMENT

Objectives of Contract Management

Before proceeding with the development of detailed documentation pertaining to the contract for centre management, a concise statement of purpose is essential. The correctional jurisdiction must clearly define the role and objectives of the centre. Key aspects covered in the provisions of the contract will include the following:

How is the yearly management fee to be escalated?

While a number of formulas are available particular attention needs to be paid to the productivity improvements required of the contractor during the life of the contract. If this is not considered, the jurisdiction could be required to absorb all cost increases incurred by the contractor during the life of the contract.

Insurance

This is a difficult issue with most governments carrying their own insurance. However, as the philosophy of user pays spreads this is becoming a less viable proposition for government. In the case of private operation of a large and expensive facility and over which the state has little or no direct control there is a case for the contractor to insure against loss or damage. This is particularly beneficial should major structural damage occurs requiring the state to find alternate accommodation for a large number of prisoners with a resulting high capital cost. There is also the issue of repairing or replacing a facility affected by major structural damage. However, obtaining insurance cover for correctional facilities has proven to be problematic for the private sector operators and self insurance by the government may prove to be the only option in the future.

Liability of the contractor in cases of escape

Escapes from secure custody invariably place an additional unforseen cost on correctional administration and the government in general. Overtime is incurred. Police are redeployed from normal duties and the public is placed at risk. Greater awareness by the contractor of its responsibility to ensure these costs are not incurred can be achieved by a penalty clause. Such a clause could take the form of either a specified fine, or a charge for specific additional costs such as overtime incurred by correctional staff and police.

In developing contracts, the Commission's approach has been:

- non-prescriptive, except when required by law;
- comprehensive — all aspects of the centre's proposed operations need to be covered;
- outcome driven — the contract specifies what needs to be done but not how to do it;
- to ensure the intent of each area of the specifications is clearly stated;
- to state the minimum standard of performance required — this forms the basis of subsequent audit and evaluation;
- to have the specification independently evaluated before issue.

Tender Evaluation

This is a critical area. All areas of government have rules and procedures for evaluating tenders and there is no reason to vary these. A number of aspects have been given special attention by the QCSC:

- ownership and financial viability. The need for continuity of operation suggests that clear lines of company ownership should be identified and provision inserted in the contract to prevent this changing without agreement from the correctional jurisdiction. A good safeguard is to build in the provision for financial responsibility to rest with the operating companies' owners;
- reference checking must be thorough and if possible include a detailed study of the company's existing operations; and
- the inclusion of independent evaluators on the tender evaluation team has been a worthwhile initiative.

COST COMPARISONS

Cost comparisons between publicly and privately managed correctional centres are difficult to make as the differences between centres need to be normalised in order to make a true 'apples and apples' comparison. Specifically, in comparing correctional centres the following factors have to be taken into account: physical infrastructure; classification mix of prisoners; functions performed by the centre; qualitative issues; and administrative overheads.

On this basis, the QCSC has made a comparison of the unit costs per offender between the Commission operated Lotus Glen Correctional Centre and the CCA operated Borallon Correctional Centre. Considering each of the above factors in turn:

- the differences in infrastructure between Borallon and Lotus Glen Correctional Centres are minimal;
- Borallon Correctional Centre accommodates mainly medium security inmates (over 80 per cent, with the remainder low and open) whereas Lotus Glen has a small number of high security inmates with approximately 40 per cent of the inmate population medium security and a further 40 per cent low and open security. Thus, it is difficult to compare the two centres on the basis of inmate classification mix as a small number of high security inmates at Lotus Glen will make for an additional drain on resources whereas the much larger numbers of low and open security inmates at that centre will have an opposite effect. On balance, it could be expected that the large numbers of low and open security prisoners at Lotus Glen Correctional Centre would at least offset the additional costs associated with the small number of high security inmates;
- Lotus Glen Correctional Centre performs a wider range of

functions than Borallon Correctional Centre. However, it is difficult to quantify what effect, if any, this should have on costs;

- qualitative issues are the most difficult to compare. However, it should be noted that Borallon Correctional Centre provides the highest program content of any correctional centre in Queensland. This is demonstrated by the number of staff employed on the 'programs' side of the centre — 49, compared with 25 management, administrative and programs staff at Lotus Glen;

- in order to complete the comparison, overhead costs need to be added back to each centre. The administrative overheads which should be distributed to Borallon from the QCSC are substantially less than for Lotus Glen as Borallon operates as a 'stand-alone' centre with only limited support from the QCSC central office. Nevertheless, some audit, prisoner welfare, transport and escort, police and operations support overhead costs have been allocated to Borallon for the purpose of this comparison. On the other hand, the QCSC correctional centres are substantially supported by administrative elements in central office and these central costs should be apportioned to each centre on the basis of the number of offenders.

In view of the above, the cost comparison between Borallon and Lotus Glen Correctional Centres is illustrated in Table 1:

TABLE 1

Borallon Correctional Centre 1992/93		Lotus Glen Correctional Centre 1992/93	
	m		m
Total cost:	$10.08	Net Budget	$8.49
Average daily offenders 235		Add Industry Expenditure Gross Budget [1]	$0.65
Unit cost per annum per offender	$42,900	Average daily offenders 234	
		Unit cost per annum per offender	$39,060
Apportioned central office overheads per offender	$1, 300	Apportioned central office overheads per offender	$10,820
Normalised unit cost per annum per offender	$44,200	Normalised unit cost per annum per offender	$49,900

Note: CCA are returning industry revenue to capital infrastructure development for industries at the centre. Thus, it is more valid to compare their costs with Lotus Glen Correctional Centre's gross rather than net budget, the former being the total cost of running the centre before industry revenue is subtracted to give the net budget.

On the basis of this comparison, the cost of Borallon Correctional Centre for 1992/93 was approximately 10 per cent lower per offender than Lotus Glen Correctional Centre.

Conclusion

Up until 1990, the management of prisons in Australia had been exclusively carried out by public sector employees. Unfortunately, in most jurisdictions, including Queensland, inefficient work practices and ineffective and sometimes inhumane methods of operation had become entrenched. For many public sector staff it was difficult to even recognise the need for change much less actively participate in it.

Contracting out the management of a number of correctional centres and community corrections centres to the private sector/community organisations has proved to be a useful tool for the QCSC in breaking the inertia of the status quo.

Competition from the non-government sector has provided motivation for the employees of the state to address their work practices. Productivity improvements in the state run operations began to be realised within a year of the commencement of private sector contract management of QCSC facilities.

Borallon Correctional Centre has provided a model for a programs-run institution. The QCSC is currently putting arrangements into place to ensure cross fertilisation of ideas from Borallon to the state system.

Redundancies associated with the contract management of the Arthur Gorrie Correctional Centre have enabled the Commission to ensure that those staff least disposed towards and able to operate in the new environment have been given the opportunity to terminate their employment with the Commission.

Significant cost savings have been achieved, particularly in the case of custodial centres, as a result of contract management.

Overall, the 'experiment' commenced by the QCSC in 1989 has proved to be an outstanding success and has already influenced other correctional jurisdictions in Australia and New Zealand to consider involvement of the non-government sector in the operation of corrections.

9

Economic and qualitative aspects of prison privatisation in Queensland

Allan Brown*

Abstract: This chapter is primarily concerned with examining the economic issues relating to the contracting out of prison services in general, and at Borallon in particular. It recognises, however, that a concentration on economic aspects alone is too narrow a focus for policy formation, and thus presents a simple framework to take account of both cost and 'quality' dimensions of prison management.

According to conventional wisdom the provision of services by private, profit-oriented firms will result in lower costs than provision by public sector enterprises. The logical extension of this argument gives rise to belief that the management of prisons by private firms will result in cost savings to governments. Empirical evidence on the experience of private prison operations in both the United States and Queensland, however, does not allow the case for the superior economic efficiency of private prison firms to be accepted with confidence.

The performance of state prisons should not be considered in static terms. There seems nothing inherent in the nature of public sector prisons to prevent improvements in both economic and non-economic dimensions of their operations. In fact, public prisons will need to improve the efficiency and 'quality' of their operations to prevent further loss of territory to private prison contractors.

The major motivation for governments to privatise prison operations is to reduce the cost of their corrective services. In this sense the issue of prison privatisation is clearly one suitable for economic inquiry. However, prison privatisation has another dimension, namely, the 'quality' or 'effectiveness' of corrective services which is not so easily amenable to economic analysis. Perhaps this partly explains the current dearth of studies by economists on the subject of prison privatisation, both in Australia and elsewhere. The literature search for this chapter uncovered only one article on the topic in professional economic journals (namely, Roper 1986).

An examination of the now quite extensive non-economic literature on prison privatisation, however, reveals that criminologists, lawyers, sociologists, bureaucrats and activists writing on the topic often involve themselves in economic considerations, generally integrating the treatment of the economic aspects of prison privatisation within their wider consideration of the issue. It is also notable that, in the fine tradition of the discipline of economics, non-economists arrive at differing conclusions regarding the economic consequences of prison privatisation.

The purpose of this chapter is to draw an outline of some of the major economic questions relating to the privatisation of prisons. These matters will then be discussed within the context of the Queensland experience, especially the Borallon prison. By way of background, some reference will be made to the history of private prison operations and to the related 'moral issue'.

HISTORY

The recent moves towards the privatisation of prisons do not represent the first experience of private involvement in incarceration. In medieval England prisons were operated to produce a profit. Prisons belonged to the crown, but were sublet to gaolers who were in effect small business operators. Income was generated by way of a fee system whereby prisoners were charged both an 'admission fee' and a 'release fee'. During their period of incarceration prisoners were also required to pay for food, water, bedding and other daily necessities — including the temporary release from leg-irons! — on a sliding scale in accordance with their social standing which was used as proxy for their capacity to pay (Borna 1986; Porter 1990; Weiss 1989). Various forms of this system — which is an early and perverse example of the 'user pays' principle — continued in England until the 1780s, when prisoners began to be transported to Australia.

The financial exploitation of prisoners was common in France and the United States throughout much of the 19th century, but was substantially extended in the southern states of the United States in response to the severe labour shortage following the Civil War. In the US convicts were either forced to work under state supervision on railroad construction, mining, lumbering and other areas where free labour was scarce, or were subleased by the state to entrepreneurs who used them, essentially as slaves, on cotton plantations and in factories (Borna 1986; Weiss 1989). This era of private sector involvement in United States prisons continued until as late as 1960 when media exposure of the harsh conditions, and the resulting public pressure, eventually brought about complete public administration of prisons and prisoners (DiIulio 1991).

The recent return of the private sector to the operation of prisons originated in the US in 1975 when RCA Service Company, a subsidiary of RCA Corporation, was contracted by the state of Pennsylvania to operate an establishment which houses a small number of juvenile delinquents (Borna 1986). Since 1975 over 20 corporations have entered the 'prisons market' as builders and/or operators of a number of US prisons — mainly in the southern states and mainly (but not exclusively) for low to medium security prisoners. By 1990 approximately 20,000 prisoners, representing almost 2 per cent of the United States prison population, were housed in private prisons (Harding 1992a).

Australia is the second country after the United States to participate in the current era of prison privatisation. In October 1988 the National Party government in Queensland decided to operate the new prison named Borallon, at Esk near Brisbane, under a management contract with a private company. On coming to power the current Labor government confirmed this decision, and has since also placed the new Arthur Gorrie Remand and Reception Centre at Wacol, a Brisbane suburb, under private management. Liberal Party governments in New South Wales and Victoria have since followed the Queensland lead in contracting to privatise part of their prison operations.

THE MORAL ISSUE

It is not suggested of course that the current trend towards the privatisation of prison operations is a return to the abhorrent systems of medieval England or 19th century America. Nevertheless, the same ethical issues associated with allowing prisons to be run by private interests, for the purpose of profit, remain.

At a very general level there is a potential conflict between the interests of society in ultimately reducing the number of people confined in prisons, and the financial interests of private prison operators in increasing the number of prisons and prisoners, and the length of sentences. While there is some doubt that what is good for General Motors is also good for the United States, there is greater doubt that what is good for the private prison industry is also good for American, or Australian, society. It should be stated that the literature reveals no evidence that private firms in recent times have in any way unduly influenced decisions to establish private prison operations. The eagerness of governments in Australia, the United States, New Zealand and the United Kingdom to move to privatised prisons has obviated the need for lobbying by private interests.

Another fundamental ideological difficulty with prison privatisation relates to the premise that the setting and enforcing of the laws of society are inherently and essentially functions of the state, and that incarceration of offenders is an integral part of the legal process which should not be delegated by the state to the private sector (Porter 1990). John DiIulio, a prominent United States opponent of the privatisation of prison operations, invokes the classical political theorist, John Locke, in support of this argument by quoting from the *Second Treatise of Government* where Locke defines political power itself as, 'a right of making laws with penalties of death, and consequently all less penalties, for the regulating and preserving of property, and of *employing the force of the community*, in the execution of such laws . . . for the public good' (DiIulio 1988, p. 81) [emphasis added]. On the basis of this conception of political power DiIulio concludes, '[i]t is not unreasonable to suggest that "employing the force of the community" via private penal management undermines the moral writ of the community itself' (DiIulio 1988, p. 81).

On the opposite side of the philosophical fence in the United States is Charles Logan who takes the view that the state does not *own* the right to punish, but that its authority to imprison derives, as does all of its powers and authority, solely from the consent of the governed. It follows, argues Logan (1987, p.36), that this authority may, with similar consent from the governed, be delegated further to subsidiary entities — provided that those entities are ultimately accountable to the people and subject to the same provisions of the law to which the state is subject. Thus, it is the law, according to Logan, not the civil status of the entity involved, that determines whether any particular exercise of authority — including the use of physical force or other coercive measures — is legitimate (see also Brakel 1992).

To be more specific, there are three potential problems associated with the notion of the state delegating the management of prisons to private interests. The first is that the management of prisons, and the functions of prison officers, cannot be reduced to the carrying out of mere administrative or routine tasks (Ring 1987). By its very nature, the operation of prisons involves the exercise of coercion by one group of people over another, and it is argued that it is simply wrong for the state to allocate the responsibility of coercion to private contractors. To quote DiIulio once again: 'to remain legitimate and morally significant, the authority to govern behind bars, to deprive citizens of their liberty, to coerce (and even kill) them, must remain in the hands of government authorities' (DiIulio 1991, p. 197).

The second problem follows from the first. The relationship between prisoner and prison officer is that of authority of one over the other. The authority of prison officers is based on an internal disciplinary system within prisons, which necessarily involves the exercise of discretion in relation to punishments such as confinement to cells, the imposition of fines and the loss of privileges: 'All of these features of prison life indicate that extensive discretion is exercised over every aspect of inmates' existence' (Weiss 1989, p. 35).

Third, behaviour in prison is one factor which is taken into account in decisions relating to classification, remissions, parole and early release of prisoners. The preparation of reports on the behaviour and attitude of prisoners also involves discretionary judgements on the part of prison officers. Moreover, there is a conflict of interest on the part of the private prison manager in providing input into this decision making process: 'It is even conceivable that an unscrupulous corrections entrepreneur would perversely rig parole recommendations to release prisoners who are troublesome, dangerous, sickly, or otherwise expensive to detain, while holding on to the more profitable inmates' (Donahue 1989, p. 176; see also Ring 1987).

There are of course safeguard mechanisms which can, and are, put in place with the aim of preventing or minimising these potential problems of privately managed prisons. There are also abuses in the operation of public prisons. Under both public and private systems inconsistencies and injustices in prison administration and decision making will not always be detected or, if detected, made public. For these reasons, and because by its very nature the issue involves value judgements, disagreement over the moral propriety of private prison operations may never be fully resolved. Moreover, once a government has set out on the road of private prison management philosophical arguments on moral issues are likely over time to have a diminishing effect on decision making.

COST EFFICIENCY

As already mentioned, the major motivation of governments to privatise their prison operations is to achieve cost savings. The 1988 Kennedy Report into corrective services in Queensland, upon which the decision to privatise Borallon was based, simply asserts that 'in some particular areas (of prison operations) the private sector can do it cheaper and better' (Commission of Review into Corrective Services in Queensland 1988, p.88). But is the assumption of lower costs justified?

It is widely believed that private companies are inherently more economically efficient than public enterprises in the provision of goods and services. Supporters of this notion argue that private owners of firms are able to appropriate profits for their own use, and that those profits are increased by minimising costs. In contrast, public sector employees generally cannot take home any monetary rewards resulting from cost efficiencies which they initiate. To the contrary, so it is argued, whereas the incentives of private firms are conducive to cost reduction, the financial rewards facing public sector managers tend to be tied to the size of their budgets thus creating the incentive to increase rather than reduce spending levels (Martin and Stein 1992, p.84-85).

Empirical evidence provides general support for the greater economic efficiency of private over public production of goods and services. A frequently cited and comprehensive review of the numerous studies comparing the relative economic efficiency of public and private enterprises was carried out in 1982 by three German economists who examined the results of 52 case studies of productive efficiency undertaken in the United States, (West) Germany and three other countries including Australia (Borcherding, Pommerehne and Schneider 1982). They found that in 40 of the 52 cases private enterprises had a lower per unit cost structure than equivalent public enterprises. With a few exceptions, subsequent studies and reviews have yielded similar results (see, for example, Pryke 1982, Millward 1982, Domberger and Piggott 1986).

These findings in favour of the superior economic performance of private firms are subject to an important qualification however. This concerns the dynamic nature of public sector management and production, especially over the past decade or so during which few areas of the public sector in developed countries have avoided the effects of 'corporatisation' and 'commercialisation'. These terms refer to a range of efficiency measures intended to reform public sector operations so as to bring their structure, management and perfor-mance more into line with those prevailing in the private sector. A recent study of the productivity of Australian government business enterprises (GBE's) gives some indication of the efficiency gains currently being achieved (Economic Planning Advisory Council 1992). EPAC found that for all Australian GBE's at state and federal government levels productivity grew at an annual rate of 4.1 per cent over the period 1979-80 to 1990-91. In comparison, productivity growth in the private sector over the same period was only 0.2 per cent per annum (EPAC 1992, pp. 26-27). Another study undertaken in the United Kingdom compared the profitability, between 1979 and 1988, of business enterprises which had been privatised with that of public enterprises *that had not been privatised.* The study found that the privatised firms increased their profits (measured as earnings before interest and tax) by some 140 per cent, while the non-privatised public corporations boosted their profits by 240 per cent! (Domberger 1993, p. 64). These two empirical studies clearly indicate that the economic performance of publicly owned providers of goods and services can be substantially improved over a relatively short space of time.

There are a number of United States studies comparing the relative costs of public and private prison operations. However, accounts of these studies vary between different interpreters of their results. After a decade and a half of private prison operations in the United States, DiIulio (1990, p. 156) summed up the comparative cost issue as follows:

> Despite a variety of claims to the contrary, there is absolutely nothing in either the scholarly or the nonscholarly literature on the subject—no journal article, no government report, no newspaper story, no conference proceedings, no book—that would enable one to speak confidently about how private corrections firms compare with public corrections agencies in terms of costs . . . or any other significant dimension. The necessary comparative research simply has not been done, and reliable empirical data are still scarce.

Thomas and Logan (1992, p. 231) are satisfied, however, that the superior economic efficiency of private prisons in the United States has been adequately demonstrated:

> . . . all of the available evidence supports the hypothesis that private management of correctional facilities is significantly less costly than is public management. The same body of research reveals that cost savings can be realized without any sacrifice being made in terms of the quality of correctional services that

are provided. Indeed, the research evidence to date reveals that operating costs can be significantly reduced at the same time that the quality of correctional services is being enhanced.

Notwithstanding the two year gap between the publication of these assessments their widely conflicting interpretation of the evidence makes it prudent to withhold judgement concerning the relative economic — and non-economic — performance of United States private and public prison operations.

There are significant methodological difficulties in comparing the costs of prisons under alternative systems. In particular, it is often difficult to identify one private and one public prison whose operations are sufficiently comparable. The location of a prison may affect wages and other costs, the age and design of a facility can have a bearing on required staff numbers, and the security classification of inmates determines the extent and cost of their custody requirements. Most importantly, the population size of a prison is a major factor affecting the 'per day per prisoner' cost of operation (Logan 1990): a prison with 400 inmates is likely to have a lower daily cost per prisoner than one which houses 200 inmates, whether private or public.

There are potential 'dynamic' cost efficiencies involved with private prisons. Costs could fall over time as private firms gain experience in prison operations, and new cost cutting approaches by the private sector may be able to be applied to public prisons. In particular, the 'demonstration effect' of lower private sector labour costs may be used by governments to reduce the bargaining power of public sector prison workers (Donahue 1989).

As in most other industries, the potential for cost savings in private prison management will depend largely upon the degree of competition in the 'prisons market'. If there are several firms bidding for contracts, and several firms willing and able to take over contracts from incumbent private firms, the consequent competition can be expected to result in economically efficient operations. On the other hand the existence of only a few private competitors in the market will be less conducive to efficiency.

A low level of competition will increase the likelihood of incumbent firms becoming entrenched, with little prospect of losing existing contracts when they become due for renewal. Under such circumstances there will be little incentive for them to control and reduce costs, and they will enjoy an enhanced ability over time to increase charges under their contracts with the state, and their profits (Donahue 1989; Gentry 1986; Porter 1990). A small number of firms also creates the conditions for the development of 'cartel' behaviour to reduce the level of effective competition among members of the industry (Ring 1987).

The economic term for governments hiring the services of private firms to carry out services previously undertaken by public sector employees is 'contracting out'. Contracting out is thus, a particular form of 'privatisation' which is the term used to refer to the more general phenomenon of shifting responsibility for economic activity from the public to the private sector. Governments considering contracting out prison operations are faced, not with a single decision of whether to contract out or not, but with a number of possible areas of private involvement in prison operations. Table 1 sets out three major areas of prison operations, namely, (1) construction of prisons, (2) detention services, and (3) other services, with (non-exhaustive) lists of 'sub-services' under each of (2) and (3). Governments can choose among numerous possible permutations of private involvement in prison functions. The contracting out of areas 1 and 3, however, are likely to be less contentious than the allocation of detention services (area 2) to private contractors (DiIulio 1991).

TABLE 1
POSSIBLE AREAS OF PRIVATE PRISON OPERATIONS

1.	CONSTRUCTION OF PRISONS	
2.	DETENTION SERVICES	
	a.	supervision
	b.	control room monitoring
	c.	gatekeeping
	d.	perimeter security
3.	OTHER SERVICES	
	a.	meals
	b.	medical/dental
	c.	counselling
	d.	drug treatment
	e.	education
	f.	prison industries
	g.	recreation
	h.	cleaning
	i.	fire protection
	j.	laundry
	k.	vehicle maintenance
	l.	property maintenance
	m.	management consultancy
	n.	escort/transport of prisoners

Governments can maximise the conditions for competition among private prison firms by separating functions 1 and 2. That is, given a decision to involve private enterprise in prison operations, there are likely to be benefits to governments in owning prisons (whether constructed by the public or private sector) and entering into contracts with private firms for their management. This will reduce the 'exit costs' of private prison operators, lessen the possibility of 'entrenchment', and thus make it easier for governments to change private operators on the expiration of contracts, or to return the operation of individual prisons to the public sector (McDonald 1990).

Another point concerning the contracting out of prison operations — or any service previously carried out by the public sector — relates to the extent of possible cost savings to the government. Shifting an economic activity from the public to the private sector involves an additional, new 'cost', namely the *profit* paid by the firm to its owners (that is, shareholders). If the payments made by the government under a contract with a private firm were equal to the total cost of providing the service with public employees, the profits of the private contractor would be exactly equal to the value of the cost savings it was able to bring about. There would be no financial benefit to the government however if its total expenditure for the provision of the service was the same, after contracting out as under public provision. The private contractor therefore, faces the task of finding cost savings sufficient to cover (a) the reduction in total expenditure to the government and (b) the payment of profit to its shareholders. It follows that any service — including prison management — will be more highly conducive to contracting out, the less economically efficient is its provision by the state. Conversely, there will be no financial benefit to governments (or private firms) in the contracting out of a service which is already provided by the public sector in an economically efficient manner.

Although the cost-effectiveness of private relative to public prisons is an important matter, it should not be considered (even by economists) as the only matter of concern. The more relevant issue is whether private contractors are more or less able than the public sector, within a range of acceptable costs, to fulfil the objectives of a government's corrections policy. Consideration must be given therefore to the performance of private prison firms in the 'qualitative' areas such as conditions of confinement (including safety, crowdedness, health care), internal security (victimisation, violence, escapes and attempted escapes), social adjustment and rehabilitation (personal, vocational and employment counselling, education, drug and alcohol programs, recidivism) and management and staffing (staff morale, staff turnover, inmate grievances against staff) (see Hatry, Brounstein and Levinson 1993).

Putting aside the methodological and practical difficulties involved in measuring both the cost and qualitative aspects of prison management, the framework for government decision makers in considering whether or not to contract out the operations of any particular prison can be formally set out as follows:

- if it is estimated that both cost can be reduced and 'quality' aspects improved, prison management should be contracted out;
- if neither cost nor quality improvements are considered achievable, prison management should not be contracted out;
- if cost savings are considered achievable but with reduced quality outcomes, the decision regarding the contracting out of prison management is not clear-cut — in this case the decision will involve a 'trade-off' between, on the one hand, the amount of estimated cost savings and, on the other, the number, extent and nature of anticipated quality reductions; similarly,
- if private operation is estimated to increase costs but to improve quality outcomes, the contracting out decision will again not be clear-cut but will involve consideration of the trade-off between cost and quality.

ACCOUNTABILITY

One of the disadvantages of contracting out any service function is the government's or agency's reduced control over the delivery process. This dilemma is addressed by specifying required quality outcomes in the contract, and by monitoring performance during the contract period. The more precisely service outputs can be defined, the easier it will be for them to be specified in the contract, and for their achievement to be monitored. Conversely, however, where outputs cannot be accurately defined, their specification and monitoring may prove problematic.

In particular, there are two aspects of service output which affect contract specification and the ability to monitor. The first is 'tangibleness': it is a relatively straightforward matter to write a contract for services with outputs that are readily identified and quantified, but less so where the output is intangible and not easily measured. The second aspect is 'product complexity': where the service output has a number of dimensions, some of which are difficult to delineate or define, contract monitoring may not be fully effective. It follows, therefore: '[t]he more complex the product, the better suited it is to public production . . . governments are more likely to contract out services that can be easily monitored, i.e. services that have tangible and simple outputs' (Ferris and Graddy 1986, p. 333). By these criteria, prison management, because of the multidimensional and highly qualitative nature of its outputs, would seem an unlikely candidate for contracting out.

When, however, prison management is contracted out the negotiation, preparation and monitoring of contracts adds an additional layer of responsibility to the administration of prisons by governments or corrections agencies, as well as additional costs. McDonald (1990, p. 188) explains that:

> In public correctional facilities, an unbroken chain of command is assumed to exist between the officer who deals with inmates on a day-to-day basis and the highest elected public official in the jurisdiction. In private firms, no such direct linkage exists. A legal barrier divides the governing entity and private correctional firms, and this divide is bridged by contractual agreements that have to be negotiated and then put in writing.

McDonald also notes that in many instances in the United States control over public prisons is neither as direct nor as effective as the ideal of the 'unbroken chain' would suggest. This gives rise to the phenomenon of 'government failure' in public sector prison operations. Other writers have suggested that government failure in the management of prisons may not be confined to the United States (Harding 1992b; Matthews 1989; Moyle 1993; Zdenkowski 1990).

As already mentioned, the mechanism designed to achieve accountability of private prison operators is the monitoring of contract performance. Requirements of the private prison operator will be detailed in the contract, and the performance of the contractor monitored against those requirements. Procedures will be agreed upon for the frequency and extent of the monitoring process, the records and information to be made available to the monitors, the reporting of the results, and the options available (including contract cancellation) in the event of the discovery of breaches committed by the private contractor.

There are possible shortcomings in the monitoring process itself however. The first is that there may be a tendency on the part of the regulatory agency to focus on the means, rather than the ends, of contract performance: 'Public organisations are notorious for evaluating performance according to inputs rather than outputs'

(DiIulio 1990, p. 162). This suggests that, as well as the regular monitoring of the day-to-day activities of the private prison firm in accordance with the requirements of the contract, the overall operations of individual private prisons should be evaluated at regular intervals in relation to government corrections policy (Keating 1990).

Second, effective monitoring is expensive and the cost could absorb much of the savings (if there are any) from contracting out (DiIulio 1991). Correction agencies will therefore have a disincentive to devote sufficient resources to the monitoring of private contractors: 'Monitoring expenditures are thus capped by a criterion wholly unrelated to prison quality' (Gentry 1986, p. 359).

A third potential problem with the monitoring of private prison operations, related to the second, is that the corrections agency may have a vested interest in not monitoring the private firm sufficiently closely or thoroughly. To the extent that the agency has promoted the concept of privatisation and/or was involved in the selection process for the awarding of the contract, it will be seen to be at least partly responsible if serious breaches of contract or other improprieties are revealed by the monitoring process. Finally, as in other areas of government regulation of private sector activity, agencies monitoring private prison contractors are potentially subject to the phenomenon of 'capture' by the regulated firm or industry (Gentry 1986).

Gentry (1986, pp. 360-67) has proposed an open monitoring system for private prisons, consisting of the following elements:

- a range of fines and bonuses to act as pecuniary incentives to the private firm for achieving and exceeding the provisions in the contract;
- guaranteed public access to relevant information concerning private prison operations;
- physical access by interested members of the public to all parts of private prisons; and
- members of the press and academic researchers to be allowed private interviews with inmates.

Gentry also argues that prison contracts should be advertised for rebidding at frequent intervals as a means of avoiding entrenchment and hence maximising the cost efficiency of private prison operations.

THE QUEENSLAND EXPERIENCE

When the Queensland government announced to Parliament in October 1988 that Borallon would be contracted out, the decision was condemned by the Labor opposition. Later, in correspondence with the Queensland State Service Union (QSSU) which represents state prison workers, the opposition leader, Wayne Goss, confirmed the opposition of the Labor Party in Queensland to the concept of private prison operations, and to the contracting out of Borallon in particular. He stated that: 'The Goss Government will move to end the privatisation of Borallon . . . there will be no renewal of the contract or extension of the experiment' (quoted in QSSU 1990).

Since coming to power in December 1989 however, the Labor government has had a change of heart. It has not only allowed Borallon to continue operations under private management, but has also contracted with another private consortium for the management of the new facility, the Arthur Gorrie Correctional Centre, at Wacol. In fact, the Wacol decision represents a considerable extension of the contracting out experiment, as it is a remand and reception centre and thus, unlike Borallon, houses inmates across the full range of security classifications. As well, the non-government staff members at the Arthur Gorrie Centre play a role in determining the classifications of inmates at the facility.

Borallon became operational in January 1990. The contract between the Queensland Corrective Services Commission (QCSC) and Corrections Corporation of Australia (CCA) was for a period of three years, with an option to renew for a further two years. The renewal option was exercised by the contracting parties in late 1992, and the contract with CCA now runs to December 1994. The QCSC has a number of options available to it in the period prior to the expiration of the current contract, including the calling for new tenders to operate the facility from 1995. The Borallon contract is costed on the basis of 100 per cent occupancy throughout the year, which means that CCA is paid the total contract fee whether or not it houses a full complement of prisoners. The QCSC thus has a financial incentive to maintain the number of prisoners at Borallon to its cell capacity. The management fee for the first year of operation was $8.2 million. Under an escalation clause in the contract the fee for the 1991-92 financial year was increased to $9.3 million, and for 1992-93 to $10.08 million (see below).

Borallon was originally designed for 84 maximum security and 160 medium security prisoners (Harding 1992a). It now houses around 90 per cent medium security, and 10 per cent low and open security prisoners. Even though intended partly for maximum security, the decision was made when it was contracted out to private management (after completion of construction) to use Borallon only for medium, low and open prisoner classifications. To the extent of the additional construction costs incurred, the maximum security facilities at Borallon — now apparently unnecessary — represents inefficient utilisation of prison capacity. It is ironic that this should be a feature of Australia's first experiment with private prison management, an experiment justified mainly in terms of economic efficiency.

The 380-person remand and reception facility at Wacol was opened in June 1992. The contract for the Arthur Gorrie Centre is let to Australasian Correctional Management, a subsidiary of Wackenhut Corrections Corporation, the largest independent private security firm in the US. The Goss government decided to contract out management of the centre following the breakdown of negotiations between the QCSC and the QSSU over staffing and operational matters at Wacol (Harding 1992b). Apart from the amount of the contract fee, around $12 million for 1992-93, little financial information is available to date concerning operations at the Arthur Gorrie Centre. The following examination of the cost of private prison operations in Queensland is therefore confined to Borallon.

QCSC data indicate that the contracting out of the Borallon facility to private operators since 1990 has resulted in efficiencies and savings relative to the cost of its publicly operated prisons. These data are summarised in Table 2 which compares, for both 1991-92 and 1992-93, the annual cost per prisoner at Borallon and Lotus Glen, which is a state operated prison situated at Mareeba in North Queensland.

TABLE 2
QCSC BORALLON AND LOTUS GLEN COST COMPARISONS:
1991-92 AND 1992-93

	Borallon		Lotus Glen	
	1991-92	1992-93	1991-92	1992-93
Total facility costs	$9.3m	$10.08m	$8.96m	$9.14m
Average daily offenders	237	235	209	234
Net annual cost per prisoner	$39,240	$42,900	$42,870	$39,060
Central office overheads per prisoner	nil	$1,300	$11,690	$10,820
Gross annual cost per prisoner	$39,240	$44,200	$54,560	$49,880

Source: QCSC data.

It was mentioned earlier that it is usually difficult to compare the costs of private and public prisons because of differences in their sizes, locations, age and the security classifications of their inmates. Nevertheless, the QCSC maintains that in the case of Borallon and Lotus Glen a meaningful cost comparison can be made. QCSC (1992) points out that both prisons have recently been constructed, differences in their infrastructure are minimal, and both cater for a similar number of inmates.

Table 2 shows that, according to QCSC calculations, for 1991-92 the net annual cost per prisoner was 9.3 per cent higher at Lotus Glen ($42,870) than at Borallon ($39,240). When QCSC head office overheads are allocated the cost advantage of Borallon increases to 39 per cent — $54,560 for Lotus Glen compared with (an unchanged) $39,240 for Borallon. These 1991-92 figures were criticised by the current writer when they were first released by the QCSC on the basis that it was 'difficult to accept the apportionment by the QCSC of $11,690 per inmate to Lotus Glen for head office overheads, and zero for Borallon' (Brown 1992, p. 10 see also Moyle 1992 who made a similar criticism earlier). Subsequently, in the preparation of the 1992-93 data, the QCSC allocated $1300 per inmate as central office overheads for Borallon, while the comparable figure for Lotus Glen was reduced from $11,690 for 1991-92 to $10,820 for 1992-93. Table 2 shows that for 1992-93 the annual net cost per prisoner at Lotus Glen ($39,060) was 9.0 per cent less than at Borallon ($42,900), but when overheads are accounted for Borallon ($44,200) shows a cost advantage over Lotus Glen ($49,880) of 12.9 per cent.

The difference in the gross annual cost per prisoner in 1991-92 was $15,320 ($54,560 less $39,240) which calculates out to a total annual cost advantage for Borallon of around $3.63 million ($15,320 per prisoner multiplied by 237 prisoners). The equivalent figures for 1992-93 are as follows: difference in gross annual cost per prisoner, $5680 ($49,880 less $44,200); total cost advantage for Borallon, $1.33 million ($5680 per prisoner, multiplied by 235 prisoners). In other words, on the basis of the QCSC figures, the annual operating costs for Borallon would have been approximately $3.63 million greater for 1991-92, and $1.33 million greater for 1992-93, if it were operated as part of the state prison system.

The QCSC is mindful of the difficulties of this type of cost comparison but defends the value of the exercise. It notes the differences in the classification of inmates between the two establishments: Borallon has approximately 90 per cent medium security, and 10 per cent low and open security inmates; while Lotus Glen has approximately 40 per cent medium security, 40 per cent low and open security, with the remaining 20 per cent being high security. The QCSC (1992) reasons that: 'On balance, it could be expected that the large numbers of low and open security prisoners at Lotus Glen Correctional Centre would more than offset the additional costs associated with the small number

of high security inmates'. The QCSC also advises that Borallon provides the highest program content of any correctional centre in
Queensland, and employs a much greater number of staff on programs
than does Lotus Glen.

A notable feature of the cost comparisons between Borallon and
Lotus Glen is the trend over the two financial years. Each figure of net
and gross annual cost per prisoner indicates an increase for Borallon
and a reduction for Lotus Glen. The 9.3 per cent advantage for
Borallon for 1991-92 in relation to net cost per prisoner became a 9.0
per cent advantage for Lotus Glen in 1992-93; and the 39 per cent
margin of Borallon over Lotus Glen for gross cost per prisoner in 1991-
92 decreased to 12.9 per cent in 1992-93. This apparent cost improvement of the state operated prison in relation to its privately managed
counterpart could be due to a range of causes, and there is no indication in the raw figures as to what factors may have been at play.
The trend in favour of the publicly operated facility is consistent with
the EPAC findings examined earlier of improved productivity by
Australian government business enterprises. Because of the short
period of only two years covered by the QCSC data however, it cannot
be assumed that the trend in the figures favouring Lotus Glen will be
maintained.

While the QCSC has altered its stance in relation to central office
overheads, and has apportioned $1300 per prisoner at Borallon for
1992-93 compared to its zero allocation for 1991-92, a more realistic
figure may be yet higher. The Queensland Public Sector Management
Commission (PSMC) carried out an extensive review of QCSC
operations in 1993, including the contractual arrangements with the
private operators at Borallon and the Arthur Gorrie Centre, and
QCSC's cost comparisons of Borallon and Lotus Glen (PSMC 1993).
In relation to the particular issue of cost allocations the PSMC noted:

> Some central office costs such as audit, prison welfare, transport
> and escort, police and operations support have been recognised
> (by QCSC). Other corporate overheads such as health and
> medical costs, legal fees and freedom of information have not
> been considered. The review considers that more refinement of
> the cost attribution exercise is required (PSMC 1993, p. 118).

There are a few other factors favouring Borallon in the cost comparisons with Lotus Glen, which are not adjusted for in the QCSC
figures. These are:

1. Because of its location in north Queensland, Lotus Glen is at a cost
    disadvantage relative to Borallon, which is near to the Brisbane

metropolitan area, at least for some of its inputs. For example, a remote area allowance is payable to Lotus Glen (but not Borallon) employees.

2. As already mentioned, Borallon was constructed as a maximum/ medium security prison, but is now utilised to house mainly medium security inmates. This may result in some savings in operating costs for Borallon which are not similarly enjoyed by Lotus Glen.

3. Lotus Glen caters for an unknown number of special protection, remand and HIV-positive inmates, whereas CCA is not obliged to accept any such prisoners at Borallon (Moyle 1994). This is likely to represent a further cost disadvantage to Lotus Glen (the amount depending upon the number of inmates and the special detention requirements involved).

Accounting for these factors will further reduce the cost advantage of Borallon over Lotus Glen represented in the QCSC figures.

The comparison of costs between Borallon and Lotus Glen is an imperfect exercise. Nevertheless, there are sufficient similarities between the two facilities for it to be meaningful and worthwhile. However, it is not entirely satisfactory for the QCSC each year to issue a brief statement of figures and to expect them to be accepted at face value. The QCSC has addressed some of the deficiencies in its 1991-92 data, but further refinement seems warranted. In terms of objectivity and transparency, greater confidence would be able to be placed in the cost comparison if it were undertaken in conjunction with some individual or small group independent of the QCSC. More importantly, as indicated earlier, any study of costs should be complemented by an examination of the 'quality' dimension of prison operations. Appropriate decisions in relation to the contracting out of prison management can only be made when both cost and quality aspects are taken into account.

In its review of the QCSC the PSMC (1993, p. 119) took a similar view. It found that 'The bases upon which quantitative and qualitative comparisons are made between contract-managed and State-managed correctional centres need to be refined'. The PSMC recommended that:

By 30 September 1994, the Queensland Corrective Services Commission, in consultation with the Office of the Cabinet and Treasury, develop a methodology for evaluating contract management of custodial and community corrections centres which includes:

- the basis on which costs should be compared;
- the basis on which quality of service can be assessed; and
- the overall financial and other impacts on the State and the State correctional system of contract-managed centres.

This proposed task has the potential to make a substantial contribution to the assessment of private prison management in this country.

The QCSC figures for 1991-92 and 1992-93 suggest that per prisoner cost at Borallon is less than that at Lotus Glen, but that the margin may be narrowing. Until a comprehensive study along the lines of that recommended by the PSMC is carried out however, the conclusion regarding the claimed superior economic performance of privately operated relative to public prisons in Queensland must be the same as that for the United States, namely, 'not proven'.

STAFFING

Staffing is the single most important issue affecting both the cost and quality of prison operations. Because facilities require to be staffed 24 hours a day, and need a sufficient number of prison officers to direct inmates and to ensure the internal security of staff, other inmates and property, prison management is a highly labour intensive activity. The major potential for savings by private prison contractors, therefore, is in relation to labour costs. This can be achieved by reducing staff levels relative to public prisons. Brakel (1992, p.254) points out that because of the round-the-clock surveillance requirement the reduction of one prison guard *position* means that five fewer guards will be needed and five fewer salaries will have to be paid.

Private prison firms can also make savings in expenditures on labour by hiring staff at a lower average hourly cost. This may mean that private prison officers are employed on terms less favourable than those pertaining in the public sector, with lower salary levels, penalty rates and/or retirement benefits. Savings in labour costs can also be achieved by private prison firms hiring a higher proportion of casual and lower ranking prison officers than their public counterparts. It is of interest in this context to refer to a 1984 examination of the performance of private firms carrying out (non-custodial) services for local governments in the US. The study found that, compared with municipalities which undertook the work with their own employees, the private contractors tended to require more work from employees (less liberal vacation and leave for equivalent salaries), use the least qualified personnel able to perform each task, use part-time labour wherever appropriate, and use less labour intensive means of producing services (see Ferris and Graddy 1984, p. 333).

Information available on staffing practices at Borallon indicates possible savings in staffing costs at that facility. CCA administrative staff members are not unionised and are on fixed contracts which have no provision for the payment of overtime (Moyle 1993, p. 243). Non-administrative staff are unionised but are members of the Miscellaneous Workers Union, not the QSSU. All prison officers at Borallon are accredited by QCSC but not all are full-time employees at the facility. The payment of overtime is minimised by means of a pool of casual workers who work at Borallon during weekends, evenings and other times when the award for public sector employees requires the payment of penalty rates (Harding 1992a). In contrast, the casual workers are on fixed rates and receive no holiday pay or the other benefits of full-time employment. Moyle (1993, p. 243) claims that, overall, the status, pay and conditions at Borallon are inferior to those for public sector prison officers.

The benefits to the government of lower labour costs at Borallon will extend to the public sector if the 'demonstration effect' reduces wages and/or conditions for state-employed prison officers. It is clear that problems in negotiating with public sector prison officers has been a major factor in the decision of the government to experiment with the private operation of prisons. To this extent the corrections policy of the Queensland government is interrelated with its industrial relations policy.

Employment remuneration and conditions less financially favourable to employees can be expected to lower total expenditure on labour and, therefore, the overall costs of prison operations. The effect that changes in employment arrangements will have on the 'quality' dimension of prison management, however, is less apparent. The relationship between prison officers and inmates, and that between officers and management, are crucial determinants of the quality of prison operations, and changes in the traditional nature of those relationships may not always be detrimental to the effectiveness of prison management. Moyle (1992, p. 115) refers to the 'quasi-militaristic' attitude of some long term public prison officers which he considers to be 'an impediment to the reform process'. (But cf with some interesting changes in work culture by public correctional officers, Moyle 1994, pp. 62-3.) In this context it is worth quoting at some length from a comparative survey study

of publicly and privately managed prisons in the US (Hatry, Brounstein and Levinson 1993, pp. 198-99):

> By and large, both staff and inmates gave better ratings to the
> services and programs at the privately operated facilities; escape
> rates were lower; there were fewer disturbances by inmates; and in
> general, staff and offenders felt more comfortable at the privately
> operated facilities.
>
> Why is this so? Our data indicate that the privately operated
> facilities had younger and less experienced personnel, and
> staff who were compensated less (partly because of their lesser
> experience), than their counterparts in publicly operated
> facilities. Does additional experience and higher wages lead
> to higher quality performance? The data we examined do
> not indicate this to be the case. We conjecture that youthful
> enthusiasm may combat 'job burnout' of longer tenured mem-
> bers . . .
>
> By and large, staff in the privately operated [prisons] . . .
> appeared to be more enthusiastic about their work, more involved
> in their work, and more interested in working with inmates than
> their public counterparts.
>
> We suspect that at least some of the advantage of the privately
> operated facilities could be regained by the public sector in these
> corrections environments if management and organisational
> hindrances, such as rigid procedures, could be alleviated.

The results of this single study do not overturn the earlier conclusion
regarding the relative overall performance of private and public prisons
in the US. Nevertheless, the above quote and the study from which it
derives does suggest that in at least some individual cases it is possible
for contracting out to bring benefits to both cost and quality aspects of
prison management.

SUMMARY AND CONCLUSIONS

This chapter has primarily involved consideration of economic factors
related to private prison operations. Too narrow a focus on economic
matters, however, carries the risk of neglecting important non-
economic issues. By applying the term 'quality' to represent the wide
range of non-economic criteria, a recurring theme of this chapter has
been that both cost and quality aspects need to be taken into account
in policy considerations relating to the contracting out of prison
management.

There are theoretical arguments and empirical evidence in support of the view that the production of goods and services by private, profit-making firms is inherently more economically efficient than their provision by public enterprises. It is a short step from the acceptance of this conventional wisdom to the belief that the contracting out of prison management will result in cost savings to governments. The cost issue was shown, however, to be somewhat more complex than first appears. First, for any prison facility the cost advantage of private over public provision of services needs to be sufficient both to allow the government to reduce its outlays for prison management and for the private contractor to generate a profit. Second, the economic efficiency of the public provision of services must be considered in dynamic, not static terms. Empirical evidence shows that in recent years Australian government enterprises have increased their productivity at a much greater rate than firms in the private sector. There seems to be no inherent factor preventing publicly operated prisons from similarly improving their economic productivity.

The Queensland government has made the correct decision in keeping open for itself the option of abandoning the privatisation experiment if it chooses to do so. By maintaining the ownership of both the Borallon and Wacol facilities, and contracting out only their management, the government has largely avoided the dangers and potential costs associated with the incumbents becoming entrenched. To date there has been a significant number of private firms tendering for prison management contracts in Queensland (Harding 1992b). This indicates that the possible inefficiencies from an uncompetitive 'prisons industry' is not currently a problem. Competition in the industry could be further enhanced by permitting the public sector, in future tenders for prison management contracts, to submit bids against those from private firms.

According to data produced by the QCSC it appears that the cost to the government of contracting out the management of Borallon is less than that for the operation of the 'equivalent' state prison at Lotus Glen, but that the cost advantage of Borallon is narrowing. The methodology of comparing the relative costs of the two prison operations, however, has not yet been sufficiently refined for these results to be accepted at face value.

The contracting out of prison operations has attractions for governments only if there are significant cost and 'quality' deficiencies in public sector corrective services — assuming government decisions are made without ideological bias. In this sense, the privatisation of parts of the prison system in Queensland and other states of Australia can be seen to be a response by governments to their perception of the poor performance, in terms of both cost and/or effectiveness, of their own public prison systems.

If the cost aspect of public prisons is able to be improved so also should the 'quality' dimension. The inertia that comes from the comfort of tradition and established practices may cause an initial resistance to change, but ultimately there is unlikely to be anything inherent in public sector prison operations to prevent change.

Indeed, with an increasing number of Australian states contracting out an increasing number of facilities to private firms, public prisons may need to adapt simply in order to survive. The onus thus lies with state operated prisons to 'compete' with the new private prison firms across the areas of cost and quality. There are indications that for some public prisons the process of change is already underway. The consequence of such a response from the public sector to the recent advent of private prison management will be not only to reduce the costs of operating prisons, but also to bring about a more effective and humane prison system.

References

Borcherding, T. E., Pommerehne, W. W. and Schneider, F. 1982, 'Comparing the efficiency of private and public production: The evidence from five countries', *Zeitschrift fur Natinalokonomie*, Supplementum 2, pp. 127-56.

Borna, S. 1986, 'Free enterprise goes to prison', *The British Journal of Criminology*, vol. 26, no. 4, October, pp. 321-34.

Brakel, S. J. 1992, 'Private Corrections', in *Privatizing the US Justice System*, (eds) G. W. Bowman, S. Hakim and P. Seidenstat, McFarlane

Brown, A. 1992, 'Economic aspects of prison privatisation: The Queensland experience', in D. Biles and J. Vernon (eds), Australian Institute of Criminology Conference Proceedings on Private Sector and Community Involvement in the Criminal Justice System, no. 23 AIC, Canberra.

Commission of Review into Corrective Services in Queensland 1988, *Final Report*, vol. 1, (Chairman J. J. Kennedy), Government Printing Service, Brisbane

DiIulio, J. 1988, 'What's wrong with private prisons', *The Public Interest*, no. 92, Summer, pp. 66-83.

—— 1990, 'The duty to govern: A critical perspective on the private management of prisons and jails', in *Private Prisons and the Public Interest*, (ed) D. McDonald, Rutgers University Press, New Brunswick, pp. 155-78.

— 1991, *No Escape: The Future of American Corrections*, Basic Books, New York.

Domberger, S. 1993, 'Privatisation: What Does the British Experience Reveal?', *Economic Papers*, vol. 12, no. 2, pp. 58-68.

Domberger, S. and Piggott, J. 1986, 'Privatization policies and public enterprise: A survey', *The Economic Record*, vol. 62, no. 177, PP. 145-62.

Donahue, J. 1989, *The Privatization Decision*, Basic Books, New York.

Economic Planning Advisory Council (EPAC) 1992, *Profitability and Productivity of Government Business Enterprises*, EPAC Research paper no. 2, August.

Ferris, J. and Graddy, E. 1986, 'Contracting out: For what? With whom?', *Public Administration Review*, no. 46, July-August, pp. 332-44.

Gentry, J. 1986, 'The Panopticon revisited: The problem of monitoring private prisons', *Yale Law Journal*, vol. 96, no. 2, pp. 353-75.

Harding, R. 1992a, 'Prison privatisation in Australia: A glimpse of the future', *Current Issues in Criminal Justice*, vol. 4, no. 1, July, pp. 9-27.

— 1992b, 'Private prisons in Australia', *Trends and Issues in Crime and Criminal Justice*, Australian Institute of Criminology, no. 36, May.

Hatry, H. P., Brounstein. B. J. and Levinson, R. B. 1993, 'Comparison of privately and publicly operated correction facilities in Kentucky and Massachusetts', in *Privatizing Correctional Institutions*, (eds) G. W. Bowman, S. Hakin and P. Seidenstat, Transaction Publishers, New Brunswick, pp. 193-212.

Keating, M. 1990, 'Public over private: Monitoring the performance of privately operated prisons and jails', in *Private Prisons and the Public Interest*, (ed) D. McDonald, Rutgers University Press, New Brunswick, pp. 130-54.

Logan, C. H. 1987, 'The propriety of proprietary prisons', *Federal Probation*, no. 51, September.

— 1990, *Private Prisons: Cons and Pros*, Oxford University Press, New York.

McDonald, D. 1990, 'When government fails: Going private as a last resort', in *Private Prisons and the Public Interest*, (ed) D. McDonald, Rutgers University Press, New Brunswick, pp. 179-99.

Martin, D. T. and R. M. Stein 1992, 'An empirical analysis of contracting out local government services', in *Privatizing the US Justice System*, (eds) G. W. Bowman, S. Hakim and P. Seidenstat, McFarlane

Matthews, R. 1989, 'Privatization in perspective', in *Privatizing Criminal Justice*, (ed) R. Matthews, Sage, London, pp. 1-23.

Millward, R. 1982, 'The comparative performance of public and private ownership', in *The Mixed Economy*, (ed) E. Roll, Macmillan, London.

Moyle, P. 1992, 'Privatising Prisons The Underlying Issues, *Alternative Law Journal*, vol. 17, no. 3, June, pp. 114-119.

— 1993, 'Privatisation of Prisons in New South Wales and Queensland, Australia: A Review of Some Key Developments', *Howard Journal of Criminal Justice*, vol. 32, no. 3, August, pp. 231-250.

— 1994, 'Private Adult Custodial Corrections in Queensland and the First Wave: A Critical Reflection on the First Three Years — Reform or Regression?' in D. Biles and J. Vernon (eds), *Australian Institute of Criminology Conference Proceedings on*

Private Sector and Community Involvement in the Criminal Justice System, No. 23, AIC, Canberra.

Porter, R. 1990, 'The privatisation of prisons in the United States: A policy that Britain should not emulate', *The Howard Journal of Criminal Justice*, vol. 29, no. 2, May, pp. 65-81.

Pryke, R. 1982, 'The comparative performance of public and private enterprise', *Fiscal Studies*, no. 3, July, pp. 68-81.

Public Sector Management Commission 1993, *Review of the Queensland Corrective Services Commission*, December, Queensland Government Printer, Brisbane

Queensland Corrective Services Commission (QCSC) 1992, Comparisons Between Lotus Glen Correctional Centre and Borallon Correctional Centre, April, unpublished.

Queensland State Service Union (QSSU) 1990, Open Letter to All Labor Members of the Legislative Assembly, 23 July.

Ring, C. R. 1987, *Contracting for the Operation of Private Prisons: Pros and Cons*, American Correctional Association, Maryland.

Roper, B. 1986, 'Market forces, privatisation and prisons: A polar case for government policy', *International Journal of Social Economics*, vol. 13, no. 1-2, pp. 77-92.

Thomas, C. W. and Logan, C. H. 1992, 'The development, present status, and future potential of correctional privatization in America', in *Privatizing Correctional Institutions*, (eds) G. W. Bowman, S. Hakin and P. Seidenstat, Transaction Publishers, New Brunswick.

Weiss, R. 1989, 'Private prisons and the state', in *Privatizing Criminal Justice*, (ed) R. Matthews, Sage, London, pp. 24-51.

Zdenkowski, G. 1990, 'Privatisation of prisons: The pros and cons', Paper presented at the Third International Criminal Law Congress, Hobart, September.

---

* This chapter revises and updates the paper, 'Economic aspects of prison privatisation: The Queensland experience', Presented at the Australian Institute of Criminology Conference, 'Private Sector and Community Involvement in the Criminal Justice System', Wellington, New Zealand, 30 November — 2 December 1992.

Part III

The New Zealand experience

10

Private sector and community involvement in the New Zealand prison system

Terry Craig

Abstract: This chapter examines current debates about whether prison services should be delivered by the public or private sector using the New Zealand experience as a basis for that examination. The existing prison system is currently fully managed by the public sector although the New Zealand government has made clear its intention to privatise the management of part of the New Zealand system.

The limited utility of a model which is essentially bipolar and focuses on public or private provision of services will be discussed. It will be argued that within a system that is managed by the state there are in fact a wide range of service providers operating from a variety of bases. That experience will be drawn upon to challenge the utility of the bipolar model.

A model will then be proposed which offers greater utility in the analysis of service provision. It will show that at a time of great change in the New Zealand prison system, with an emphasis on clarity of results and efficiency of processes, value has been found by having a mix of providers including profit oriented providers, private practitioners, not-for-profit organisations, agencies of state and volunteers as well as the prisons providing its own services.

Issues raised by having a mix of service providers will be examined with particular reference to responsibility, accountability, cultural issues and the implementation of a management structure appropriate to ensure that desired results are obtained so that services are integrated.

The relationship between the Department of Justice and the providers of programs and services (be they private or community organisations) is a complex one. It is also a developing relationship involving, on the department's part, an opening up to new ideas and new ways of working, a desire for more understanding of responsibilities, constraints and accountabilities, and the need to be able to monitor results against clearly defined objectives.

This chapter will outline the nature and extent of private sector and community involvement in New Zealand's prisons. The discussion will canvass the rationale for the current levels of involvement, the organisational structure of that involvement; its contribution to the prison system's goal of reducing reoffending; the issues raised by the involvement and future developments planned in this area.

The paper will largely focus on these interactions in the area of programs and services provided to inmates. This is because these are the areas where interactions are most developed and, more basically, because they are the areas about which the author is best informed.

It must be stated 'up front' that this article is from a prison management perspective. It does not, and should not, try to look at the issues from a community or private sector perspective. That is an area which needs to be developed with the organisations concerned. However it does aim to clarify the objectives, issues and constraints of the prison system, to suggest ways in which the input of those wanting to be involved might be most welcomed and most effective.

TYPOLOGY OF PROVIDERS

A particular concern of this chapter is the vagueness of the terms 'private sector' and 'community involvement'.

The terms overlap and the way they do depends very much on the individual's own point of view. For example, one person may regard the term 'private sector' as referring to the total privatisation of functions currently provided by the state; another may see it as the contracting to other than state systems of certain functions or inputs; yet another may see it as integrating state and private sector endeavours to enhance the greater good of society. 'Community involvement' is a similarly confusing term. To one person it may mean the utilisation of volunteers, to another the use of community based agencies to provide certain goods and services. Another concern of the chapter is to address the very significant relationships between agencies of state which, though supposedly reflective of the community, are not usefully addressed by the term community involvement.

The aim is to identify the range of organisational relationships in the prison system and to consider the issues they raise at a more sophisticated level than is suggested by the use of the term 'private sector/community involvement'. The author has attempted to group the existing relationships in a way which illustrates the range of interests that have to be addressed in the process of policy development and implementation.

THE NATURE AND EXTENT OF PRIVATE SECTOR COMMUNITY INVOLVEMENT

The range of programs and services provided in New Zealand prisons is very wide indeed as is the nature and number of service providers. Increasingly the department is placing an emphasis on establishing those services which can show a capacity to contribute to the achievement of its stated mission and in particular to a reduction in reoffending.

Profit Oriented Providers

There are no readily identifiable examples of program and service providers which fit the standard private sector objective of existing to generate a financial return, although they are common in other areas of prison operations such as capital works. Their absence in delivery of programs and services is not because the prison system is averse to such relationships but because at this time such organisations who can make a contribution have not been identified. There are some indications that organisations are beginning to see prisons as a potential customer. These most frequently have a product which has been developed overseas and which has been imported into New Zealand.

There have been some instances of private sector groups involving themselves with prisons and inmates. A recent example is a timber company which had the facade of a Maori meeting house carved for an international display. The display subsequently won an international award. The prison was given a valuable set of carving tools and has received positive publicity for its participation. The real gain however has come to the company which as well as the positive public relations it has generated also became aware through the exercise that they needed to enhance their own policies and procedures to incorporate a cultural perspective.

Private Practitioners

This group is made up of individuals or small groups of individuals who provide programs and services within prisons in return for payment. The distinction between them and profit-oriented groups is a fine one, but I have made it because concerns for social service are significant factors in their opting to involve themselves in this area. The range of services provided by this group cover all aspects of programs and services in the prisons. They include medical officers, psychologists, social workers, educationalists, vocational trainers, cultural tutors and a range of specialists in areas such as anger management and substance abuse treatment. Usually services are provided on a fee-for-service basis and are the subject of individual contracts between the prison and the practitioner.

Not-for-Profit Organisations

These are organisations which are set up specifically to provide certain services or to address the needs of particular groups of people. They may be local organisations, such as trusts, set up in particular areas, but they often have a national structure as well. Of particular note in this capacity are those organisations set up with a specific focus on the needs of prisoners. In New Zealand the largest of these is the Prisoners' Aid and Rehabilitation Society. This is a national organisation whose work is recognised as being of such significance to criminal justice functions that most of its funding is provided by way of a payment on behalf of the Crown made through the Department of Justice. Other organisations such as Marriage Guidance and the Plunket Society provide their services on an as required basis in areas of special relevance, such as relationship and parenting training. They are generally engaged on a contractual fee-for-service basis.

Agencies of State

These are governmental agencies which receive specific funding from the state to undertake work with inmates. There are two major examples. The first is Area Health Board forensic teams which have been established to provide psychiatric services to offenders, including prisoners. They receive their funding from the Department of Health and are fully independent of the Department of Justice. The second is polytechnics which are responsible for the co-ordination of educational services to inmates, and in some cases are major suppliers of the services themselves. In the case of polytechnics the funding is held by the Department and contracts for services are negotiated on an annual basis.

Volunteers

These are individuals, groups of individuals or organisations which provide programs or services to inmates without an expectation of payment, although in some cases there may be recovery of expenses such as travel costs. Most frequently these are church-based endeavours, the most extensive being chaplaincy services provided to all prisons by the Catholic Church and general spiritual services provided by Prison Fellowship. There are, however, sizeable contributions made from other sources, and culturally based organisations are of special relevance in this regard. Support groups such as Alcoholics Anonymous also have a significant presence in activities. The growing role of inmates as volunteers is especially noteworthy. Currently inmates provide voluntary services in the areas of educational tutoring, including literacy training, as course managers for the lifestyle changes programs (developed to address HIV/AIDS issues) and as sports coaches.

RATIONALE FOR INVOLVEMENT

There is a widespread belief that an extensive network of relationships which extend beyond the prison walls is important if prisons are to meet their stated goal of contributing to a reduction in reoffending. This has been expressed in departmental documents, including Prisons in Change (the departmental submission to the Ministerial Committee of Inquiry into The Prisons System, 1988), Te Ara Hou (which was the report of that committee, 1989) and in overseas documents such as Prison Disturbances April 1990 (the Woolf Report, 1991). Most commonly the support is provided as a 'given' with relatively little exposition of its rationale. Common themes however are the need to provide for as normal an environment as possible within prisons and the desirability of facilitating post release support.

From another perspective there is increasing emphasis on the need to provide a competitive basis for the provision of services in order to maximise efficiency. There is also increasing recognition of the need to ensure that programs and services are provided by competent people who are fully informed on developments in their particular area of expertise. While not impossible to achieve, that can often be difficult to maintain without significant ongoing contact with colleagues working in the same field.

The rationale for choosing whether to have the prison itself provide a particular program or service or whether to seek alternative providers will vary according to the nature of the particular program or service. The same will apply if a decision is made to seek alternatives.

THE ORGANISATIONAL STRUCTURE FOR INVOLVEMENT

New Zealand's prison system has undergone major organisational change in the last three years and though the principal elements of the changed organisation are now in place, there are still changes to be made. Of most significance to the subject matter of this paper are the changes which have taken place in the management structure, in inmate management, in community involvement in the prisons and in regional prison policies.

The Management Structure

All prisons in New Zealand have a management structure consisting of three levels rather than the previous seven levels. This has been achieved by managing work which only needs supervision. The new structure has a general manager leading the prison with a common second tier made up of a manager administration who is responsible for corporate services, a manager custody who is responsible for containment and meeting the basic needs of inmates and a manager programs who is responsible for the provision of inmate programs and services. At the third tier are unit managers responsible for custodial duties and, in the programs area, a nurse in charge who is responsible for the health care of inmates.

The manager programs is primarily responsible for managing the involvement of the individuals and organisations discussed in this paper.

Inmate Management

Two principal management strategies related to inmate management have been developed by the Department of Justice for New Zealand prisons. Case management involves the effective planning and co-ordination of programs and services to ensure the fair and humane treatment of offenders to assist them in preparing for effective return to the community. It is a continuous process aimed at assisting offenders through both imprisonment and parole.

To facilitate the delivery of programs and services each prison has a case management planning committee chaired by the manager programs and including both custody and programs staff from the prisons, representatives of Community Corrections (Probation) and representatives of significant community groups including Maori. It is the role of this committee to identify the types of programs and services required to meet the identified needs of inmates. It is important to note that it is needs, not wants, which are to be addressed.

It is then the responsibility of the manager of programs to ensure that those programs and services are provided so far as is possible given the availability of resources.

The other major inmate management strategy is unit management which is currently being introduced into New Zealand's prisons. Essentially this involves a more stable staffing of units and residence of inmates within units.

Community and Cultural Involvement in Prisons

Changes in the management structure have also involved changes in the ways that prisons relate to the community. In particular there is a need to ensure that expertise from the community is available to advise on the development of prison processes. This comes in part through the Department's own community based agencies, notably Community Corrections, but it also comes more directly through involvement of community groups in management planning. A key element is the participation of community groups in the case management planning committee outlined above.

Complementing that participation has been developments in the cultural area of prison life. Recognising that Maori make up 42 per cent of inmates and the requirement of the Treaty of Waitangi to develop partnership between the Crown and the Tangata Whenua, the Department has placed emphasis on developing its processes in a culturally appropriate way. To assist in this it has established certain rules of procedure (for example that Maori must be represented on all appointment panels) and has established procedures to ensure that cultural elements are addressed in all processes. The latter has mainly been through the establishment of cultural development groups in each institution which includes both institution staff representatives of all cultures and Maori. In some prisons inmates are also part of these groups.

Our community in New Zealand has a unique cultural make-up and history. Our prisons, originally based on a British military style approach, are at last developing into a system which responds to that uniqueness.

For inmates, this has meant more emphasis on programs, custodial policies and case management plans which incorporate cultural needs in education, spiritual areas, health, employment and opportunities for reintegration into the community. Prison staff are also looking to establish Maori and community contacts to support inmates in the event of incidents such as suicides, and for activities such as temporary home leave.

This integration of the inmate with the Whanau and community is not something that should occur in the last few months of an inmate's sentence, but as an integral part of the case planning process, and may include Maori support, social support, sporting contacts, stable family relations and, if possible, employment opportunities.

Regional Prison Policy

Following the Report of the Penal Policy Review Committee in 1981 a pilot scheme was established to investigate the utility of a regional prison policy, that is a policy aimed as far as possible at retaining inmates in their area of origin. A key purpose of that policy was to enhance reintegration of inmates into the community through the maintenance of community linkages. Though a formal evaluation of that pilot was never carried out the policy has been extended to cover all prisons and the goal is now to retain inmates in their area of origin wherever possible. An objective of that policy is to maintain and, if possible, enhance inmates' relationships within the community.

THE SUCCESS OF THE INVOLVEMENT

While it is possible to outline in broad terms the rationale for differing forms of involvement, and the recent developments in New Zealand's prison management systems, it is difficult to say at this time what the relative pros and cons of the varying forms of involvement might be. A core consideration has to be the effectiveness of the programs and services delivered in terms of their capacity to reduce reoffending. That is of course a major problem of evaluation for every correctional agency in the world and is neither simple to undertake nor useful in determining what choices should be made about current needs because of the long-term evaluative approach.

Therefore it is too early at this time to say what relations have been particularly successful or unsuccessful in helping attain the prisons' mission. In process terms however there have been clear advantages. The prisons are now much more exposed to a range of beliefs and ideas on how they should manage themselves and on how they should relate to other social agencies and groups. Equally those agencies and groups are better informed about prisons and their purpose.

Issues raised by Involvement

The increasing involvement of individuals and community groups in the provision of prison services has been welcomed by the department, mainly because of the widespread belief that an extensive network of relationships which extend beyond the prison walls is important if prisons are to meet their stated goal of contributing to a reduction in reoffending. This goal leads to the need to establish a positive environment within prisons and improve post-release support — both areas where the community and the private sector can play a major role. However involvement does raise several key issues. From the department's perspective these include:

- the selection of providers. Increasingly prison management must choose whether the prison itself should provide a particular program or service, or whether to seek alternative providers (and if so, which type). The rationale for these decisions will vary according to the nature of the particular program or service. However a major factor to be considered, whatever the arrangement, is the ability of the service provider to deliver the Departments requirements effectively. Other factors to be considered include cost (particularly in the light of prison budget constraints), the capacity to work within a prison environment, and availability. These factors may mean that compromises have to be made in the choice of provider;
- the increasing emphasis on the need to provide a competitive basis in the provision of services, in order to maximise effectiveness;
- the need to ensure that programs and services are provided by competent people who are fully informed of developments in their particular area of expertise;
- for those prisons in rural areas, the question of whether they can actually locate the services they have identified as needing;
- issues related to funding, or more particularly its continuity, given the yearly funding cycle. To allow prisons to be more responsive to such practical issues there has been considerable decentralisation of funding in the last two years. However each prison still has to make decisions on priorities among a wide range of needs and possible programs;
- accountabilities and responsibilities (see below).

ACCOUNTABILITY AND RESPONSIBILITY

Accountability and responsibility are the 'thorniest' issues raised by the involvement of community and private organisations and individuals as providers of programs and services. Traditionally there have been questions asked about the right of prison management to require accountability, in other than security terms, of agencies providing programs and services on a voluntary basis. That tension has varied proportionately to the level of financial support provided by the prison.

The argument is sometimes put forward that prison management has no right to seek accountability from volunteers who do not call on the resources of the Department. However it needs to be recognised that *all* programs have some cost to the prison, and even those provided on a voluntary basis may involve staff supervision and overhead costs.

In the past that confusion has reflected the lack of clarity within prisons about what goals they are seeking to achieve and in particular whether they have any role in rehabilitation. The Penal Division of the Department of Justice now clearly states that it *does* see itself as having a role in this regard, and therefore it must develop its programs and services in a way which enhances that role. A major effort has been made to identify the characteristics of programs and services which do reduce the likelihood of reoffending. The first exercise was a review of the international literature to identify general characteristics of successful programs. This report has been published (McLaren 1992). Additional work is being done to relate this to specific offender groups including violent offenders, rapists, alcohol and substance abusers, long-term inmates and pre-release program needs.

Increasingly, program and service providers are being asked to show how their approach relates to those *principles of effectiveness* identified in that report. The acceptance of programs into prisons which 'seem like a good idea' but which may lack research or theoretical support is being increasingly questioned. The vulnerability of inmates (literally a captive audience) to the effects of sometimes quite ill-conceived programs provides a compelling argument for accountability.

In asking for accountability the prisons have a responsibility to ensure that potential program providers are fully informed about what they are being asked to do. A feature of some prison/provider relationships is that organisations or individuals have seen the primary reason for involvement as the achievement of *their* desired outcomes rather than the desired outcomes of the corrections system. The two are not necessarily incompatible, but there needs to be more clarity to avoid confusion and discord. For example, prisons must provide clear statements of desired outcomes.

Prisons must also ensure that the potential providers have an understanding of the prison environment and of the limitations this may place on their desired ways of operating. We also have to inform providers of the standards we expect and how we believe they can best be met.

For those reasons, we are currently working on induction programs for service providers and 'user friendly' documentation of the research evidence on what has been shown to be effective in reducing re-offending. We are also working on standardised process evaluation documents which we believe will be of assistance to program participants, providers and prisons in program development. This is not to increase control over providers, but to ensure that standards are high and programs are as successful as possible. The days of 'gut feelings' and 'common knowledge' about what works and what doesn't are no longer appropriate.

CONCLUSION

This paper has examined the complexity of the relationships between prisons and providers of programs and services. It has looked at the ways those relationships are organised and at the issues of management which they raise. The focus of this chapter has been on prisons and how they achieve their desired outcomes. Program providers will have their own concerns, only a few of which are likely to have been touched on in this paper.

However, there is one element which should be given further consideration and that is what such relationships actually contribute to the community. Obviously the business of reducing the likelihood of reoffending is not just the concern of prisons but of all society. What else is in it, perhaps more directly, for the program providers? Obviously in many cases there is money and the achievement of their own goals whether they are organisational or personal.

The largest return though is recognition that the business of reducing the likelihood of reoffending is not just the responsibility of prisons but of all society. From more and better involvement in prisons, the community can hope to get the substantial long-term benefit of reduced offending.

References

Department of Justice 1988, *Prisons in Charge*, Submission to the Minister, Committee of Inquiry into the Prisons System, Department of Justice, Wellington.

McLaren, K. L. 1992, *Reducing Reoffending: What Works Now*, Penal Division, Department of Justice, New Zealand.

Ministerial Committee of Inquiry into the Prisons System 1989, *Te Ara Hou; The New Way*, Department of Justice, Wellington.

Penal Policy Review Committee 1982, *Report of the Penal Policy Review Committee 1981*, Government Printer, Wellington.

Woolf, Rt. Hon. Lord Justice and His Honour Judge Stephen Tumim 1991, *Prison Disturbances April 1990*, HMSO, London, February.

Part IV

International perspective

11

Private prisons in the United Kingdom: radical change and opposition

Mick Ryan*

Abstract: This chapter sets out to detail the extent of private sector involvement in financing, building and managing private prisons in the United Kingdom. A preliminary assessment of the private sector's performance is offered. Comparisons with the experience of other countries such as Australia and the United States are made. Opposition to the introduction of private prisons is also explored.

The prison service in England and Wales was nationalised at a stroke in 1877. Thereafter, it was strictly controlled from the centre. The conditions of service enjoyed by prison officers, the daily regime and diet of prisoners, all these things became subject to the detailed scrutiny of the Home Secretary who was accountable, in theory at least, only to Parliament. This highly centralised, some would argue, insular service is now undergoing fundamental change in three quite different, but related, ways.

First, the government has granted the prison department agency status as part of its Next Steps program which is aimed at reducing the size of central government and making the services it offers both more efficient and more sensitive to consumer preferences. The service is now once removed from the Home Office and the Home Secretary only requires the agency to report to him or her on a very restricted range of issues, such as serious prison disturbances (Home Office 1993a, p. 2). As if to symbolise the agency's independence in terms of the day-to-day running of the service and its control of important policy matters, including industrial relations, parliamentary replies to Members' questions now come directly from the Director General of the new agency and are printed in Hansard. In addition to this significant, if not total, decoupling at the centre, the agency itself is set to pursue a vigorous policy of decentralisation giving, for example, area managers far more autonomy under yearly negotiated contracts and allowing individual prison governors more control over local health care budgets, and even in some respects, more freedom over staffing.

Second, the central services which the agency itself provides, and some other services which have remained in the Home Office, are being market tested. That is to say, under tender documents drawn up largely at the centre, the private sector is being invited to bid to run a whole range of previously government operated services, including prison education, the assisted visits scheme, headquarters training schemes and even the administration of the prison service super-annuation scheme (Criminal Justice 1993a). For those who remain as agency staff — or as civil servants for that matter — a whole new battery of management techniques borrowed from the private sector is being put into place, including performance related pay and staff appraisal, techniques which are enshrined in the Citizen's Charter (Home Office 1993b, p. 34).

Finally, the Conservative government has sanctioned private prisons. These were first given the green light in March 1989 (Hansard 1989) when the Home Secretary announced that as an experiment the private sector would be allowed to build and/or manage remand prisons. Before the 'experiment' was fully underway, let alone evaluated, permission to extend privatisation to the rest of the prison system was unexpectedly introduced at a late stage in the passage of the Criminal Justice Act (1991). Private prisons are now in place.

Taken together, these changes have radical potential. A once hierarchical public service in which competition had little or no place is being transformed into two significantly decentralised systems operating in direct competition and each offering different conditions of employment, possibly even different conditions of confinement. It is in this wider and rapidly changing context that the introduction of private prisons in England and Wales needs to be situated. (The Scottish prison system is administered separately and legislation to facilitate private prisons there was signalled in the Queen's speech in November 1993.)

PRIVATE PRISONS; LEARNING FROM ABROAD

The idea of private prisons in the United Kingdom was largely the inspiration of the New Right. Michael Forsyth, now a Cabinet Minister but then a backbencher, first put the issue on the Conservative Party's agenda, building on previous publications from the Adam Smith Institute which had begun to explore how to radicalise the entire criminal justice system — including police — as early as 1984 with the launch of its Omega Project (Ryan and Ward 1989, p. 45).

To a government already in favour of reducing big government at the centre, and which had already sold off a range of public utilities to the private sector, the idea of private prisons had a strong ideological appeal. However, the Conservative Party, like the intellectual New Right, is hardly a homogeneous entity and there were senior Conservatives who were all too aware that championing the free market had already unleashed strong social and political movements which the forces of law and order had been stretched to contain. Policing the miner's strike would be one example; the opening of former army camps to house the influx of those imprisoned after the inner city uprisings in the early 1980s is another.

The government was thus initially cautious about tampering with the apparatus of law and order, and the Home Secretary of the day originally ruled out private prisons (Hansard 1987), only to change his mind two years later following the publication of a Green paper, Private Sector Involvement in the Remand System (Deloitte, Haskins and Sells 1989). We have traced the many pressures which led to this change elsewhere (Ryan and Ward 1989, chapter 3) and it is not the intention to detail them again, other than perhaps to sketch out the role of the House of Commons Home Affairs Select Committee in order to illustrate how the experience of other countries was employed to facilitate this change of heart.

The role of select committees is fairly straight forward, namely, they shadow individual policy areas and enable backbench MPs to question Ministers and civil servants and to make their own judgements and recommendations on subjects and issues within their respective fields of competence. In the course of their enquiries they can call for Ministerial papers, travel abroad and hire expert research assistance.

It was in 1986 that the Home Affairs Select Committee decided to investigate the state and use of prisons in England and Wales and as part of its enquiry travelled abroad to the United States where its members were invited to visit private prisons, two of which were run by the Corrections Corporation of America. Some members of the Select Committee were surprised at this invitation as the subject of private prisons had not been on the committee's agenda. Nonetheless, it was on the basis of this one visit that the committee produced a bitterly disputed report which recommended that private prisons be introduced into the United Kingdom as an experiment (HMSO 1987). This report was used by a small but well connected group of Conservative backbenchers in a concerted attempt to change the Home Secretary's mind, actively supported by the Adam Smith Institute which by then had produced its own widely publicised report on the virtues of American private prisons, The Prison Cell (1987).

The quality of the committee's report was poor, not to say disingenuous. For example, it carefully used the plural form to conceal the fact that it had only visited one private prison and more or less ignored the detailed opposition of the Howard League which had been called to give evidence, and which was opposed to privatisation. It also seemed to heap undue praise on the Corrections Corporation of America which was mentioned no less than seven times in a report of only three pages. The tactic of referring, and often in quite misleading ways, to the experience of other countries was a feature of the pro-privatisation lobby. For example, in response to a challenge from a Labour spokesman on the threat to prison officers' pay, the Conservative member for Thurrock claimed:

> The Right Hon. and learned Gentleman's point about wages is not relevant to the debate about the way forward for the prison service. If he believes that lower wages for employees would be detrimental to the service provided to prisoners, he should consider events in the United States and Australia. Private sector prisons there have lower rates of recidivism than those in the public sector. (Hansard 1991)

The fact that Borallon (Australia's first private prison), for example, was only just up and running then was conveniently ignored. The government was not above such obfuscation itself. In the Green paper, for example, it was simply asserted that the problems which had surrounded the introduction of private prisons in the US had already been overcome, a claim which many American critics would dispute even now (Ryan and Ward 1989, pp. 31-38). (To be fair to the government, it later commissioned accountants Deloitte, Haskins and Sells to look in more detail at the feasibility of private prisons and court escort services and their report made little of experience abroad).

We shall probably never know which of the many pressures on the Home Secretary were decisive, but certainly the lobby in favour of private prisons was well organised and had ready access to those in power. For example, Sir Edward Gardner who chaired the Home Affairs Select Committee persuaded the junior Minister directly responsible for prisons to discuss the idea of privatisation with over a hundred guests, including city bankers and property developers' at the Carlton Club in 1988. It was even rumoured that Mrs Thatcher had intervened in support of privatisation (Ryan and Ward 1989, p. 47). Whatever the truth behind this particular story, the lobby for private prisons got its way, and what had once seemed like a 'wacky' idea even to the director of the Adam Smith Institute was, by 1991, not only on the political agenda, but actually in place (Criminal Justice 1993b).

EXTENT AND PROSPECTS

The extent of prison privatisation in the UK can be quickly detailed.

There is Britain's first privately managed prison for over a century, Wolds. This is a newly built secure prison for those prisoners awaiting trial or pending sentence with a capacity of 300. A second privately managed prison has recently opened at Blakenhurst in the West Midlands. This new establishment is designed for both sentenced and unsentenced prisoners. A third new prison at Doncaster is scheduled to go out to private tender later this year. The money to build each of these prisons came from the government.

Only one established prison has so far gone out to tender. This was Strangeways, a prison recently re-opened after major refurbishment following the serious disturbances which took place there in 1989. It is expected to operate with a capacity of 500 sentenced and unsentenced prisoners. Prison officers' who cannot tender to manage new prisons, put in a bid to manage Strangeways in direct competition with the private sector, including Group 4. This bid—with the active but somewhat rueful support of the national Prison Officers Association—was successful and the new contract will formally come into operation later this year. According to a Prison Officers Association (POA) spokesperson no redundancies are anticipated, but existing work practices are to be modified.

In a major new development the government has recently announced that it will shortly publish a tender document for six new prisons, that is, in addition to the existing building program, which it will invite the private sector to finance as well as to build and manage. A public enquiry aimed at securing planning permission for the first of these six new prisons at Fazakerley on Merseyside is currently in progress.

In addition to prisons, the government is also intent on privatising the task of escorting convicted and unconvicted prisoners to and from the courts, a job previously undertaken by prison officers and police. The government believes that these escort duties take up too much time, that experienced and highly trained prison and police staff would be better employed elsewhere. So far these services have only been privatised in the Humberside and East Midlands region, though according to the prison service's corporate plan tenders are shortly to be invited for some of the London courts (Home Office 1993b, p. 33). More progress has been made in market testing, and then privatising, a range of prison services such as catering and education in state run prisons. Only one service — warehouse and distribution — has so far been market tested and retained in house (Criminal Justice 1993a).

Looking even further into the future the government has also declared its intention of putting out to private tender the construction and management of up to 65 new secure units for young offenders following the suicide of 15-year-old Phillip Knight in Swansea Prison. The cost of this projected program is currently estimated at £3.75 million. The voluntary sector is being encouraged to bid for the management of these units in competition with the private sector.

Finally, it should be remembered that in the UK, government has for some years contracted out the arguably more sensitive task of locking up immigrant detainees to private interests (Ashford 1993). Small scale reception facilities at Heathrow, Gatwick and Stanstead airports are operated by the private sector, as is the long stay detention centre at Harmondsworth close to Heathrow. During the unexpected influx of Tamil refugees in 1989 the government hired a de-commissioned channel ferry, the Earl William, to house detainees until the ship broke its moorings and was driven aground during a severe storm in 1990. The decision to hire the private sector to guard detained immigrants was first taken by a Labour government in the 1960s (Ryan and Ward 1989, p. 67-68).

Given that one of the virtues of privatisation is seen to be competition, the number of successful private operators in this area of service provision is so far quite small. Group 4 Remand Services Ltd, a subsidiary of a Netherlands Antilles based multinational, manages the Wolds prison, which though paid for with government money was actually built by UK Detention Contractors, a consortium of two UK construction firms Mowlem and McAlpine, with the Corrections Corporation of America as consultants. Group 4 also has the contract for the Humberside and East Midlands prison escort service and manages all the government's immigrant detainee reception and detention centres. Blakenhurst is being managed by UK Detention Services (UKDS), a consortium headed by the Corrections Corporation of America (CCAm) and supported by building contractors Mowlem and McAlpine. The project director of Blakenhurst — rather than its site manager or governor — is an American, Sharon Johnson. She is forthright in her view that Blakenhurst is a CCAm prison, and this perhaps helps to explain why its current director, although very experienced at running British prisons, has recently been seconded to the US for a training course only months after taking up his appointment.

While it is not the intention to go into great detail about trans-continental links in this paper — others are monitoring this in some depth (Lilley and Knepper 1992) — it is important to point out that apart from running prisons in both the UK and the United States, CCAm also has a stake in managing Borallon, Australia's first private prison near Brisbane in Queensland. It is involved too, with Chubb Holdings in a bid to build a private prison in New Zealand where Group 4 has also teamed up with Fletcher Construction for the very same purpose (*The Listener* 1993). Security and construction companies are thus gearing up for what is perceived to be an expanding and highly lucrative global market.

However, while the private sector's optimism may be a pointer to the future, it is very important that its share of the market is not exaggerated. In the US, for example, the number of adult prisoners — as opposed to immigrant detainees — held in private prisons is still not much above 30,000 out of a total prison and jail population of well over one million. This is a remarkably little advance on the figure a few years ago. The truth of the matter is that privatisation in America, where private operators sometimes own as well as manage prisons, has stalled. Similarly, prison privatisation received a serious setback in the UK when the former Home Secretary Kenneth Clarke, an enthusiast for bringing in the private sector who was reported to be planning the privatisation of some 20 prisons early in 1992, ran foul of the European Transfer Undertaking Protection of Employment (TUPE).

What this requires under European Community law is that existing pay and conditions, including pension rights, of public service employees must be guaranteed when, and if, their enterprise is taken over by private operators. This makes existing prisons much less attractive to the private sector, though they are being encouraged to bid for them, in order, we suspect to sustain the veneer of competition. The UK government is thus having to wait until new prisons come on stream to give its privatisation scheme the dynamism it would like. Michael Forsyth, significantly, is campaigning to repeal TUPE on the grounds of inefficiencies.

THE PERFORMANCE OF THE PRIVATE SECTOR

How well is the private sector performing in the UK? This is a genuinely difficult question to answer for a number of obvious reasons.

First, are privately managed prisons in the UK more cost effective than those in the public sector? We have no means of deciding this in the UK because the government, Group 4 and UKDS are unwilling to release the full terms of their contracts. Commercial confidentiality is apparently sacred, even where taxpayers are expected to meet the bill, although we have — thanks to the recent Chief Inspector of Prisons Report — discovered that in the case of the Wolds utility services — gas, electricity and water — are currently being paid for by the government (Home Office 1993c, p. 19). Yet even if there was full disclosure, it has to be admitted that separating out the cost of managing a single state prison from the rest of the national system to make a sensible comparison with a similar private prison possible is an extremely difficult exercise, one which is riddled with uncertainties. As in the US and Australia, the truth of the matter is that whatever the private sector may claim in the UK to the contrary, the jury is still out on the issue of costs (Brown 1992, see also chapter seven).

Second, the UK's experience of private prisons is fairly limited. Blakenhurst, for example, is really very new, and as yet operating well below capacity. To be sure, there are aspects of its management which cause concern, particularly its over reliance on technology, including the use of electronically sensitive 'smart cards' to monitor prisoners' whereabouts. But in fairness to those running Blakenhurst, we shall have to wait a little longer to see how the regime is working out in practice. As to whether the provision for it to sub-contract out prison labour to commercial companies contravenes the International Labour Organisation's convention on forced labour as the POA claims, this is also something which we shall have to wait to see tested (POA 1993).

There is more substantial evidence on Wolds. True, the government's own in depth evaluation of Wolds being carried out by the nearby University of Hull is not due to be published until the middle of 1994, but we have at least now had both the Chief Inspector's Report and one carried out by the Prison Reform Trust (PRT 1993), as well as the views of the many hundreds of prisoners who have already passed through Wolds. The prisoners offer contrasting opinions. For example, one former inmate claimed that in the Wolds: 'the atmosphere is terrible. It's a violent place. There's knives floating about, people getting beaten up with table legs or snooker balls in socks. Don't get me wrong—it happens in other prisons, but I noticed in the Wolds it's like an everyday occurrence' (New Statesman and Society 1993).

Balanced against this, the PRT quoted one prisoner who said: 'I know what the Wolds is like because I am here. They (the Prison Officers Association) are not. Of course there are scrapes and arguments, because you are seeing each other all the time. But there is nothing wrong with this prison. As far as I am concerned, the staff treat us as we should be treated, innocent until proved guilty. We have good food, the officers are courteous and I have no complaints at all' (PRT 1993, p. 8).

The PRT did not find it difficult to reconcile these sharply contrasting views in the sense that it agreed that the newly recruited and mainly non-unionised guards did indeed treat their charges with courtesy and respect, but the Trust was very sceptical about the ability of the management to effectively police the prison given its high staff-prisoner ratios. The governor even admitted that his staff had been 'seriously depleted on occasions' (PRT 1993, p. 25).

Living in Wolds is thus, as one prisoner put it, rather like living on a tough housing estate. This is compounded by the fact that under the terms of its contract Group 4 Remand Services has to guarantee that its prisoners are released from their cells for at least 14 hours a day, a laudable provision provided that prisoners are offered a wide range of constructive activities. Regrettably they are not, according to the PRT, and the impression is of large numbers of prisoners milling about without much purpose, a recipe for trouble, and something which perhaps explains why Wolds has a higher than average number of recorded assaults. While it is true—as the Chief Inspector has pointed out—the ways in which such offences are recorded varies between prisons, this evidence nonetheless needs to be set against the complacent comments of the new Director General of the Prison Service who boasted that: 'Commercial enterprise would be a better enterprise for prisoners. We have the concept of the prisoner as a customer. If they get the service they are promised, they are easier to deal with. If you remove petty restrictions and remove avoidable tensions and make the place less stressful, there will be less potential danger for staff and prisoners' (*The Independent* 1992).

The Chief Inspector's report largely confirms the findings of the

PRT. That is to say, there are good things happening at Wolds. A committed, hard working, predominantly non-unionised workforce is apparently working conscientiously under the glare of hostile publicity to operate a decent, open regime.

However, it is also clear that there is little purposeful activity for prisoners and that important elements of the contract like the provision of a bail information scheme had not been met at the time of the Chief Inspector's visit. In addition, both reports confirmed worries over the availability of drugs, including hard drugs (Home Office 1993c, chapter 6). Apparently security had been very lax on this front, even in the supposedly drug free unit which the Inspector recommends should be closed. One prisoner has even complained of being tortured and forcibly injected with heroin. At one stage a group of prisoners petitioned the governor to implement drugs counselling. Part of the difficulty was said to have been that officers were insufficiently knowledgeable about drug cultures and dependency and outside help had to be called in. Staff were also reputedly inept at body searches and it was apparently easy for visitors to bring a wide range of substances into the prison, including alcohol. Fortunately the Chief Inspector was able to report that security has been significantly improved.

While both these reports have gaps, and methodologically speaking would dismay analysts such as Charles Logan, they contain the best information we have and both, mercifully, ignore the wild rumours which have surrounded the operation of Wolds since it opened, some of which have been far from innocent (Logan 1992). But what are we to make of this 'experiment'?

It has hardly been an unqualified success. Of course conditions may have improved since these reports were published, nor can it be denied that prisoners are shooting up in other prisons all around the country, that most prisoners in the state system are under occupied, or that Wolds is not the only prison where lapses in security have led to escapes. But Wolds does appear to share much the same problems as state prisons. And where it does seem to do better — that is to say in its routine face to face contacts with prisoners, its sensitivity over prison visits to give another example — progressive prisons in the state system, Blantyre, for example, are said to do equally well.

This suggests that there is nothing that private prisons do well that cannot be matched in the public sector. Significantly, this conclusion is confirmed by Australian research which compared the privately run Borallon prison in the south eastern part of Queensland with the state managed prison, Lotus Glen. Both were judged to operate reasonably tolerant, flexible regimes, albeit with somewhat different inmate populations, Lotus Glen taking on the more difficult prisoners (Moyle 1993a). What is even more revealing, however, is that the basis for Moyle's research indicates that improvements at Lotus Glen took place before Borallon came on stream, and were largely the result of sweeping administrative and management changes within the Queensland Correctional Services Commission (a regulatory agency entrusted with the role of administering Queensland's correctional system). This raises the interesting question, is there nothing the public sector cannot do as well as the private sector if properly managed, and are the changes outlined in part one necessarily the right ones in the particular context of the UK?

Finally, if Group 4 is sensitive about its management of Wolds, it has even greater worries about the public perception of its escort business, Group 4 Court Services, where things seem to have occasionally gone disastrously wrong. A number of prisoners have been lost or have escaped. There are also claims that secretarial staff have been drafted in to cover staffing shortages, and the inquest is awaited on Ernest Hogg who had apparently drunk large quantities of alcohol in the Wolds before his transfer to court, a transfer which ended in his death. Hogg apparently slipped to the floor of the van transporting him from Wolds, and he went to and from court before the private security guards noticed him.

Guarding prisoners, convicted or otherwise, has turned out to be a far more taxing business for Group 4 than guarding immigrant detainees. While this latter function has not been carried out without complaint, not least from those Tamils who complained of racism while imprisoned aboard the Earl William, it did not arouse such public concern, or indeed, such public ridicule. The point to be made here is that the company's perceived incompetence has led to it becoming the butt of cartoons and jokes. A Group 4 managed operation is close to becoming a metaphor for incompetence. Indeed, it is reported that a tabloid newspaper, *The Sun*, paid its readers £10 for every Group 4 joke submitted and published (Kelsey 1993). This has so worried the company that it has appointed a public relations firm to improve its image. The company is fortunate that the government continues to defend it, and Group 4 has declared that it has no intentions of pulling out of the prison business. And no doubt with experience Group 4 will do better.

This survey suggests that the private sector has not performed brilliantly, but on the other hand, delivering pain is a difficult as well as unpleasant business and it could have arguably done far worse. And in fairness to those involved, these are early days.

RESPONSES TO PRIVATISATION

The penal lobby in the UK has been almost universally hostile to the idea of private prisons. Leading the campaign against dismantling the existing prison service has been the POA, supportedly more recently by the Civil and Public Services Association (CPSA) whose members are now being directly affected by market testing. While the POA has voiced ethical objections to privatisation, its opposition rests mainly on the quite reasonable assumption that the new policy will cost its members their jobs and/or worsen their conditions of employment. In a series of manoeuvres the POA has avoided cooperating directly with the private sector, but its threatened strike against privatisation was dealt a body blow in the High Court in November 1993 when Mr Justice May ruled that under 1992 trade union legislation prison officers had exactly the same privileges and duties as police constables and were thus not entitled to take strike action, and that if they did, their leaders could face fines or imprisonment.

The Howard League's response was arguably more principled. In its evidence to the Select Committee which originally considered privatisation the league was adamant that the state could not, in principle, give up the role of running our prisons. And yet in almost the same breadth the league went out of its way to support the use of non-custodial sanctions, some of which were not only fairly intensive, but also managed by the private sector.

Exactly why the state could easily give up its power to administer non-custodial punishments but not prisons was never made clear. This argument was glossed over, it is suspected, because in theory at least the distinction is hard to maintain. Once it is accepted in principle that the state can delegate the delivery of pain then there is surely no logical reason in theory or in principle why this cannot be applied right across the penal system, even at the deep end, that is, in the running of prisons, provided that those private interests are subject to the community through Parliament and the rule of law.

But, and here it gets a bit closer to the nub of the issue, it might be argued that however theoretically consistent it might be, private prisons are undesirable for the very simple reason that communal or parliamentary accountability, like the rule of law, is far from perfect in most liberal democracies, including Britain. And to take away the running of our prisons from those civil servants who notionally run them on our behalf, and who are directly accountable to our elected representatives in Parliament, and instead, hand them over to private interests whose structure of accountability is likely to be — at best — less direct, is surely to diminish an already imperfect system of communal accountability in a particularly sensitive area of social regulation, i.e. punishment.

While one may sympathise with this line of argument, the difficulty is that in principle the same reservations surely also apply to handing over other, 'lesser punishments' like community service to private interests. If privatised, these too would be once removed from direct communal accountability. We are thus still left asking why it is that the Howard League — and many other lobby groups share their position — is only really concerned to keep prisons under direct state control.

On its own, the accountability argument is surely insufficient.

The real case against private prisons it is suggested, though often more implicitly implied than explicitly argued, is that where force is required on a routine basis, sometimes deadly force, this is more properly employed by state agencies and their employers. This is not just because they are more accountable, which is the admittedly important argument we have just considered, but even more importantly because they are exercising powers on our behalf, sometimes deadly powers, which we only surrender willingly to the state under the terms of the social contract — and certainly not to some private body — in order to better regulate the social order. Of course, the argument that only the state can be involved at the deep end of the system where force is routinely involved applies as much to charities or non-profit making bodies as it does to corporate or profit making bodies. In other words, The Howard League should no more run prisons than Group 4.

The argument, then, seems to be not so much about whether or not the state can or should delegate the delivery of punishment — it can and clearly does — but more about the proper limits to this delegation, limits which some wish to set where the delivery of pain requires more or less routine force. Such powers, it is argued, are not properly trusted to private bodies.

ACCOUNTABILITY

The issue of accountability is something which Nils Christie has written passionately about in his recent book, Crime Control as Industry (1993). He argues, 'The servant of the state is . . . under greater responsibility and control than those who only serve the private firm' (p. 102). Again, we have much sympathy with this argument, but the difficulty is that it carries far more weight in theory than when translated into practice. UK prison activists will not need to be reminded that it was civil servants in the form of basic grade prison officers who systematically attacked and humiliated prisons after the Hull prison disturbance in 1976; it was Prison Department civil servants at all levels who turned a blind eye to their illegalities, and it was elected politicians, Labour politicians, in office who seemed powerless to get to the bottom of what had actually taken place (Ryan 1983, pp. 62-63).

Christie is right to argue that all these parties, not least the civil servants involved, represent 'the community', that is us, and to this extent their abuse of power is a more serious matter than if private interests had committed them (p. 102). But it must be reiterated that where the moral force of this argument is seen to amount to little in practice, then it is certainly easier for those who argue in favour of private rather than communal responsibility to make their case: and conversely, why opponents of privatisation find the accountability argument so difficult to advance with real conviction when they debate the issue with the private sector in empirical rather than principled terms.

The UK government claims to have taken the accountability issue seriously. So, for example, Boards of Visitors which report directly to the Home Secretary operate in private prisons in exactly the same way as they do in state prisons. But in addition, private prisons also have a resident controller who is also the Home Secretary's representative and whose function is to adjudicate in respect of disciplinary matters which carry a penalty of loss of remission up to 28 days, and to oversee the running of the prison generally in the terms of the specified contract, So it is argued, private prisons are even more accountable then their public counterparts. They are supervised not only by Boards of Visitors and the Chief Inspector, but also by a resident controller — a sure guarantee against misconduct.

This claim is far from convincing. Some time ago it was argued that it was difficult to believe that an on site controller in a total institution like a prison would become colonised by the disciplinary staff (Ryan and Ward 1989, p. 75). And this suspicion has been reinforced by the Chief Inspectors Report on Wolds which tells us that they have rooms along the same corridor, and that the governor or director is far more senior in rank and experience than the controller (Home Office 1993c, p. 2). It is also worrying that the controller's financial oversight is apparently cursory, but that is another issue. In Australia, the role and effectiveness of the controller is far from certain (Moyle 1992).

THE PENAL-INDUSTRIAL COMPLEX

Other arguments against the intervention of corporate or profit making organisations in running prisons stem from the premise that in any society there are rules, and unfortunately people break these rules and have to be punished. Punishment is therefore an unfortunate social necessity. However, or so the argument runs, it is morally questionable to make money out of the delivery of punishment. True, probation officers and prison guards make money out of inflicting pain, but there is surely a distinction between those who make a modest living wage out of such an activity — somebody has to undertake this unfortunate social duty and live at the same time — and those who seek to secure riches. Furthermore, there is the contingent argument that corporate interest will grow richer as the quantum of pain is increased, and it would therefore be in the interests of private entrepreneurs if punishment at the deep end of the penal system was increased. This concern was expressed by Brian Sedgemoor MP who suggested that: 'It would be in the interests of the prison entrepreneurs to support longer sentences and have more people put in prison. That would be disaster of the highest magnitude as sentencing policy is already excessive in this country' (Ryan and Ward 1989, p. 71).

This line of argument has some force, but requires two important qualifications. First, Christie is surely right to remind us that an expanded state prison system is likely to be of great benefit to the private sector (Christie 1993, p. 98). In the UK for example, private interests have always had a role in building state prisons, supplying locks and other essential materials and services. A larger prison stock under state control, the increasing contracting out of prison services, these developments would all enhance the profits of private companies like Tarmac, Mowlem and Shepherd in their various corporate identities. To this limited extent, whether prisons are privately or publicly owned is irrelevant. The scale of the private sector's involvement in the UK's state building program, the biggest since Victorian times, can be gauged by the following detailed table to a recent parliamentary question about the extent of private sector involvement.

A second qualification is that while financial backers of the Conservative Party like McAlpine, Tarmac and Shepherd (Labour Research 1993) would be well placed to encourage an expansion of the prison population by lobbying for more private prisons, the real pressure on prison numbers is surely likely to come from elsewhere. For example, one of the major themes of Nils Christie's book is that in many western countries, including the US, the increase in prison numbers is largely explained by the strong reaction of governments and the press to drug related offences (Christie 1993). In the UK, to take a rather different example, the government is planning for an increase in the prison population of several thousand during the next two years as a result of unfavourable public and press reaction to changes in the Criminal Justice Act (1991) which, among other things, has allowed magistrates to ignore previous offences when considering a sentence, a reductionist measure which the government now feels forced to abandon. Indeed, magistrates seem to have been issued with new and even tougher guidelines which seem likely to undermine the very philosophy of the 1991 Act.

TABLE 1
SCALE OF PRIVATE SECTOR'S INVOLVEMENT IN THE
STATE'S PRISON BUILDING PROGRAM

Prison	Date of opening	Estimated total cost (£K)	Main construction contractor
Wayland	January 1985	22,365	Carters of Norwich
Stocken	June 1985	17,182	Miller Construction
Thorn Cross	July 1985	13,014	Shepherd Construction
Full Stutton	September 1987	40,020	Monk Construction
Littehey	January 1988	34,002	Bovis Construction
Mount	March 1988	28,185	Wimpey Construction
Garth	July 1988	45,110	Tarmac
Swaleside	May 1990	33,539	Mowlem
Belmarsh	April 1991	161,273	Wimpey Construction
Moorland	July 1991	55,219	Higgs and Hill
Whitemoor	September 1991	54,100	Monk Construction
Brinsford	November 1991	45,563	Taylor Woodrow
Elmley	February 1992	82,782	Mowlem
Bullington	March 1992	64,339	Kier Construction
Wolds	April 1992	36,880	UK Detention Contractors (Consortium: Mowlem and Sir Robert McAlpine)
Holme House	May 1992	66,184	Sir Robert McAlpine
Woodhill	July 1992	117,753	Higgs and Hill
High Down	August 1992	91,058	Alfred McAlpine
Lancaster Farms	March 1993	73,150	AMEC
Blakenhurst	May 1993	80,432	Tarmac
Doncaster	April 1994	94,730	Shepherd Construction

*   Includes capital cost, claims and property services agency's resource costs.

These examples illustrate that sentencing policy is determined by many factors, and it would be quite erroneous to suggest a simple and direct relationship between the lobby power of private prison operators and the overall level of the prison population at any given time. This is not to suggest that public image and profit motive will not add new forces which may influence levels of accountability and monitoring (see Moyle, chapter 5). The argument against crude determinism was well made in the Australian context by Richard Harding, who reminded critics of plans to open a private prison in New South Wales that the rapid increase in prison numbers there was driven by 'truth in sentencing' policies which had pre-dated the debate over Junee Correctional Centre (Harding 1992a).

But having made this important caveat it is still possible to argue that the claims by private operators that they deliver incarceration more cheaply than the public sector, and/or that they are well placed to meet any sudden, unexpected emergency, are obvious incentives for governments to keep expanding the prison estate. Recall, for example, the six new privately financed prisons which the UK government has recently announced (see above). These are in addition to the existing prison building program. It is extremely doubtful if these would have been contemplated at the present time when the UK government is facing a huge fiscal deficit if the private sector had not been prepared to foot the bill. Significantly, this expansionary potential is implicitly conceded elsewhere, even by Harding, who while reiterating that it is governments which make policy, also acknowledges that the private sector will lobby to 'seize the available opportunities' (Harding 1993b, p. 6).

REFORM

There is also, we must not forget, the attractive claim that private prisons are agencies for reform. It is argued that not only do they reform their own inmates, and at low cost, but to the extent that their good practices spread to the state sector, mainstream prisons and prisoners also stand to benefit. About the Australian experience, Harding has recently claimed that: 'cross fertilisation is occurring so as to improve the whole system . . . Of course comprehensive evaluation is needed of whether such improvements feed through into lower recidivist rates, higher post-employment rates, less family breakdowns and so on. But prima facie the evidence so far is promising' (Harding 1993b, p. 3-4). Other Australian researchers are sceptical about such claims, and there is no hard evidence in the UK or the US to suggest that this miracle is happening elsewhere (Moyle 1993b), least of all in the UK.

Apart from anything else, Wolds and Blakenhurst have been operating for too short a period for any proper evaluations to be made, and to the extent that other British prisons have adopted similarly relaxed regimes there is no evidence that they were to any significant extent influenced by what was happening in the private sector. This is not to suggest that cross fertilisation might not take place. Both systems will now influence each other, and it's even possible that in the long term public sector prisons will benefit most, but to use privatisation as a metaphor for reform, to even go so far as to suggest that after nearly two centuries mechanisms for reform have at last been found, is likely to turn out to be a fantasy, yet another (ig)noble lie.

While on the subject of innovation it is relevant that when the private sector was in charge of juvenile institutions in the UK on a regulatory basis its record was far from impressive. Indeed, apart from holding many juveniles who had only been involved in minor infractions of the law — many had not even broken the law at all — it was the failure of these private institutions to innovate and change which led to increasing state intervention. True, these institutions were not run for profit, and therefore not subject to the discipline of the market place, but they were at least free from the 'stultifying' hand of the state which, if today's private sector is to be believed, is one of the main barriers to innovation.

LOOKING AHEAD AND ELSEWHERE

In spite of the limitations imposed by Transfer Undertaking Protection of Employment (TUPE), and the problems experienced by Group 4, the introduction of privately managed prisons is likely to continue at a steady pace in the UK. The Home Secretary's recent speech to the Conservative Party conference (November 1993) has made this clear. However, given the POA's opposition, and in order to end the isolation of privately run prisons, the process could well go forward on a regional basis. So, for example, Doncaster is to join the north east region which already has Wolds and its privately run escort system in place.

Some opponents of private prisons believe that their progress in the US is likely to be more dramatic than in Britain, and with unfortunate consequences. Christie, for example, believes that they will help to expand America's already excessive levels of incarceration. He is persuaded that politicians will accept the logic of Charles Logan's arguments, namely, that the growing demand for prison places should — in the name of justice — be met, even at the risk of over supply (Christie 1993, pp. 109-110), and that state governments will increasingly turn to the private sector to provide these places, not just because of their alleged competitiveness but also because it means state governments can bypass the taxpayer who will no longer be called upon to directly bear the capital cost of building new facilities (Christie 1993, p. 111).

Inasmuch as this scenario suggests a rash of speculative prison building in the US by the private sector, this is unlikely. In the first place, private prisons have been around for sometime now, and yet as we pointed out earlier, the number of adult prisoners held by private contractors is still only a tiny fraction of the overall US adult prison population, a far smaller proportion than in Australia which leads the field.

Second, if there is to be any expansion in the provision of private prisons, Carter's scenario of targeted marketing is the more likely one. Carter does not believe that private sector involvement is likely to expand, or that it is necessarily desirable that it should expand, in the US, through speculative building for the mainstream prison population. Rather, he argues that in association with government the private sector should seek to offer specific, licensed facilities for women, sex offenders, substance abusers and the mentally ill (Carter 1992). While there is no firm evidence that this is yet an established trend, the idea of separating out these categories from the prison population as a whole is more likely to win political support, and engender less union opposition, in the US than farming out mainstream prisoners to privately built and/or operated prisons.

Nothing that has been argued here gainsays the possibility — even the probability — that the state sector system will expand in the US, or that private interests will not greatly benefit from such an expansion in terms of prison building and the provision of a whole range of services. It is suggested that there is unlikely to be a runaway, speculative provision of private facilities for the mainline adult prison population.

CONCLUSION

As in most other liberal democracies the relationship between the state and the penal system in the UK is not a fixed one. For example, in the 18th century the penal system was largely in the hands of private operators before a period of central inspection and state involvement lead to its nationalisation in 1877. It is also true that, as in most other liberal democracies, the private sector has always had some role to play in the UK's management of offenders. As nationalisation was tightening its grip on the adult penal system, for example, reformatory schools for juveniles were being run in the UK by private voluntary bodies in the reform movement inspired by Mary Carpenter who was keen to keep the state at arm's length. Given this established and long standing mixture of the public and the private in managing the UK's penal system, why has there been so much opposition to the introduction of private prisons?

In the first place, and as Janet Chan wisely reminds us, significant shifts in social and penal policy are nearly always contested (1992 Chan). Not unreasonably, trade unionists like the POA and the CSPSA fight hard to secure their jobs and conditions of employment against entrepreneurs who seek to reduce costs and maximise profits. And there are those like Nils Christie who fear that private prisons will contribute to higher levels of incarceration. Likewise, there are those who can see that there is a case for delegating the delivery of punishment to private interests, but not at the deep end of the system where the use of force — sometimes life taking force — is routinely applied and human rights systematically abused. However, while these concerns have been sufficient to generate intense debate, there is a strong moral anxiety underpinning most of these positions that it is wrong in principle to benefit, that is to make a profit — as opposed to a living wage — out of the unfortunate social necessity of inflicting pain. It is this anxiety which has really fuelled the debate in the UK.

If we add these concerns together the issue becomes not so much a crude struggle between the public and the private, but rather a debate about exactly where, and on what terms, private interests should be involved.

Finally, the recognition that the debate is a complex one will be welcomed by some post modernist theorists who see the state as nothing more than a powerful rhetorical device or discursive resource (Melossi 1991), or perhaps at best, as a mere collection of power circuits, discreetly organised and largely autonomous (Stenson and Cowell 1991). For such theorists the exercise of power in modern societies is highly fragmented and the boundary lines between the public and the private by no means clear and, above all, subject to negotiation; where pragmatism and process in a slightly uncomfortable way take over from a priori reasoning which traditionally has as its first or organising principle, some notion of the social contract. All this is a far cry from the liberal democratic discourse of the Howard League, a striking irony which deserves further elaboration, as has been pointed out elsewhere (Ryan 1992).

References

Adam Smith Institute, 1987, *The Prison Cell*, London.

Ashford, M. 1993, *Detained Without Trial; A Survey of Immigrant Detention*, JCWI, London.

Brown A. 1992, 'Economic Aspects of Prison Privatisation; The Queensland Experience', in *Private Sector and Community Involvement in the Criminal Justice System* in (eds) D. Biles and J. Vernon, Australian Institute of Criminology, Canberra (forthcoming).

Carter, S. A. 1992, 'Will Privatisation Impact Forecasting for Correctional Services?' in *Private Sector and Community Involvement in the Criminal Justice System*, (eds) D. Biles and J. Vernon, Australian Institute of Criminology, Canberra (forthcoming).

Chan, J. 1992, 'The Privatisation of punishment; A review of the key issues', *Australian Journal of Social Issues*, vol. 27, pp. 223-47.

Christie, N. 1993, *Crime Control as Industry*, Routledge, London.

Criminal Justice 1993a, Howard League Newsletter, London, vol. 11, no. 4, p. 17.

— 1993b, Howard League Newsletter, London, vol. 11, no. 2, pp. 6-7.

Deloitte, Haskins and Sells 1989, *Report on the Practicality of Private Sector Involvement in the Remand System*, Prepared for the Home Office, unpublished.

Hansard 1987, House of Commons, July 16, col. 1303.

— 1989, House of Commons, March 1, col. 278.

— 1991, House of Commons, January 31, col. 575.

— 1993, House of Commons, October 19, col. 214-215.

Harding, R. 1992a, 'Private Prisons in Australia', *Trends and Issues*, no. 36, Australian Institute of Criminology, Canberra.

— 1992b, Privatising Prisons; Principle and practice, (unpublished).

HMSO 1987, *Contract Provision of Prisons*, Fourth Report of the House of Commons, Select Committee, Home Affairs, Session 1986/87, London.

Home Office 1993a, Framework Document, HM Prison Service, London.

— 1993b, Corporate Plan, HM Prison Service, London.

— 1993c, Report by the Chief Inspector of Prisons, Wold Remands Prison, London.

Kelsey 1993, Privatised Justice; One Experiment too far, Alan Nixon Memorial Lecture, Wellington, New Zealand, unpublished.

Labour Research 1993, July, London.

Logan, C. 1992, 'Comparing Quality of Confinement in Public and Private Prisons', *Journal of Criminal Law and Criminology*, vol. 83, no. 3.

Lilley, R. and Knepper 1992, 'An International Perspective on The Privatization of Corrections', *The Howard Journal of Criminal Justice*, vol. 31, no. 3, pp. 174-191.

Melossi, D. 1991, *The State of Social Control*, Polity Press, Oxford.

Moyle, P. 1992, 'Privatising Prisons The Underlying Issues', *Alternative Law Journal*, vol. 17, no. 3, June, pp. 114-119.

— 1993a, 'Privatisation of Prisons in New South Wales and Queensland: A Review of Some Key Developments in Australia', *The Howard Journal of Criminal Justice*, vol. 32, no. 3, pp. 231-250.

—— 1993b, 'Research Note — Private Prison Research in Queensland, Australia; A Case Study of Borallon Correctional Centre', Paper presented to the British Criminology Conference, Cardiff, Wales, August, *British Journal of Criminology*, (forthcoming).

New Statesman and Society 1993, March 19, p. 18.

Prison Officers Association (POA) 1993, *The Case Against Privatisation in Britain*, London.

Prison Reform Trust (PRT) 1993, *Wolds Remand Centre, Contracting Out; A First Year Report*, London.

Ryan, M. 1983, *The Politics of Penal Reform*, Longman, London.

—— 1992, 'Some Radical and Left Responses to Privatising the Penal System in England and Wales', in *Private Sector and Community Involvement in the Criminal Justice System*, (eds) D. Biles and J. Vernon, Australian Institute of Criminology, Canberra, (forthcoming).

Ryan, M. and Ward, T. 1989, *Privatization and the Penal System; The American Experience and the Debate in England*, Open University Press, Milton Keynes.

Stenson, K. and Cowell, D. 1991, *The Politics of Crime Control*, Sage, London.

The Independent 1992, April 14.

The Listener 1993, Auckland, New Zealand, March 27, p. 22.

---

* While this article contains new material and has been adapted to incorporate the Australian context, it inevitably draws directly on material from a series of seminars given in Prague and London in the Summer and Autumn of 1993, and which were later combined in an as yet unpublished paper submitted to the *International Journal for the Sociology of Law*.

Part V

Private police

12

The legal powers of private police and security providers

Rick Sarre*

Abstract: Private police and security providers find their legal power in the law of contract, the law of property, and industrial law. The 'special' power which is exercised by them emanates from little more than a combination of their principals' powers and intimidation by appearance. The presence of security providers' badges and weapons is thus little more than a facade of legal power. It does not derive from any unique authority granted by statutory nor common law to private security personnel, but rather it is found in the perception of those at whom it is directed. Private security providers face no readily accessible mechanisms of accountability, unlike their public counterparts.

There is much confusion in the minds of those whose actions are governed and monitored by private police on a daily basis. This confusion will persist while the distinction between public and private policing operatives remains blurred.

Increasing demands for protection of people and property together with financial constraints on governments have greatly expanded the role of modern private security providers, inquiry agents and private police in Australian and New Zealand societies. Thus policing, far from being the exclusive preserve of public functionaries, is an activity undertaken by a host of private operatives. This resurgence of private policing (which pre-dated modern policing) has attracted an array of literature in recent years exploring its implications for the sociology of policing and public versus private relations in the late 20th century (Heald 1985, Marx 1987, Nemeth 1989, Shearing 1992, Shearing et al 1980, South 1988, Stenning and Shearing 1991, US Private Security Advisory Council 1977, Walsh 1989).

However there is rarely any discussion of the more fundamental and basic questions concerning the legal basis of their authority. On many occasions each day shoppers, travellers, students, tenants and workers are confronted by these 'private' individuals. Requests may be made for searches of their property. Questioning may occur. Exit or entry may be denied. Arrests may be effected. These interactions occur both on private property (for example indoor shopping malls) and in public areas (such as parks). In very few cases does anyone stop to question whether there is any basis in law for the requests or the orders made. What legal authority do security agents have? In what circumstances can force accompany non-compliance with a request? In what situations can an arrest occur? What avenues for legal accountability exist in the event that authority is exceeded? An accurate legal answer to each of these questions is elusive. Yet the implications for civil liberties are significant.

There is little doubt that the legal authority of private security providers, that is, those to whom we have entrusted much of our day to day policing and protection responsibilities, is determined more by a piecemeal array of legal rights, privileges and assumptions than by clearly defined law. This chapter is designed to explore these issues and attempt to define the parameters. It is clear, from a cursory glance, that the uncertainty reported by Canadian researchers 17 years ago has not altered significantly since then:

> At the very least it is necessary to clarify the powers presently held by private citizens, a matter which, because of the relatively recent upsurge in the size of the private security industry, and the tendency of the legal superstructure to lag behind social reality, has only received very limited consideration, either in the legislature or in the courts. (Freedman and Stenning 1977, p. 66)

There are a number of reasons for the limited consideration that continues to this day.

First, it is not difficult to imagine that there is perennial confusion among the general public in differentiating between private security personnel and public police officers, given the similarities in dress, the comparable numbers of both in the 'security' trade, and the ability of both (in certain circumstances and subject to licensing requirements) to wear exposed firearms. Indeed, it is in the best interests of private security providers not to discourage the confusion, as this enhances their appearance of authority:

> Despite the fact that private agents . . . do not possess police powers, it is probably true that most individuals when confronted by a uniformed guard or a man stating that he is a 'detective' or 'investigator' naturally assume he has some kind of legal authority. Public misunderstanding of the law undoubtedly gives private agents an additional advantage. (Scott and McPherson 1971, p. 272)

Second, there is a general reluctance by private security providers to have their powers tested in the courts. Whenever objections to their actions are raised, it would not be foolish to suspect that many matters are quietly discussed behind closed doors and compromises are encouraged, for one would anticipate that private property owners are anxious not to threaten their rights as owners. An essential ingredient in loss prevention (typical of the function of private security) is lack of publicity. Investigations and security checks will proceed as quietly as possible if wrong-doing is suspected. If a culprit is apprehended, private security will first enquire into the possible ramifications for business interests prior to contacting the public police. Arguably, only if there is no risk of damage, bad publicity or loss of company secrets are the public police invited to participate in the process:

> Hence the great importance . . . of the 'unique access to private places' which private security personnel enjoy. On the one hand they are in a unique position to observe and detect criminal activity on private property. On the other hand, the rights of private property ownership, which they enjoy by virtue of the fact that they act as agents of the owner, leave them with a virtually unfettered discretion as to whether they will invoke the criminal justice process in dealing with such activity, or attempt to deal with it in some more private fashion. (Stenning and Shearing 1979-80, p. 235).

Finally, it is no longer as easy to differentiate between private property and public areas as it once was. The boundaries have well and truly merged. Our cities have typically moved towards converting formerly open and 'public' areas (like shopping streets, markets and housing estates) into closed 'private' property (like indoor shopping malls and monitored and patrolled living areas, in housing 'compounds' or high-rise apartments for example). Shearing and Stenning describe this latter phenomenon as 'mass private property' (1981, p 229). This gives rise to unfortunate theoretical difficulties, for the law often differentiates between these areas in order to determine when powers and rights begin and cease. The dividing lines are not evenly drawn nor clearly visible, for example, where an arrest for a 'public' offence takes place on ostensibly private property (see *Semple v Howes* (1985) 38 SASR 34). For these reasons a degree of cooperation has been forged between the two policing sectors, in no small measure because many security personnel are ex-police officers. In those circumstances it is not difficult to imagine that, to the public, there is no distinction in law between the powers granted to all sectors of the 'law and order' industries.

It may not be surprising that little academic attention is paid to this important aspect of order maintenance. The phenomenon of private security cannot be examined using traditional tools commonly employed for the study of the 'public' police, since private security personnel are neither enforcing public law privately, nor are they public police merely acting privately. This chapter will explore the roots and manifestations of the authority assumed by the private sector in an endeavour to clarify the questions raised earlier.

ORIGINS OF THE LEGAL AUTHORITY OF PRIVATE POLICE PERSONNEL

What legal authority do security providers have? Unlike the public police, whose power is found generally in the various law enforcement statutes, the powers of private security personnel derive principally from their being legal 'agents' of those who control and own private property.

True, there has been legislation passed in a number of jurisdictions concerning the registration, employment and training of private legal personnel (discussed below), but none of the pieces of legislation delineates or grants legal authority. Thus, whatever coercive powers private security personnel assume, they are not based in statute. Nor does any law confer any extraordinary powers upon them beyond the powers of the ordinary citizen. Indeed the criminal law seems 'to have been drafted in complete ignorance of the existence of the huge army of specialised private security officers . . . because these laws . . . were devised long before the phenomenon of private security as we know it today came into existence' (Shearing and Stenning 1982, p. 3).

Security agents are able to draw, arguably, upon three fundamental areas of the common law to enhance their position vis-a-vis the rest of the world: the law of contract, the law of property and industrial law, each of which will be examined in turn. Following this examination, the chapter continues with an examination of three specific powers: forcible ejection, search, and arrest. It will conclude with a review of the mechanisms of accountability which may exist.

The law of contract

From the law of contract private security personnel derive their right to contract as agents for their principals, and thus to act upon their instructions within the scope of their authority. The 'agent' status of private security personnel allows them access to, and control over, places where the public police may not routinely go. By virtue of their being contractual agents, they are able to exercise, in so far as they remain within their scope of authority, the powers possessed by the owner of the property.

Putting to one side employment contracts (discussed below), the contractual power of owners or managers of private land and their legal agents over visitors is extremely problematic. Those who challenge shoppers and request a search of their belongings, for example, may find it difficult to locate the legal 'consideration' required for there to be a contract between manager and shopper. Visitors who pay for the privilege of residence (tenants for example by the payment of rent) or entertainment (by the purchase of a ticket) may, however, find that a contract does now exist. Visitors may therefore be subjected to express (written and verbal) and implied contractual terms upon the payment of rent or the purchase of a ticket. They will, at law, be deemed to have consented to these terms in so far as the terms (for example, the requirement of a search of a bag at a concert which may contain recording equipment) have been clearly brought to their attention and thus incorporated into the terms of the appropriate contract.

Such tenants or visitors enter the premises or entertainment venue on the basis of not only express contractual terms but also the following implied terms — that in return for the entertainment, and the provision of a safe environment in which to be entertained, the visitor agrees (impliedly) not to behave in such a way as to threaten or disrupt the integrity of the apartment or presentation, and to obey any directions of the managers or promoters or their legally appointed agents. The person who is in charge of premises has the capacity, and thus is under a legal duty, to make those premises safe. In return, the visitors agree to abide by the rules and may have their privileges withdrawn in the event of a breach. Whether withdrawal can be enforced by physical means is a matter of debate.

So while there are rights under contract for parties to enforce compliance under contract law (which rights are extended to legal security agents), these rights are seriously circumscribed in certain situations, for example, where no contract exists or where force is contemplated to enforce the contract (discussed below).

The law of property

From the law of property, private property owners and their agents receive great power. The influence of capitalist economics upon the notion of private property has entrenched the concept that each person's home is his or her castle (Stenning and Shearing 1979-80, p. 233 quoting the famous dictum — in gender neutral terms — of the judges in *Semayne's Case* (1604) 77 E. R. 194).

It is clear that the law grants to the owner (or legally appointed agent of the owner) of the 'castle' power to require visitors to leave premises, or to subject invitees and visitors to stipulations prescribed by the property owner. Both invitees and strangers will have to follow the directions of those charged with the responsibility of 'security', particularly if there are clear directions (to which notice has been drawn) of the terms of the implied 'licence' to enter.

Like the situation in the law of contract, fundamental to this area of law is the issue of consent. Where there is consent by the invitee to the terms of the licence, there is no problem. Anyone who dissents, however, before entry or during the visit is in a different and far more contentious position. That person is unlikely to be invited or, if they are already present, will be ordered off the property with the legal authority of the owner to use whatever force is necessary and reasonable in the circumstances, and furthermore to be subjected to any requirements of entry (for example a search) that were drawn to their attention upon entry. Such a proposition of law, of course, still leaves open the question of the 'reasonableness' of the force used.

It is important to reiterate at this stage of the argument that private security personnel possess no greater powers than those of the property owner. Like any citizen, property owners or their agents have limited rights to make a 'citizen's arrest' in circumstances where they perceive that a crime (such as larceny in a shopping centre, for example) has been committed. The only limitation is that citizens have to be right about their suspicions or face a civil suit (for false imprisonment or assault) if they are wrong, or unable to prove their case. Off private property, the right of the property owner or agent to enforce the criminal law becomes even more delicate.

Industrial law

The law of contract would appear to have more 'bite' in the field of industrial law and industrial relations. Employees may be required to agree to undergo searches and credit reference checks (subject to strict privacy laws such as those that came into effect on 24 September 1991 under the Commonwealth *Privacy Amendment Act* 1990) in order to remain employed, since that condition may be a part of their employment contract. While formal negotiation regulates and justifies the bargains struck between employers and employees, it is often doubted that the final workplace agreement is, in all respects, fair. In theory, it can only operate with the consent of both of the parties, but, in reality, consent is usually deemed to have been given or put in the form of an offer that cannot be refused, particularly in times of high unemployment and under what is known as 'enterprise bargaining'. Infused in this relationship is the fundamental 'master and servant' doctrine. In that environment, workers have little choice but to comply with requests by security providers for them to submit to searches and to answer (subject to equal opportunity laws) certain questions if they wish to remain employed.

For example, there is an implied term in the employment contract that one should be honest. There follows a 'right' granted to employers ('masters') to ensure honesty (of 'servants'). If the request for a search is reasonable in the circumstances, then a search of a person's belongings while they are on the property of the employer (or leaving it) would be entirely appropriate. In *Latter v Braddell* (1881) 50 LJQB 448 (C.A.) it was held that no assault was committed when a mistress required her maid to be medically examined to see whether she was pregnant. Although under protest, the maid complied, and it was held that her consent negatived any action in the tort of 'battery'.

Nevertheless, there are good public policy reasons why consent should be regarded as nullified in certain circumstances (Williams 1962, p. 75 ff), for example, in relation to breaches of legislatively prescribed occupational health and safety requirements. In other words, it should not be possible to allow a person to consent to being injured. The object of industrial legislation is to keep these hazards to a minimum and to ensure that a person is protected even if it appears, *prima facie*, that consent to a danger was present.

In all of this, however, the difficulty arises in relation to the ability of security personnel to use force to ensure worker compliance. The political dimensions of this situation cannot be understated. Industrial conflicts questioning the right of management to use force to ensure compliance by staff raise an entirely new set of questions, outside the parameters of this chapter.

Having considered the contractual, proprietary and industrial dimensions of the legal authority of private security providers, it is possible to reach an early conclusion. The presence of security agents' uniforms, their badges and weapons is little more than a façade of legal power. The 'special' power which is exercised emanates from little more than a combination of their principals' powers (primarily under property law and in some limited respects contract and industrial law) and intimidation by appearance. It does not derive from any unique authority granted by statutory nor common law to private security personnel, but rather it is found in the perception of power by those to whom it is directed.

In other words, if one adds to the general power of property owners to control conduct on their property a right to allow their agents to wear uniforms, the ability to engage in legal 'control' activities on a paid full time basis, the ability to require searches (with implied and unchallenged consent) of those who enter that property, the availability of sophisticated surveillance equipment and the privilege of carrying firearms, it is not surprising that there is a perception by the general public that 'private' security providers have the same powers as public police. The argument is simply that this power is found more in fact than it is in law.

POWERS

At this point it may be instructive to examine some of the more common and specific legal powers often exercised by security providers: forcible ejection (for example, by 'bouncers'), search (for example, by airport security) and arrest (for example, by store detectives). To what extent is there more power in the 'fact' than in the law? The powers of the two 'forces' will be compared where it is appropriate to make a comparison.

Forcible ejection from property

As discussed above, there is arguably a right, under contract law, property law and industrial law in some circumstances, for owners or managers of property (and their security 'agents') to require invitees, visitors and strangers alike to leave that property. While consent is present there is no problem. But to what extent can force be used to ensure compliance by those who refuse? Does the existence of implied consent extend to the use of force, and if so, to what degree?

There are many difficult legal questions surrounding the common law right of a person in Australia (including a police officer) to go on to private property for the purpose of arresting someone on a criminal charge (*Halliday v Nevill* (1984) Aust Torts Reports 80-315) or intervening in a personal dispute (*Panos v Hayes* (1987) 44 SASR 148) (cf the UK position in *McConnell v Chief Constable of Greater Manchester* CA, 1988, reported in Johnston 1992, p. 206). Thus the power of the land-owner remains *prima facie* paramount. The law has been made somewhat clearer in Australia since the High Court's decision in *Plenty v Dillon and Others* (1990-1) 98 ALR 353. In that case police officers wished to enter a house in order to serve a summons on one of the occupants. Their implied licence to approach the house was withdrawn by the occupier and verbal notice of that withdrawal was given unequivocally. The question was whether the police were entitled to remain on the land after the implied permission had been withdrawn. The court decided in the circumstances that an officer (or indeed any person) is not authorised to enter private land without the consent of the owner in the absence of any implied 'leave' or licence to remain. Having said that, however, the law does allow any police officer or citizen to enter premises to prevent the commission of a felony and indeed that may include breaking into premises once permission to gain entry without breaking has been refused. However, there is no power to enter premises without permission merely upon suspicion that something is amiss (per Gaudron and McHugh JJ in *Plenty* at 361), and there was certainly no element of that in this case.

The question that has not been answered definitively by the courts is the extent to which force may be used in order to facilitate compliance with the request to leave. The answer quite simply (if that ever be possible) is that reasonable force is be used, and the determination of what is 'reasonable' will turn on the facts of each individual case. For example, had the owner of the house in *Plenty's* case fired a rifle and killed one of the officers, then he would have been charged with a serious offence. Appearing with a fierce dog and threatening them if they remained on the property may, however, have been deemed reasonable.

In South Australia the common law power of property owners to defend their territory from uninvited 'guests' has been reinforced by statute. An Act to amend the *Criminal Law Consolidation Act 1935* (s15) was passed into law in December 1991 adding a subjective component (in the determination of the availability of a defence to a criminal charge) to the current common law test of 'reasonable' force. Whether it applies, of course, beyond the home-owner to encompass security officers is another question and one that has not been tested in the courts.

How such legislation will affect one's common law liability in *tort* is another interesting question. In *Hackshaw v Shaw* (1984) 155 CLR 614 a farmer defending his supply of fuel from thieves injured a thief when he fired recklessly at their car. The High Court found that the injured person (in the car) should be compensated for her injuries because it was reasonably foreseeable that an injury was likely to result. In the words of Justice Murphy, to fire bullets at a car in this way 'is not merely extra-hazardous, it is ultra-hazardous'. So while the farmer may have had a right to protect his property, which would extend to his legally appointed agents, and may have had a defence to a criminal charge, it is possible that using reasonable force may still render him liable for injuries caused if those injuries were reasonably foreseeable. It is important to remember that an occurrence can still be 'foreseeable' notwithstanding that it may be more probable than not that the occurrence will not occur (*Commonwealth of Australia v Introvigne* (1981) 41 ALR 577).

Search

The law allows a person with the proper contractual rights to request a search of a person coming on to or leaving private property. Fundamental to this question once again, however, is the issue of consent. If the person gives a valid and informed consent to being searched, then there is no problem. Consent can be expressed ('Yes, I will do as you ask') or implied ('Yes, I saw the sign when I entered and agreed then to be bound by it while I remained in the shop'). But if there is no consent, the issue becomes quite uncertain.

The common law right to use force to secure compliance with the terms of a contract (even if it can be established that a contract exists) is extremely equivocal. By contrast, force may be used in order to preserve the integrity of a proprietary, as opposed to contractual, right, at which time it becomes a question of the reasonableness of the force used. For example, courts could find a qualitative difference between a bag inspection undertaken by force (as a reasonable condition of one's exit from a store), and a personal search undertaken by force (an unreasonable condition). The law could also differentiate between places where the request is made. Perhaps a cursory search upon entry into an alcohol-free concert could be distinguished by the law from a more invasive search required upon entry to a prison visitors' centre where questions of public safety and security are more acute. Once again, there are very few cases in the law reports which provide any guidance on these issues.

In the final analysis one might suspect, from the arguments presented above, that the private security guard or store detective who does not obtain a warrant or express and informed consent, and who cannot imply consent, cannot search any person against their will or use force to ensure their compliance without *running a risk* of being sued for (civil) assault, which risk may still persist (depending upon the force used in the circumstances) even if it turns out that their suspicions (that an offence has been committed) are confirmed. The public police, by contrast, can detain any person upon suspicion of an offence by virtue of the criminal statutory codes or other regulations. The powers are quite dissimilar, although they do differ from jurisdiction to jurisdiction, making anything less than broad statements of principle problematic.

Arrest
This is another large and difficult area of law because the variations on the laws of arrest change from jurisdiction to jurisdiction also. For example, in all states of Australia the common law rights of private arrest have been supplemented and even expanded by statute (NSW and South Australia allow arrest in circumstances where there is a mere 'reasonable cause' to suspect the commission of an offence for example), yet in one state these powers have been abrogated. The Victorian government passed the *Crimes (Powers of Arrest) Act* in 1972 to limit the availability of a 'citizen's arrest' to situations beyond mere suspicion. How can a citizen, security guard or private detective know precisely which statutes apply in which jurisdictions? While the common law power of arrest exists, the situation is clear. But in circumstances where that has been modified the situation becomes unclear. Even the High Court's ruling in the case of *R v Iorlano* (1983) 50 ALR 291 (which held that the common law power of arrest can continue alongside any statutory modification of the common law) is not entirely helpful.

The difficulty in this area is to balance the citizen's or private security person's right to enforce the law with the danger that officious intermeddlers might abuse others' rights. The conflict is resolved by judicial limitations on the privilege, assuming, of course, that matters such as these ever get to court.

In circumstances where a person is held against their will, there may arise a case of false imprisonment. In the case of *Robinson v Balmain Ferry* [1910] A.C. 295 an extraordinary situation arose. Robinson missed his Sydney Harbour ferry and attempted to go back through the turnstiles at which he had already paid his fare. Unfortunately, his retreat required the payment of another fare, since passengers alighting from the return trip were not charged at the dock where they boarded. Robinson refused to pay twice for a trip that he was denied, and was 'held' (albeit passively) by the ferry agents against his will. He sued in the tort of false imprisonment. He failed. The court said that his imprisonment was justified since Robinson was well aware of the rules under which the ferries operated. The judges added, however, in passing, that the non-payment of the fare would not have justified the use of force to restrain Robinson. The common law protected the ferry company from civil suit only in so far as they legitimately blocked Robinson's exit *without* the use of force. There is no common law power to justify *force* to ensure the payment of any debt (*Sunbolf v Alford* (1838) 150 E.R. 1135) and it is highly likely that this principle applies to all contractual duties and undertakings.

The position has been somewhat clarified more recently in Australia by the decision of the Federal Court in *Brown v GJ Coles* (1985) 59 ALR 455. Brown was detained by a store detective under suspicion of having shoplifted. Later the police arrived and formally charged him with larceny (a felony). He was later acquitted of the offence and brought an action for false imprisonment saying that his arrest and detention by the store was unlawful in the circumstances, particularly given that it was unduly lengthy. The test applied by the court was whether the arrester (the store) could show that they had had reasonable and proper cause to suspect that a crime had been committed. They were assisted by the decision in *Rejfek v McElroy* (1965) 112 CLR 517 which held that a party in such (civil) proceedings need only establish this belief upon a balance of probabilities, not proof beyond reasonable doubt. In the circumstances the court was satisfied that the store detective had been able to show that she had had reasonable and proper cause to suspect, on the balance of probabilities, that an offence had been committed and thus the arrest and subsequently undue detention had neither been unlawful nor unreasonable.

In the United States, laws concerning citizen's arrest 'privileges' (US National Advisory Committee 1976, pp 392-3) have been specifically enacted in over half of the states. Like the situation in the English common law tradition, the difficulty remains in determining the reasonableness of the suspicion that an offence has been committed. Recent legislation in Britain may have assisted in this respect. The

Police and Criminal Evidence Act 1984 (UK) s24 allows a citizen to arrest without a warrant 'anyone whom he has reasonable grounds for suspecting to be committing (an arrestable) offence'. The case of *Graham Self* (1992) 95 Cr App R 42 illustrates the complexities of the legislation. The alleged shoplifter was acquitted on the charge of theft, and thus the court held that since the commission of an arrestable offence was a pre-condition to a valid arrest, then the arrest was not warranted and the charges of assault (an attack by the accused upon the store detective while being arrested) could not stand.

Suffice to say for our purposes that under normal circumstances the powers of the private citizen (and consequently private security) to arrest someone without a warrant are more limited than those of the public police who have the right in most cases to arrest on suspicion of the likely commission of an offence which may be about to occur. For example, in some jurisdictions the right of a private person to make such an arrest is limited to felonies and not misdemeanours or summary matters, assuming that the person understands the distinction! In other jurisdictions the powers are quite straightforward. In sections 271-2 *Criminal Law Consolidation Act* (SA) and 76-77 *Summary Offences Act* (SA) there are statutory powers of arrest and search by any person who reasonably suspects that another person is committing, will commit or has committed a felony or misdemeanour. National security firms would do well to study the differences which exist from state to state.

Where deadly force is used in order to effect an arrest, the problem is compounded (Elliot 1979, pp. 72 ff). The case of *Hackshaw v Shaw* (discussed above) makes it clear that there may be tortious (as well as criminal) liability in the event of injury to any person involved, or indeed a bystander. The danger is not only to citizens but also to the security officers and public police. In many jurisdictions security personnel and police officers have the privilege of carrying firearms, the former regulated by licensing requirements and the latter by police regulation, (in SA by *Police Issue* 3375). Further debate concerning the use of deadly force by public and private police is required, given that there is some evidence of an increased likelihood that police or security officers will be shot if wearing a firearm (McCulloch 1992, p 136, Boyanowsky and Griffiths 1982, p. 406).

Private security personnel remain constantly at risk in many jurisdictions of being sued for assault or false imprisonment either for their initial action (where they were wrong in their assessment), or in circumstances where they do not hand that person over to a member of the police as soon as possible after apprehension.

272 Private Prisons and Police

ACCOUNTABILITY

Breaches of authority give rise to the question: what mechanisms of accountability exist in relation to private security providers? Although it is clear that the extent of the proper accountability of public police is far from unequivocal (Hogg and Harker 1983, Sarre 1989), it is strongly arguable that the formal accountability mechanisms that exist within that sphere (for example, ombudsmen, police complaints authorities, criminal justice commissions, disciplinary codes and internal investigation mechanisms) outstrip the more *ad hoc* mechanisms of accountability of private security. The private sector is not dependent upon the state for its authority and the state has little power to control or require accountability, having merely granted contractual and proprietary rights and then left them alone. Private protection providers, therefore, are accountable chiefly to private interests, such as industry associations, stockholders and owners. 'The accountability of the state through the ballot box is more achievable than the accountability of corporations which, although theoretically accountable to the state, are beyond the reach of the public' (McCarthy 1992, p. 113).

The common law, in circumstances where private property is involved, favours the privacy of the property owner above the privacy of the individual. There is a paradox here, since the very agents responsible for the protection of privacy must invade others' privacy in order to complete their task (Reiss 1987, p. 20). So when things go wrong, what can be done to redress the mistakes? As one can imagine, poorly delivered protection services are a risk to the safety of people and the protection of property. In *Photo Production v Securicor* [1980] AC 827 things went horribly wrong for the Securicor company when one of its own guards, lighting a fire for a cup of tea, allowed the fire to rage out of control thereby seriously damaging the factory under guard. In the end, the security company was able to resist suit by pointing to a carefully worded exemption clause.

Essentially the private security industry in Australia and New Zealand is unregulated apart from the requirements under some state legislation to license its operatives, companies and businesses. There is no consensus view on the form and extent of government (or industry-based) regulation of practitioners and firms. There, indeed, may be very little interest (Swanton 1993, p. 4). It is instructive, however, to look at some of the legislation and other regulations that provide some forms of accountability.

Through the civil law

The civil law only provides a mechanism of accountability if the party aggrieved by the excesses of private security can establish a cause of action, finance their law suit and prove their case. The *Securicor* case (above) provides a good example of the way in which even the most blatant mistakes made by security firms can be excused in circumstances where a contract has been cleverly drawn. The House of Lords in their judgment found that the exemption clause was clearly intended to cover incidents such as the one which occurred. If the hirer was unhappy with the clause then it was in a position to negotiate alternative wording.

Duty of care cases, admittedly, are having something of an effect upon the excesses of security providers. Indeed, there is some suggestion that private security firms in the US owe a duty of care to their clients for acts of criminals whose conduct they ought to have foreseen (Schiller and Harris 1988)! But despite the growing number of cases which are finding firms liable for their breach of tortious or contractual duty (*Reg. Glass Pty Ltd v Rivers Locking Systems Pty Ltd* (1968) 120 CLR 516; *Williams v Peters and Peters* No. A562/77 of 1982 in the High Court of New Zealand; *Chanel v Remath* No. 050153 of 1989 Supreme Court of New South Wales) these cases do little to provide systematic mechanisms of accountability. They merely indicate that the private security firm has to undertake its private responsibilities well, or risk being sued by those with whom it has contracted or to whom it owes a duty of care. In addition, the healthy competition keeps margins low with the inevitable consequence that low wages for operatives are the order of the day. The poor operational quality of many operatives reflects this point (Swanton 1993, p. 6). Furthermore, market forces and the risks of civil suit are poor forms of accountability where a non-contractual party, a by-stander or a trespasser is involved. The last of these is especially interesting. *Hackshaw and Shaw (above)* aside, it is unlikely that a trespasser will bring an action (assuming he or she is still alive) given the fact that they were trespassing, even though there may be evidence that the security officer used more force than was necessary in attempting apprehension.

Civil accountability is quite *ad hoc*, and relies upon the injured person undertaking expensive civil litigation. Comparisons with the North American situation (the availability of protections under a Bill of Rights or a Charter of Rights and Freedoms, and the greater accessibility to the courts by potential litigants in the North American tradition) are not particularly useful in the Australian and New Zealand context.

Through government regulation

The security industry statutes exist chiefly to regulate the persons who operate within the industry and who wish to enter it. There is no national code in Australia, rather the codes are piecemeal operations of the states. None of the codes mention anything to do with powers of security operatives. Indeed, the South Australian *Commercial and Private Agents Act 1986* (administered by the Minister of Consumer Affairs), for example, specifically excludes the possibility of it being read to create powers: 'S19 (1) A licence . . . [under the Act] does not confer upon an agent any power or authority to act in contravention of, or in disregard of, any law or any rights or privileges guaranteed or arising under, or protected by, any law'.

Similarly the Victorian *Private Agents Act 1966* requires annual licensing of guards (companies) and watchmen (personnel), although on some evidence unlicensed workers outnumber registered ones by two to one (Johnston 1992, p. 84). Even this Act has its limitations. By virtue of initiatives of the Law Reform Commission, the state government after 1989 introduced a policy of de-regulation of the industry.

Some governments do prohibit conduct by security providers which may be interpreted as holding them out as having more legal authority than they actually possess. Consider the following offence in South Australia: S19 (2) 'A person licensed as an agent who claims or purports to have by virtue of the licence any power or authority that is not in fact conferred by the licence shall be guilty of an offence against this Act and liable to a penalty not exceeding $2000'.

However, while these sections are common in such legislation, governments have been more generally concerned only with the suitability of applicants as holders of licences (once there has been the payment of a fee). Generally speaking a person with a criminal record would be unable to obtain a licence as not being a 'fit and proper person'. Consider the following requirement (clause 10) from the Queensland Security Providers Bill 1993. In addition to being over 18 years of age, and having successfully completed a training course, the applicant must be deemed an 'appropriate' person by the Department of Consumer Affairs, namely one who has not,

(3)   (a)   (i) shown dishonesty or lack of integrity
       (ii)   used harassing tactics
       (b)   . . . [or who] associates with a criminal in a way that indicates involvement in unlawful activity . . .
       (e)   . . . [or who] has been convicted of an offence.

In addition to the above legislation, each state, the Northern Territory and New Zealand has its own private security legislation. The picture is piecemeal. The regulating authority too varies from jurisdiction to jurisdiction (see appendix).

A person refused a licence can appeal against a decision but there is good reason to suspect that licences are not given out easily. In *Pav v Commercial and Private Agents Board (SA)* (1988 no. 3145/87) Justice Perry said that the Board had erred in questioning the applicant about alleged offences which had not resulted in a conviction, but that the Board's decision to refuse the licence was not inappropriate. However, in *Tremelling v Commissioner for Consumer Affairs* (SA) (1991 no. 1622/91) and *Walker v Commissioner for Consumer Affairs* (SA) (1991 no. 1260/91) Justice Olsson allowed an appeal by persons who had been refused 'crowd controllers' licences because of old convictions for assault and marijuana offences, and in the second case previous convictions arising out of provoked confrontations with police.

Through industry self-regulation

There are a number of employer and trade organisations in Australia and New Zealand (as well as representatives of American organisations) which represent the interests of retail security, mercantile agents and private detectives (amongst others) and which insist that self-regulation is sufficient as a form of accountability. But not all businesses and companies are affiliated with these groups. Furthermore, few employer organisations would have codes of conduct and fewer would act upon complaints through a public complaints mechanism in respect of their members or affiliates. In any event the most severe sanction imposed would be revocation of membership. The British experience indicates that that rarely if ever occurs (Johnston 1992, p. 87).

Through the criminal law

There is little doubt that should a private security officer engage in conduct that amounted to criminal conduct then the appropriate action would be to prosecute through the relevant public prosecution channels. Unfortunately, private security often equates with private outcomes. It is not uncommon for dishonest operatives in private business, once discovered, to face dismissal rather than public opprobrium because of the dishonour that such an action would bring to the company. It is not unlikely therefore that serious breaches of conduct by security officers may never see their way into the public courts. Criminal proceedings against a security officer are unlikely in the absence of strong evidence of criminal conduct. In July 1987 a shopper was accidentally hit by a stray bullet fired by a security guard who had disturbed two intruders in an Adelaide city premises. At the committal hearing seven months later a magistrate denied that the guard's actions amounted to criminal conduct sufficient to put him on trial. While he had been 'criminally stupid', said the magistrate, there was insufficient evidence to mount a case that he had been guilty of unlawful and malicious wounding since it would have been difficult for the prosecution to prove the requisite intent.

The criminal law is a crude tool with which to deal with misconduct, and certainly it has grave limitations as a tool of accountability.

Through 'market forces'

There has been a suggestion that market forces which drive the private sector act as a mechanism of accountability. That is, the poor performer will not survive in any business where client confidence is important. There is good evidence to suggest, however, that shoddy performers still exist notwithstanding.

In summary, then, given the rather *ad hoc* way in which private security providers are regulated by the legal and administrative process, it is somewhat anomalous that the general public pays greater attention to the accountability of the public police (or lack thereof) than it does to accountability questions affecting the private police. Armed with different, less overt, power, private security personnel use broad coercive powers and in some cases physical force in the absence of any forum of accountability with barely a whimper from the commentators. This issue requires immediate attention by policy-makers, notably through the expansion of powers of the regulating authority.

CONCLUSION

Private policing derives its *de jure* power from an admixture of the law of agency and contract (in certain situations), the law of property, and industrial law. Its *de facto* power (by virtue of its apparent authority) allows it to have the appearance of a force equal to public police.

The power of the public police is found in the system of rules and laws promulgated by statutes and regulations and the common law which finds its way from the courts into the law reports. Since exceptional authority was to be bestowed upon those who are to administer public justice, there has been a need for extensive public debate (see Shearing and Stenning 1983, p. 11). The rules regulating the public sector of policing are used prospectively to authorise the taking of particular action, and then retrospectively in showing to interested others, such as the courts and superiors, that the action was justified in the circumstances (Ericson 1982, p. 15). It is arguable that none of this happens with private security providers. Little debate has accompanied the conferring of legal and *de facto* powers on them. Nor are private security guidelines tested and interpreted by the courts on a regular basis if at all. Arguably, if no written law or legal interpretation grants them power, private security personnel are not constrained by that power. Test cases are avoided. Thus, the legal authority is more subtle than overt, and the power is wielded quietly and without fanfare. An added complication to regulation is the fact that many private security firms are transnational corporations, and therefore any national attempt to set rules which transcend international boundaries would be difficult to implement.

Each of the two sectors of policing, private and public, is premised upon different legal bases. But it is too simple to allege that one has authority over private land and the other authority over everything else. It is too simple to assume that one is involved purely in loss prevention and detection and one is solely concerned with investigation and the administration of the criminal justice system. It is much too simple to adopt any model of relationship which suggests that the two sectors are either neatly compatible or overtly hostile and suspicious.

What we are left with at the end of the day is a scene of two forces; one a highly trained, directed and accountable (to the state) public force and the other a conglomeration of professionalised quasi-forces which, in most instances, are less trained and much less accountable to the general public. Together they move around both public and private areas, in a sea of misconceptions about their various functions, engaging in a tight-lipped dialogue which hides more than it states, and using each other only when the economic and commercial assessments have been concluded. Until the powers of both are more tightly defined and delineated, the confusion which currently exists in the minds of those whose actions are governed by both on a daily basis will persist.

APPENDIX

The various Acts and their regulating authorities (in addition to those mentioned in the text) are:

New South Wales:
   Commercial Agents and Private Inquiry Agents Act 1963
   Security (Protection) Industry Act 1985
   Regulating authority: the police

Victoria:
  Private Agents Act 1966
  Regulating authority: the police or a magistrate

Western Australia:
  Security Agents Act 1976
  Inquiry Agents Licensing Act 1954
  Regulating authority: the police

Tasmania:
  Commercial and Inquiry Agents Act 1974
  Regulating authority: the Department of Justice or a magistrate

Northern Territory:
  Commercial and Private Agents Licensing Act 1979
  Regulating authority: the police

New Zealand:
  Private Investigators and Security Guards Act 1974
  Regulating authority: the police

References

Boyanowsky, Ehor and Griffiths, Curt 1982, 'Weapons and Eye Contact as Instigators or Inhibitors of Aggressive Arousal in Police-Citizen Interaction', *Journal of Applied Social Psychology*, vol. 12, no. 4, pp. 398-407.

Elliot, Ian 1979, 'The Use of Deadly Force in Arrest: Proposals for Reform', *Criminal Law Journal*, vol. 3, pp. 50-88.

Ericson, Richard V. 1982, *Reproducing Order: A Study of police patrol work*, University of Toronto Press, Toronto.

Freedman, David and Stenning, Philip 1977, *Private Security, Police and the Law in Canada*, Research Report of the Centre of Criminology, University of Toronto, Toronto.

Heald, David 1985, 'Will the Privatisation of Public Enterprises Solve the Problem of Control?', *Public Administration*, vol. 63, no. 1, pp. 7-22.

Hogg, Russell and Harker, B. 1983, 'The Politics of Police Independence', *Legal Service Bulletin*, vol. 8, pp. 160, 220.

Johnston, Les 1992, *The Rebirth of Private Policing*, Routledge, London.

McCarthy, Kath 1992, 'Privatising Punishment for Profit', *Alternative Law Journal*, vol. 17, no. 3, June, pp. 111-113.

McCulloch, Jude 1992, 'Heroes and Martyrs in the 'War' on Crime?', *Alternative Law Journal*, vol. 17, no. 3, June, pp. 135-137.

Marx, Gary 1987, 'The Interweaving of Public and Private Police in Undercover Work', in *Private Policing*, (eds) Clifford Shearing and Philip Stenning, Sage, Newbury Park, California, pp. 172-193.

Nemeth, Charles P. 1989, *Private Security and the Law*, Anderson, Cincinnati, Ohio.

Reiss, Albert J. 1987, 'The Legitimacy of Intrusion into Private Space' in *Private Policing*, (eds) Clifford Shearing and Philip Stenning, Sage, Newbury Park California, pp. 19-44.

Sarre, Rick 1989, 'Towards the notion of policing by consent: Implications for police accountability', in *Australian Policing: Contemporary Issues*, (eds) Duncan Chappell and Paul Wilson, Butterworths, Sydney.

Schiller, Jonathan and Harris, Gary 1988, 'The Legal Liability of a Private Security Guard Company for the Criminal Acts of Third Parties' in *The Private Security Industry: Issues and Trends, The Annals of the American Academy of Political and Social Science*, (ed) Ira A. Lipman, vol. 498, July, Sage, Newbury Park, pp. 91-97.

Scott, Thomas M. and McPherson, Marlys 1971, 'The development of the Private Sector of the Criminal Justice System', *Law and Society Review*, vol. 6, pp. 267-288.

Shearing, Clifford D. 1992, 'The Relation Between Public and Private Policing' in *Crime and Justice—An Annual Review of Research*, (eds) Michael Tonry and Norval Morris, vol. 15, University of Chicago Press, Chicago, pp. 399-434.

—, Farnell, M. B. and Stenning, Philip C. 1980, *Policing for Profit: A study of contractual security in Ontario*, University of Toronto Press, Toronto.

Shearing, Clifford D. and Stenning, Philip C. 1981, 'Modern Private Security: Its Growth and Implications' in *Crime and Justice—An Annual Review of Research*, (eds) Michael Tonry and Norval Morris, vol. 3, University of Chicago Press, Chicago, pp. 193-245.

— 1982, 'Powers of Private Security Personnel', extract from Private Security and its Implications: A North American Perspective, unpublished.

— 1983, 'Private Security: Implications for Social Control', *Social Problems*, vol. 30, no. 5, pp. 493-506.

South, N. 1988, *Policing for Profit*, Sage, London.

Stenning, Philip and Shearing, Clifford 1979-80, 'The Quiet Revolution: The nature, development and general legal implications of private security in Canada', *Criminal Law Quarterly*, vol. 22, pp. 220-248.

— 1991, 'Policing', in *Criminology A Reader's Guide*, (eds) Jane Gladstone, Richard Ericson and Clifford Shearing, Centre of Criminology, University of Toronto, Toronto.

Swanton, Bruce 1993, 'Police and Private Security: Possible Directions', *Trends and Issues in Crime and Criminal Justice*, no 42, Australian Institute of Criminology, Canberra.

US National Advisory Committee on Criminal Justice Standards and Goals 1976, *Private Security—Report of the Task Force on Private Security*, Washington D.C., U.S.

US Private Security Advisory Council (Dept. of Justice LEAA) 1977, *Law Enforce-*

ment and Private Security: Sources and Areas of Conflict and Strategies for Conflict Resolution, Washington D.C., U.S.

Walsh, William F. 1989, 'Private/Public Police Stereotypes: A Different Perspective', *Security Journal*, vol. 1, no. 1, pp. 21-27.

Williams, Glanville 1962, 'Consent and Public Policy', (1962) *Criminal Law Review*, p. 74.

* This chapter has its origins in a Paper presented to the Australian Institute of Criminology Conference entitled Private Sector and Community Involvement in the Criminal Justice System held in Wellington, New Zealand, 30 November-2 December 1992. The author is grateful for the research assistance of Bill Moore LLB.

13

Private policing:
the major issues

Paul Wilson, Donna Keogh and Robyn Lincoln

Abstract: Growth in crime rates and the fear that has accompanied it have created an environment in which the private security industry has been able to expand exponentially. Though there is a dearth of documented data, it is evident that the industry has become increasingly powerful and yet remains largely unregulated and unaccountable. This chapter will examine the social, economic and political forces that have led to the increase in the private security industry in both its form and extent; analyse the various components of the industry as it operates currently; examine the question of regulatory requirements for both training and account-ability; and conclude by looking at issues for the future.

While we do not wish to further the view that 'crime is out of control', for this chapter on private policing it is sufficient to note that we now have more crime than ever before and that there is a greater focus on crime and its prevention. Australia has experienced recent periods of growth in either the perceived rates of crime or in actual increases in some offences. It has been suggested that Australia ranks high among similar industrialised democracies for assaults, minor sex crimes, burglary and motor vehicle thefts (Walker et al 1992). In short, for both personal and property victimisation we experience levels approaching those of the United States and Canada. While warranted criticism has been levelled at these cross-national surveys of self-reported victimisation, it is evident from the official crime statistics that some areas of violence and property offences have increased in Australia, even after accounting for reportability. From 1980-81 to 1988-89 the number of reported crimes in Australia rose by 66 per cent (Mukherjee and Dagger 1990). There are a variety of explanations for this increase, some of which are canvassed below.

In addition, we endure high levels of fear of crime especially for particular social groups such as the elderly and women. One study in South Australia found that 42 per cent of residents felt unsafe on their streets at night (Frank Small and Associates, 1988). Levels of public fear and anxiety are mediated by recent events, such as a gruesome murder, and are therefore fairly unstable measures. However, the fear of crime is a more relevant indicator when examining the perceived need for private security. When citizens are fearful of becoming victims or when they experience generalised fear at increasing levels of crime, then they will turn to personal and household crime prevention measures and the same psychology applies to small businesses and large corporations.

These factors create a law-and-order environment in which the private security industry is 'expanding rapidly and massively' (South 1987, p. 156). The industry has become increasing powerful and yet it remains largely unregulated and unaccountable. Indeed, there is a dearth of documented data to allow us to examine the industry in any rigorous manner. This chapter will examine the social, economic and political factors that have led to the increase in the private security industry in both its form and extent; analyse the various components of the industry as it operates currently; examine the question of regulatory requirements in terms of both training and accountability; and conclude by looking at issues for the future.

WHY THE INCREASE IN PRIVATE SECURITY?

In addition to the real and imagined increases in crime, there are a number of social, economic and political factors that have led to a growth in the private security industry. Below we canvass some of these factors, with the caveat that they are not necessarily causative, nor is our list exhaustive.

1. There has been a move from an industrial to an information society. By the year 2000, more than 60 per cent of Australians will work in information service occupations — bankers, lawyers, insurance agents, programmers and so on (Wilson 1992). No longer is it physical property alone that requires guarding but the

more intangible assets of information produced by corporations and government enterprises (Wilson 1992). Traditional policing methods are incapable of tracking and guarding the vast array of information that has been produced as a result of expanding communications networks and new technologies.

2. Demographic shifts have also influenced the levels of crime and fear of crime generally that are related to the growth in private security measures. The baby-boom echo, as it is called, means that we have recently experienced a second wave of large numbers of our population falling within the 15-21 years age group — the peak period for both property and violent offences (Walker and Henderson 1992).

3. Along with the demographic shift has come social and economic changes that have led to higher rates of youth unemployment and a rise in the proportion of working women. These changes mean that more young people have limited funds and more leisure time; while the changes for women mean that our homes are now left unguarded for longer periods each day.

4. Another trend is towards 'mass private property' (Shearing and Stenning 1983) seen by the growth in the number of commercial centres that cover hectares of land, such as shopping malls and industrial parks. Also, there has been a continuance of urban sprawl and a majority of housing estates are deserted for long periods. As a result alternatives to these detached wastelands have emerged in the form of compound-style living in town and cluster housing developments which require permanent protection in the form of technology or personnel. And with new household technologies comes the increased availability of saleable goods to steal, such as VCRs and mobile phones.

5. At the political level there is a trend towards privatisation of public enterprises such as airlines and prisons. Despite the overall increase in police personnel in Australia — up 59 per cent between 1973-74 and 1987-88 (Walker and Henderson 1992) — more areas of security have devolved to the private sector so that policing has become more and more a commodity that is offered for sale in a free-market economy (Hinds 1992).

6. Finally, the new communications technologies enable us to monitor and respond to emergencies more quickly than ever before. Since the 1960s alarms and other equipment have created the ability to deliver services that were previously impossible and thereby have led to totally new enterprises (Swanton 1993). John Cochrane of Wormald (cited in Cowan 1991) notes that more

opportunities are likely to open especially with companies using in-house security changing over to contract security because of their technological back-up.

These social, economic and political forces provide an opportune climate for the private security sector. It has grown to the extent where private security operators outnumber public police personnel, certainly in the US and Canada (Shearing and Stenning 1983). Private security now pervades all aspects of living—health, education, travel, housing, finance, workplaces, recreation facilities—and it is unavoidable (Shearing and Stenning 1983).

WHAT IS PRIVATE SECURITY?

While it is not the intention of this chapter to offer a neat label for private security, Wilkins (1970, p. 147) rightly argues that 'terminology is of serious practical significance, as pervasive concepts influence the nature of perception and the structure and action of communities'. Most definitions of private policing are predicated on the perceived role of the public police (Nalla and Newman 1990), at least in the first instance. They are seen as a wholly privatised version of uniformed police who perform the same functions and carry out similar duties. So the framework for describing the private security industry is conceptualised generally from what we know of state police forces.

Yet it is argued that private and public police operate in two different domains. Private security is not part of our mainstream criminal justice system for in pluralist societies there are many avenues for social control (Shearing and Stenning 1983). Nor should private police be seen as adversaries of state police forces. While some public police functions are transferred to the private sector in times of funding cutbacks, there is not a huge territorial battle taking place in Australian policing at present. Indeed as Chan says for private prisons (1992, p. 244), to dismiss them as 'simply another product of the crisis-ridden welfare state and its culture of economic rationalism is to fail to recognise the duality of social and ideological structures'.

In addition to the commercial sector where catch-phrases such as 'rent-a-cop', 'protection-for-hire' or 'policing-for-profit' abound, there are numerous voluntary or non-profit organisations involved in social control practices. These include religious orders, consumer rights groups, neighbourhood watch and similar schemes. By and large however, we refer to private policing as the commercial services offered within the private security industry that have rarely been exclusive state police nor voluntary functions.

There is also a tendency to assume that the role of private policing is relatively new. Yet forms of private policing actually predate those of public policing. It was only with the development of a more egalitarian welfare state that the emergence of the public police systems actually began. In this light 'privatisation' is often seen as a regressive step symbolising the eschewing of the welfare state and the wholesale abandonment of civil servants (Donahue 1989). But the privatisation process does not apply to private security in the same way as it does to corrective services, where there is a move to transfer prison management into private hands but to retain government control (Chan 1992).

Private and public policing nevertheless tend to mirror each other to a certain extent (Nalla and Newman 1990). Often the dichotomy of proactive versus reactive is used to delineate the divergent functions of private compared with public police. The private officers are seen as agents who deter crime while public officers are there to detect crime. However, this proactive-reactive delineation is too simple an approach. State police officers certainly are involved in preventing crime (see Career Information Brochure, Department of Employment Education and Training, 1992) and large private security companies certainly have aims both to detect and deter (see Wormald Security leaflet). Similarly, a passive versus active dichotomy is used to differentiate the functions of private and public policing. In this light private security is seen as comprising passive guardians (as in the use of cameras, guards outside banks and other surveillance measures), while public security is active (patrol cars, beat police and other crime-seeking methods). However, this dichotomy is also false when we examine the full range of public and private security activities.

One way of segregating private from public policing relates to their differing objectives. Indeed, the means of financing the two services — through individual fees or via collective taxes — highlights this divergence (Donahue 1989). While public police are expected to act in the public interest, private security is expected to act in the private interest of its clients. Private security is seen by some as a shift from a focus on crime to a concern with loss (Institute for Research on Public Policy 1983). It is viewed as being in the business of protecting corporate interests rather than fighting crime and is termed 'commercial justice' (South 1987, p. 151) or 'private justice' (Henry 1978, p. 123). Rather than being an act injurious to public welfare, 'crime' then becomes more concerned with an act against the ability to make profit. This not only includes theft, but also employee compliance in the face of alcoholism, absenteeism or strikes (Institute for Research on Public Policy 1983).

Crime and deviance are shifting concepts anyway. They vary across time, settings and cultures and new forms of crime are regularly codified (date rape, tax avoidance, stalking). Nevertheless, private crime — the target of private security — is qualitatively different from public crime. And the ways in which it is sanctioned and controlled also differ. This leads to the main distinction between public and private policing and that is the presence or absence of legal powers to detain, search or regulate citizens (Dance 1991).

Private security, on the one hand, is more extensive than public policing because it is concerned with behaviours that are against client interests (such as absenteeism). At the same time it is more limited because it is not concerned with a range of violations against the law nor norms of society (like drug taking) unless such behaviours threaten client profits (Shearing and Stenning 1983).

A further differentiation between private and public is the level at which policing takes place. Traditional policing was done at the neighbourhood level and still is in many countries. Indeed, there is now a return in Australia to community-based policing in the face of evidence that large state police forces have 'lost touch' with the communities they were designed to serve. While larger national bodies do operate for specific purposes (such as drug enforcement and organised crime control), public policing generally is targeted at the local level. By comparison, the private security industry is increasingly in the hands of overseas-owned multinational companies (Cowan 1991). It operates not just at a national level but at an international level. The American District Telegraph Company (ADT) for example, established in the US in 1874, is now making in-roads into Australia and claims to be one of the top four security organisations (Cowan 1991). However, the paradox is that the industry is also disparate, with 92 per cent of its operators being small businesses having less than 20 employees (Australian Bureau of Statistics 1990, p. 2).

Swanton (1993) characterises the policing domain as comprising three elements — assets, threats and controls — and it is the differences between these that distinguishes public and private policing. The former focuses on intangible assets like 'peace', it targets offenders as threats, is accountable to governments and utilises coercive powers for control. The private sector concentrates on material assets (including information), focuses on threats to assets and has no special powers although sanctions are nevertheless imposed.

So how do we characterise the private security industry? It predates the public version but has many similarities in terms of functions and roles and indeed many services are provided concurrently from the two domains. It is both proactive and reactive and passive and active. It has a focus on loss rather than on crime per se and is client-centred. It is increasingly international in its orientation but paradoxically run largely by single or small operators. Also, the industry is described as non-specific (Shearing and Stenning 1983) because it encompasses such a wide range of functions but other commentators (Dance 1991) highlight its specialised nature, such as in the protection of art collections, for example. The private security industry covers a wide variety of occupations such as locksmiths, building security staff, patrol officers, crowd controllers, bouncers, alarm and security door installers, private detectives, control room operators, transport staff, communications experts and consultants. Its three main elements comprise suppliers of hardware, guardians and investigators. Because of its diversity the industry is difficult to regulate and control and its heterogeneity makes standardised training programs almost impossible to implement.

THE QUESTION OF REGULATION

There are three options for standardising private security industry practices — a wholly deregulated free market, the introduction of government controls and licensing, or self-regulation by the industry (Swanton 1993). At its present stage of development the industry and some of its critics generally favour self-regulation with varying degrees of government oversight. Despite the debate about how a regulatory body will be structured it is evident that regulation is sorely needed to provide standardised training programs and to ensure quality of service.

Self-regulation

The statutes governing private security, especially who it covers and who is the controlling authority, vary considerably across Australian jurisdictions. At present in Queensland, for example, there are no real regulatory provisions governing the industry except for the *Invasion of Privacy Act 1971* and the *Auctioneers and Agents Act 1971* to govern investigators and security agents. A Security Providers Bill has been drafted for some time but as at early 1994, has failed to materialise as legislation. Even in the draft bill 'in-house' security (hospital, retail, hotel and government departments) remains unlicensed. In Western Australia, the *Security Agents Act 1976* and the *Inquiry Agents Licensing Act 1954* cover guards, investigators and security agents and are controlled by the police. In other states, magistrates or government departments are the responsible authorities. (See Swanton 1993, for an excellent summary of existing legislation.) Despite both government and industry attempts to 'clean-up private security' real gaps exist in the regulation of large sections of the industry.

Given existing problems within the industry, and that 'self regulatory bodies merely possess standards and codes of ethics which may not be implemented by the wider industry' (Hinds 1992, p. 2), the inadequacy of self-regulation is highlighted. This scenario is inevitable given that 'the overwhelming majority of practitioners are not members of the industry representative bodies' and there is a plethora of such organisations operating in Australia (Swanton 1993, p. 6). And as the industry consists of either small business or internationally controlled agencies, external controls are imperative.

There is always a tension between demands for industries or professions to regulate themselves and the contrary pressure for more stringent government regulation. Shearing and Stenning (1982) argue that self-regulation has some merits. With in-house auditing, private security companies are, at least in theory, under close scrutiny by regulatory bodies who have familiarity with their operations (Shearing and Stenning 1982). In the case of who regulates the regulatory bodies, 'direct regulatory enforcement by prosecution, license suspension, adverse publicity or other means is one outstandingly important way of putting pressure on companies to self-regulate' (Shearing and Stenning 1982, p. 244). While a number of bodies, such as the Australian Security Industries Association Limited (ASIAL), currently exist and argue largely for self-regulation, in reality the notion of self-regulation is, from the community's viewpoint, inadequate. To be fair however ASIAL has sought further strengthening of licensing requirements, involving a government statutory body.

The criminal element

Swanton (1993, p. 6) suggests that 'the poor performance demonstrated by many small private security operators is almost legendary' and has produced a 'lack of credibility' that has harmed the industry. Even though most private security jobs are fairly mundane, there is room for rorts. Problems begin even at the recruitment phase, or where independent operators set themselves up as security experts. In the past billions of dollars have been lost through misjudgment in the selection of personnel (Grau 1990). The vice-president of ASIAL publicly admitted 'that from time to time, the odd person with a criminal background does bob up' (*Melbourne Truth*, 12 December 1992). Aardvarks Security, which specialises in manpower and alarm response agrees that there are 'disreputable elements' in the industry (Cowan 1991, p. 18). Aardvarks' manager, Mal Paton, said that while 'shonks are generally becoming a fringe element, they are still there' (Cowan 1991, p. 18). The police have also had numerous complaints filed by crime prevention squads from concerned persons relating to the activities of various security firms (Altschul 1991).

Take for example current problems concerning the engagement of bouncers at pubs and clubs. A survey of serious assault by the Victorian Ministry of Police and Emergency Services found that an increasing proportion of reported serious assaults occurred at entertainment venues and 21 per cent of the reported incidents involved bouncers (National Committee on Violence 1990). The National Committee on Violence (1990) also received anecdotal evidence about alleged assaults by bouncers in Queensland. Bouncers are now licensed in Victoria and draft legislation is in place to ensure that they are in Queensland. Other states are contemplating similar licensing requirements.

One of the most widespread rorts is not fulfilling contracted services, such as patrol visits. Already some patrol companies are recognising the need to patrol their own security guards. Charles Blinkworth, director of Kingsecurity, has initiated a computerised system of reporting on patrolling activities to provide 'an internal management tool to monitor patrol staff efficiency, and [prove] . . . to our clients of proof that patrols are carried out and fulfilled as per contracts' (cited in Cowan 1991, p. 36). However, as competition keeps margins low (Hinds 1992) it is not uncommon for companies to resort to unscrupulous tactics in poor economic times.

More sophisticated examples abound of illegal activities through electronic surveillance and industrial espionage within the industry. According to Hinds (1992), the same firms that hire security companies to guard their secrets are usually not too scrupulous about gaining access to their competitors' secrets and the security industry provides such counter-intelligence. While no one can document the number and nature of complaints against the industry, widespread anecdotal evidence would suggest that there are many. This then raises the question of what regulatory body hears and investigates these complaints. It is doubtful that the security industry can adequately investigate itself so that the argument for a quasi-government standing commission to take on this role becomes even more compelling.

Training

Issues of training also need to be adequately addressed. As general problems in the industry will no doubt increase as private security grows, special concerns with respect to training for private security personnel will also emerge. Security is not a matter for intuition nor commonsense. It requires a complex body of knowledge, analytical abilities and the know-how to prescribe suitable security measures for specific circumstances (Criscuoli 1988). Some would argue that many industry personnel are drawn from the ranks of former state police or military officers and that their training has already been undertaken at the state's expense. Yet, the private security industry operates under different conditions and fulfils different functions. Therefore, specific training should still occur.

ASIAL believe that training standards must be decided by the industry itself, as the industry is best placed to determine what those requirements might be. ASIAL agree this should be on a consultative basis with such bodies as the police, unions and training boards (ASIAL 1992). They also argue that the marketplace should determine how many skills a guard should have beyond the core requirements of his/her job (Bright 1993). However, the marketplace does not always have adequate means for enforcing standards as all too often standards are discarded in the face of economic pressures.

Currently, many courses in this country (if they exist at all) are only two days in length. A report by the Police and Emergency Services Advisory Committee in New South Wales found that current courses are inadequate and suggested evacuation procedures and first aid be included in the programs (Bright 1993). Walsh (cited in Grau 1990) has claimed also that it is doubtful whether the industry has any objective standards for evaluating professional competence. In rebuttal, ADT's Managing Director, Lindsay Brooks (cited in Cowan 1991, p. 21), believes training legislation and the efforts of industry associations have engendered improvements to the industry. He adds though that 'it is probably fair to say that (the industry) still has a long way to go'. Undoubtedly, there needs to be greater supervision and enforcement of basic training which only comes about through either government run or regulated courses.

As Prince (1979) points out, the haphazard growth and development of the security industry has highlighted the need for some form of recognised qualification to be available as a basis for selection. Since large security companies operate in all states of Australia and internationally, it is not feasible to expect them to comply with separate training requirements across all jurisdictions. In this regard, a national initiative needs to be undertaken with regards to formal training procedures. While some elements of the industry will no doubt argue that the time and expense involved in training employees is uneconomical, in the long term formal training will heighten both professional competence and public credibility of the industry.

There are several workable models for training. Already the possibility of involving Technical and Further Education (TAFE) has been toyed with in New South Wales. In Queensland however, TAFE involvement is limited to an Associate Diploma in Business (Justice Administration). Offered at selected colleges around the state (Bayside Community College, Gold Coast Institute of TAFE and Sunshine Coast Community College), the course is designed for 'continuing professional development of personnel employed by the Departments of Police and Justice and Corrective Services' (TAFE Student Handbook 1992, p. 68). The Bachelor of Arts in Justice Administration at Griffith University does include a concentration in 'non-police law enforcement', but again the course generally is aimed at training prospective state police officers. These courses are not, therefore, structured to cater for the needs of private security personnel. On the more positive side some universities are actively planning degree or diploma courses specifically designed for the industry.

Training courses must pay special attention to the use of firearms. Given the concern with state police forces about the use of 'deadly force' and several recent Australian examples of police shootings, combined with an increasing stock of firearms in this country, it is likely that instances will occur where private security personnel confront citizens with lethal force. Over and above training in the use of firearms, regulations should specify where and when guards can be armed. In every state in Australia concerns have been expressed about issues relating to firearms and their use by private security personnel.

The American Society of Industrial Organisations has established a professional certification program for private security. In the United Kingdom there is a syllabus for a diploma course in security management. Similar courses, in consultation with tertiary providers, should be developed in Australia specifically aimed at this market. Indeed, Swanton (1993) predicts further growth in the number and variety of diploma and certificate courses available in particular topic areas (e.g. security management or tactical intelligence) but also full degrees that will cater to the industry as a whole. These courses should address pragmatic issues but also the social, ethical and legal ramifications and responsibilities of pseudo-police work. As the complexity of security work increases, a more systematic approach to formal education and training is warranted.

ISSUES FOR THE FUTURE

Because of the diversity of the private security industry it is impossible to generalise about its advantages and disadvantages. However, issues for the future include efficiencies, evaluation, accountability, use of force, public access, standards and fee setting.

With increasing crime rates and fear of crime citizens increasingly accept private security. As South (1987, p. 153) comments, 'in one sense, private security is accepted simply because it is there'. The public perception that state police forces are overburdened and the system is becoming 'bureaucratically ossified' (Spitzer and Scull 1987, p. 26) will only contribute to this trend. The reality is that the private security industry is growing in numbers and functions. Training and regulation are therefore vital. It smacks of hypocrisy for security practitioners or for criminologists to raise the question of the efficiency of public police without at the same time expressing concern about the low standards of training and performance in contract security.

There is a strong argument for the establishment of a government standing commission on private security in each state. A central body would oversee not only companies but also individuals employed in the industry. This would allow a system of vetting and inspection with the possibility of any security company or individual who failed to meet the required standards being removed from the register. The standing commission could comprise representatives from the police, the industry and civil libertarian groups and funding could come from annual fees for security licensing.

The legal liabilities of private security require close examination. Those involved in the industry should be giving attention to legal liability as a potential source of business loss. One way to avoid such loss is to have security professionals well acquainted with their legal rights and obligations (Nalla and Newman 1990). The legal ambiguities regarding any misuse of power have profound implications for the continued operation of security companies.

The extent to which misuse of power may impinge upon civil liberties has serious consequences for society as a whole. While the industry derives its power from a mixture of property, agency, contract and industrial law, little sustained debate has addressed the de facto powers of private security personnel. Given the engagement of private police at public venues and the use of intrusive technology, the extent to which private policing will control and regulate society is an issue of increasing concern. As Swanton (1993) points out few security personnel possess powers not possessed by citizens generally — even though security personnel not infrequently overreach these boundaries.

Private security must be evaluated in regard to its wider social impact. Chan (1992) questions whether we should allow profit-motive to capitalise on the fear of crime and the demand for tougher law-and-order strategies. The industry undoubtedly makes a contribution to crime prevention — at least for most of its clients most of the time. Yet, the extent to which those less able to pay for additional security become more heavily victimised is not known but is probably significant (South 1987). Neither the security industry nor its clients are under any obligation to evaluate the effects of private security arrangements on the problems of crime prevention and order in the wider community (South 1987). Displacement to unsecured businesses or households may well occur; the presence of bouncers may incite violent actions that need not have taken place without their presence. There are few data to support a conclusion either way on these issues. And in terms of its user-pays structure, not only is displacement at issue, but more importantly access to such services needs to be considered. As Berwick (1988, p. 11) notes, 'any limitation of access is incompatible with the delivery of public goods, yet another flaw in the private policing protagonists' argument'. Even within the private security industry there is a technological push where guards are replaced by cameras and electronic system thereby removing its human face. Yet neither the people nor equipment have been adequately evaluated.

As governments procrastinate over the role private security should play in our society, and the regulatory and training standards by which they operate, the industry is slowly taking over the role of justice arbiters. For who ever controls policing to a large extent determines the criminal justice system of any given society. In this regard, the growth of private security raises the possibility of power and authority over criminal justice shifting from the state to private corporations not only in their national, but as Shearing and Stenning (1983) point out, their international guises. This is clearly not a desirable situation. Private security is most typically a form of policing for profit: that is policing which is tailored to the profit making objective of its corporate and individual clients (Shearing and Stenning 1983). Hence, it is doubtful that private security could ever truly represent a broadly based social service.

On a more positive note, the security industry is beginning the process of introspection. Much has occurred to advance the profession by way of several published 'in-house' magazines such as *Security Management, Security World and Australia Security*. However, editorial and other comment in these magazines is often too defensive and dismissive of critics.

It is true also that a code of practice for guards and patrol sections of the industry has been introduced by ASIAL and that this organisation (and others) has attempted to strengthen the licensing requirements of certain personnel in the industry. ASIAL have also argued for a security industry board which would have a similar role to what we have called a government standing commission on the security industry. However, no state in the country has satisfactorily regulated the industry. Nor would such a board (or commission) deal with the wider issues that revolve around the growth of the industry and the implications of that growth for society as a whole. In addition, though both public police and private security occupy 'a largely common functional domain' (Swanton 1993, p. 2) a considerable degree of tension exists between the two sectors — tension that could well exacerbate over time.

References

Altschul, P. 1991, 'Industry Heal Thy Self', *Security Australia*, vol. 11, no. 5, June, pp. 10-15.

Australian Bureau of Statistics 1990, *Security/Protection and Other Business Services Industries, Australia*, Commonwealth Government Printer, Canberra.

Australian Securities Industries Association Limited (ASIAL) 1992, 'Training: Friend or Foe?', *Security Australia*, vol. 12, no. 10, November, p. 8.

Berwick, D. 1988, *The Application of the User Pays Principle to the Policing of Sporting and Entertainment Events: Principal Considerations*, National Police Research Unit, Adelaide.

Bright, G. 1993, 'Mutch Report Recommends Commissioner for Security', *Security Australia*, vol. 13, no. 2, March, pp. 1-2.

Chan, J. 1992, 'The Privatisation of Punishment: A Review of the Key Issues', *Australian Journal of Social Issues*, vol. 27, no. 4, pp. 223-47.

Cowan, R. 1991, 'Guards and Patrols', *Security Australia*, vol. 12, no. 3, April, pp. 16-36.

Criscuoli, E. J. 1988, 'The Time Has Come to Acknowledge Security as a Profession' in *The Private Security Industry: Trends and Issues*, (ed) I. R. Lipman, Sage, Newbury Park, pp. 98-103.

Dance, O. 1991, 'To What Extent Could or Should Policing Be Privatised?', *Australian Police*, January-March, pp. 9-13.

Donahue, J. 1989, *The Privatisation Decision: Public Ends, Private Means*, Basic Books, New York.

Frank Small and Associates 1988, *Fear of Crime Survey*, Research Report for the Australian Institute of Criminology, Canberra, December.

Grau, J. 1990, 'Security Education: Something to Think About' in *Security Training: Readings from Security Management Magazine*, (ed) S. M. Gallery, Butterworths, Boston, pp. 1-10.

Henry, S. 1978, *The Hidden Economy: The Context and Control of Borderline Crime*, Martin Robertson, London.

Hinds, S. 1992, 'Public Safety and Security: Who Is Responsible?', Paper presented at NZSIA Conference, Rotorua, 23 June.

Institute for Research on Public Policy 1983, *Private Security and Private Justice*, Institute for Research on Public Policy, Montreal.

Mukherjee, S. K. and Dagger, D. 1990, *The Size of the Crime Problem in Australia*, 2nd edition, Australian Institute of Criminology, Canberra.

Nalla, M. and Newman, G. 1990, *A Primer in Private Security*, Harrow and Heston, Albany.

National Committee on Violence 1990, *Violence: Directions for Australia*, Australian Institute of Criminology, Canberra.

Prince, L. 1979, 'Time for a Professional Approach to Security', *Police*, vol. 12, no. 3, November, pp. 22-23.

Shearing, C. D. and Stenning, P. C. 1982, *Private Policing*, Sage, Newbury Park.

— 1983, 'Private Security: Implications for Social Control', *Social Problems*, vol. 30, no. 5, June, pp. 493-506.

South, N. 1987, *Policing for Profit: The Private Security Sector*, Sage, London.

Spitzer, S. and Scull, A. T. 1987, 'Privatisation and Capitalist Development: The Case of the Private Police' in *Private Policing*, (eds) C. D. Shearing and P. C. Stenning, Sage, London, pp. 18-28.

Swanton, B. 1993, 'Police and Private Security: Possible Directions', *Trends and Issues in Crime and Criminal Justice*, no. 42, Australian Institute of Criminology, Canberra.

Walker, J. and Henderson, M. 1992, 'Understanding Crime Trends in Australia in *Issues in Crime, Morality and Justice*, (ed) P. R. Wilson, Australian Institute of Criminology, Canberra, pp. 17-29.

Walker, J., Wilson, P., Chappell, D. and Weatherburn, D. 1992, 'A Comparison of Crime in Australia and Other Countries' in *Issues in Crime, Morality and Justice*, (ed) P. R. Wilson, Australian Institute of Criminology, Canberra, pp. 1-16.

Wilkins, L. T. 1970, 'The Concept of Cause in Criminology' in *The Sociology of Crime and Delinquency*, (eds) M. Wolfgang and L. Savirz, 2nd edition, Wiley, New York.

Wilson, P. R. 1992, 'The Australian Private Security Industry: The Need for Accountability, Regulation and Professionalisation', Paper presented at the NZSIA Conference, Rotorua, 23 June.

Conclusion

Future directions and reforms for private sector involvement in prisons and policing

Paul Moyle

Private sector involvement in prisons and policing has raised unique issues within Australia and New Zealand. Three issues are highlighted as themes in these chapters. The first is the lack of accountability of private companies and their consequent failure to provide adequate information about their involvement in policing and prisons. The second is the area of legal ambiguity in which regulatory agencies and even the companies themselves often operate. They sometimes assume the power to arrest, conduct disciplinary proceedings and use force, but the legal basis for such actions is often unclear. The third is a lack of consultation with the community, often characterised by poorly organised bureaucracies which often give overriding priority to powerful business interests.

It is alarming that state governments are introducing private sector involvement in prisons and policing without adequately addressing important issues. Before embarking on these policies, a framework for how the private sector should be involved in these areas needs to be outlined. The examination of difficult theoretical and practical areas should not be devalued because of a group's desire to implement a rapid agenda for change. Citizen's rights to participate in governmental decisions should not be devalued if we are to maintain the institution of democracy. Consultation and research is a critical precursor to the successful implementation of policy initiatives. These chapters illustrate many examples of haste at the expense of careful and well reasoned policy development.

To solve difficult issues it is first necessary to admit their complexity. It is ironic that before the Australian Institute of Criminology Conference on private sector and community involvement in the criminal justice system in 1992, many of the preliminary issues associated with private sector involvement in prisons and police had not been discussed. This was despite private sector involvement in police and prisons occurring for many years. Some glaring deficiencies at the conference which gave need for this book included: a need for a theoretical core or unifying criteria to identify the role of private prisons and police within society; clarification of various definitions of private sector involvement; discussion on liability and accountability issues; identification of justifiable objectives of imprisonment which includes industrial, political, management and community interests; evaluation of the success or otherwise of the legal and practical aspects of implementing contract management; and justifications of what role governments should play in administering punishment (see Moyle 1993a, p. 42).

Further research in private policing and prisons is necessary. Parliamentary sovereignty and its meaning within modern constitutional democracies such as Australia and New Zealand must be related to private sector involvement. Will this involvement lead to a shift in power from the Parliament to private sector interests? Will private sector involvement lead to genuine reform of the operation and delivery of services within prisons and police? If so, how will this reform emerge and develop? Will private sector involvement provide opportunities to change custodial and management approaches and personal and work ethics within correctional and policing organisations? Will it enhance accountability by providing greater public access to policy, operational and contractual information? Alternatively, will commercial secrecy increase the transparency of prison rules and policing procedures? How can researchers understand historical similarities and differences with private sector involvement in corrections and policing, therefore enabling them to develop a more sophisticated understanding of trends and issues? How is liability apportioned for injuries to persons through negligent actions by private companies? How can we adopt the best practices by building a typology from various jurisdictions in a way that is culturally sensitive? (See Moyle 1993b.)

The chapters in this book begin to address these issues. Effective and accountable implementation of private sector involvement in corrections and policing requires strong regulatory agencies which have the *technical, legal and policy expertise* to identify and implement a consistent framework. The contributors to this collection have raised many fundamental issues that require further investigation. Before this can be done, it was necessary to identify some important issues raised by private sector involvement. This collection of papers begins this important process. The next step is to provide coherent solutions to the vast array of legal, administrative, technical and philosophical issues which will require specific jurisdictional work.

With such a vast array of possibilities this type of involvement raises, we should not close our minds to the enormous range of problems and solutions raised by this initiative. The development of theoretical and policy issues must, in the final analysis, be related to empirical experience. Much more work is needed if we are to achieve sustained correctional reform within constitutionally acceptable limits. For a long term improvement in the quality of corrections and policing there must be constructive and open debate across various sectors of the criminal justice system.

References

Moyle P. 1993a, 'Private Sector Involvement in Criminal Justice: Explorations in recent developments', *Socio-Legal Bulletin*, no. 9, Autumn, pp. 41-42.

—— 1993b, 'Review Article *Privatizing Correctional Institutions*', Paper presented to the Annual General Meeting of the American Society of Criminology, Arizona, October 27-30.

Index